IMAGES
of America

TUSKEGEE

ON THE COVER: This interior view of the reading room of the Carnegie library on the campus of Tuskegee Institute shows female and male students seated at tables. The photograph was taken in 1902 by Frances Benjamin Johnston. (Courtesy of the Frances Benjamin Collection, the Library of Congress Prints and Photographs Division.)

IMAGES of America
TUSKEGEE

Amalia K. Amaki and
Amelia Boynton Robinson

ARCADIA
PUBLISHING

ISBN 978-1-4671-1035-8

Published by Arcadia Publishing
Charleston, South Carolina

Printed in the United States of America

Library of Congress Control Number: 2013932730

For all general information, please contact Arcadia Publishing:
Telephone 843-853-2070
Fax 843-853-0044
E-mail sales@arcadiapublishing.com
For customer service and orders:
Toll-Free 1-888-313-2665

Visit us on the Internet at www.arcadiapublishing.com

Contents

ACKNOWLEDGMENTS

The authors are grateful to many individuals who provided assistance and support toward the completion of this book. We are grateful to the staff at the Manuscript, Archives, and Rare Books Library at Emory University, especially Randall Burkett; the Tuskegee University Archives, especially Dana Chandler; the estate of Prentice Herman Polk; the Robert W. Woodruff Library in the Atlanta University Center; and the Birmingham Civil Rights Institute, especially Lawrence J. Pijeaux.

We are thankful for the assistance of Harriett Ann Peek, Deborah Peek Crockett, Amma Malik Kehana, Peter Brighton Jackson, Carolyn Golowka, and Charles S. Johnson. A special thank-you to our editor Jason Humphrey at Arcadia Publishing for his patience, assurance, and guidance throughout the research and writing process.

Unless indicated otherwise, images are courtesy of a private collection. Helpful research sources included the Library of Congress Historic American Buildings Survey and the Library of Congress Prints and Photographs Archive.

INTRODUCTION

Prior to the first removal of Native Americans with the 1814 Treaty of Fort Jackson, the land in and around present-day Tuskegee was home to the Tuskigi (or Taskialgi) warriors, Creek Indians who lived in the area within the triangle formed by the point of convergence of the Coosa and Tallapoosa Rivers. While Creek remained in the region over subsequent decades, their numbers fell considerably and they virtually disappeared after the final removal of March 24, 1832.

As the Creek made their way to the far side of the Mississippi River, white settlers took immediate possession of the territory of east-central Alabama, in the heart of the Black Belt, along a historic Indian trail that later became the 40-mile highway between Fort Mitchell and Montgomery. Planters discovered rich soil and compatible conditions for growing preferred crops, with cotton high on the list among them. The city of Tuskegee being situated on a high, dry ridge was often noted as a plus towards good health as well.

Thomas Simpson Woodward was one of the earliest white settlers in the region. He had coexisted well with native groups and understood their culture, although he commanded whites in battles fought against Indians under Andrew Jackson. When the Alabama legislature created Macon County on December 18, 1832, Woodward was commissioned to plan a seat of government for the county in 1833. When the city of Tuskegee was incorporated in 1843, Woodward built the first house in town, soon followed by James Dent, who constructed his home on the town square.

The city was settled largely by men of means, who owned rich lands on the creeks and streams and in the prairie section of the county. They designed impressive homes for their families, oversaw large parcels of real estate, and brought in increasing numbers of slaves to do the fieldwork and other labor. They encouraged the establishment of churches and schools to provide congenial social company and to give their children educational advantages. A notable number of the earliest settlers of prominence had some training in the legal field, which may explain why the first law school in Alabama was located in Tuskegee.

Attention was also given to educating women. The Baptist College for Women was founded in 1848. The Tuskegee Female College opened in 1856 before later moving to Montgomery and eventually becoming Huntingdon College. East Alabama Female College, founded in 1852, burned down completely in 1865 and was never rebuilt. In addition, the Tuskegee Military Institute for Boys, later known as Park High School for Boys, joined the ranks of early schools operating in the city before the public school system was established in 1898.

Early leaders did not want a railroad bisecting the town, believing it to be an interruption, even though Tuskegee had emerged as an important trade center. Rail service would not be available for a few decades, and even then, it was only a short run between the outskirts of Tuskegee and Chehaw. Macon County suffered economic decline in the late 1850s because county land was exhausted from two decades of vigorous use by large planters, and land to the west was acknowledged as being more conducive to plantation agriculture. The local economy continued to decline in the 1860s, as it was further affected by the Civil War.

The war took its toll on Tuskegee, as it did on other areas of the South. Members of some of the most prominent and popular families returned as former Confederate officers to resume law practices, mercantile businesses, and different legal relationships with former slaves. Some returned to homesites where properties had been burned to the ground during Union surges. Some had spent much of their war time in Union prisons, while others sustained varying degrees of physical injuries.

All of these factors contributed to a climate of racial hatred and heightened tension. Above all else, whites became aware that the huge population of free African Americans could alter their way of political life like never before because of voting power. Reputable citizens such as the Cobbs, Battles, Abercrombies, and others engaged in intimidation tactics that were not atypical for the deep South but contradicted the professed interest of certain local leadership in Tuskegee to represent a kind of model community. For example, in 1870, the home of state legislator James Alston was shot up and he was forced to flee with his family. Leading the violence was Cullen Battle, Alston's former master. James Edward Cobb utilized his authority as a judge to order harsh sentences for African Americans who appeared in his court, especially elected officials and those who were politically active.

National attention came to the city a few years after the establishment of Tuskegee Normal College for Colored Teachers (now Tuskegee University) in 1881. Founded as the result of political agreements orchestrated by Lewis Allen, the support of Allen's proposal by George Washington Campbell, and the implementation of the agreements by Booker T. Washington, the first principal, the school became essentially synonymous with the city in which it was established. Washington was hired on the strong recommendation of Hampton Normal and Agricultural Institute founder and principal Gen. Samuel Chapman Armstrong. Washington, a Hampton graduate, had returned to his alma mater in 1879 on Armstrong's invitation to run the night school and, later, to supervise the dormitory for recently admitted male Indian students. Assuming the position of principal at Tuskegee Institute, Washington embarked on a mission that became his life's work.

Washington started the school armed with a vision and $2,000 from the state legislature for salaries—no land, buildings, or campus. A $200 loan from Hampton Institute treasurer—and Washington's finance mentor—James F.B. Marshall allowed him to purchase initial land on the outskirts of town for a campus. He endeared himself strategically to local whites, recruited and enrolled the first students, and opened the institute in a shanty. Students erected the first buildings and worked the farm areas that supplied food for the dormitory kitchen. Upon his death in 1915, the campus had 100 buildings on 2,000 acres, the faculty numbered nearly 200, there were more than 1,500 students, and the institute had a $2 million endowment.

Washington hired a stellar faculty, most notably botanist and agricultural researcher George Washington Carver, who left a teaching position at Iowa State to direct the department of agriculture. Carver's expressed intent was to share his knowledge with African American students and work to help alleviate debt and poverty among black farmers in the county, who had been restricted by sharecropping and cotton dependency. Carver's fame grew rapidly, with Pres. Theodore Roosevelt praising him at Washington's funeral.

The year 1895 was transformative for Washington. His views on race relations, emphasis on developing industrial skills and character, track record for effective philanthropic engagement, and the death of Frederick Douglass in February, positioned him to become a spokesperson for African Americans. He gained favor from many whites for a 10-minute address at the Atlanta Cotton States and International Exposition in September and sparked debate with W.E.B. DuBois and others who considered his positions too accommodating to whites to improve the situation for blacks.

The city of Tuskegee played a role in the later civil rights movement. Voting rights and equal education were guaranteed through important court cases such as Gomillion v. Lightfoot (1958) and Lee v. Macon County (1963). Tuskegee is the birthplace of Rosa Louise Parks, and is where Samuel Younge Jr. became the first African American student killed due to his involvement in the civil rights movement. The city is also the birthplace of popular syndicated radio host Tom Joyner, singer Lionel Richie, NBA player Rory White, baseball's Andre Thompson, and Chief National Guard Bureau Commander Lt. Gen. Russell C. Davis.

One

LAND

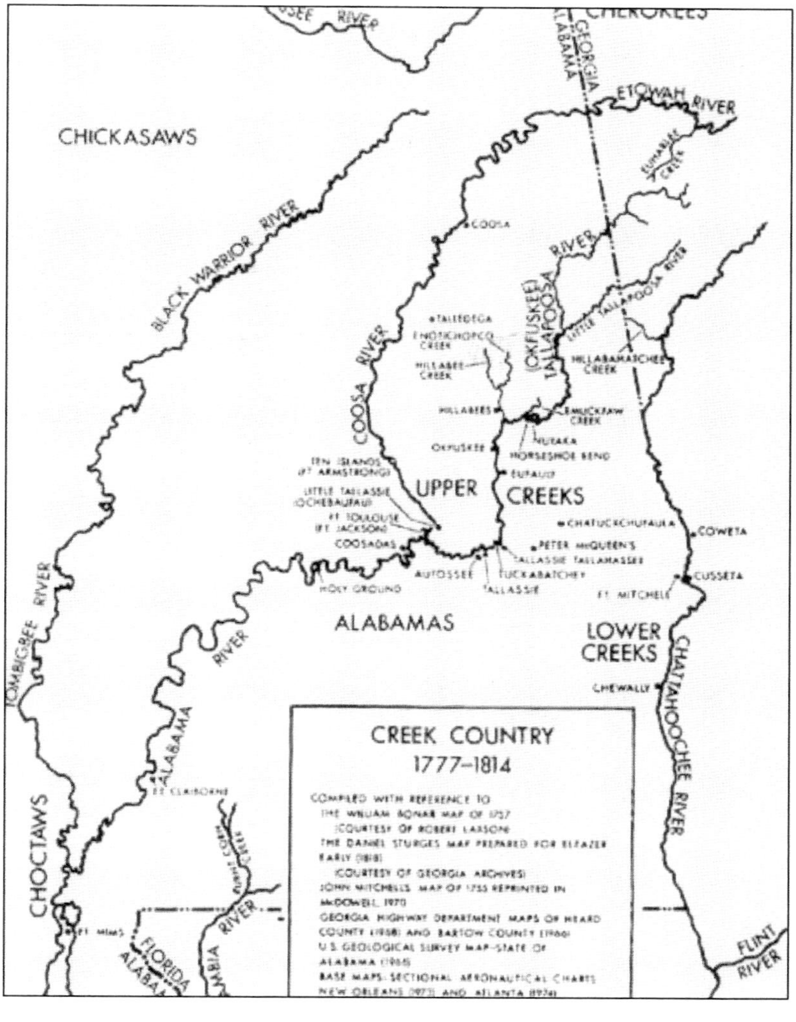

This map of the Creek nation between 1777 and 1814 in present-day Alabama underscores the significance of 1814 as a transformative year in the history of Muscogee Creek people and the evolution of the 22nd state. This change in land-based identity includes the redefinition of the "town of the Upper Creek," Taskigi, on the east bank of the Coosa River where it forks with the Tallapoosa River.

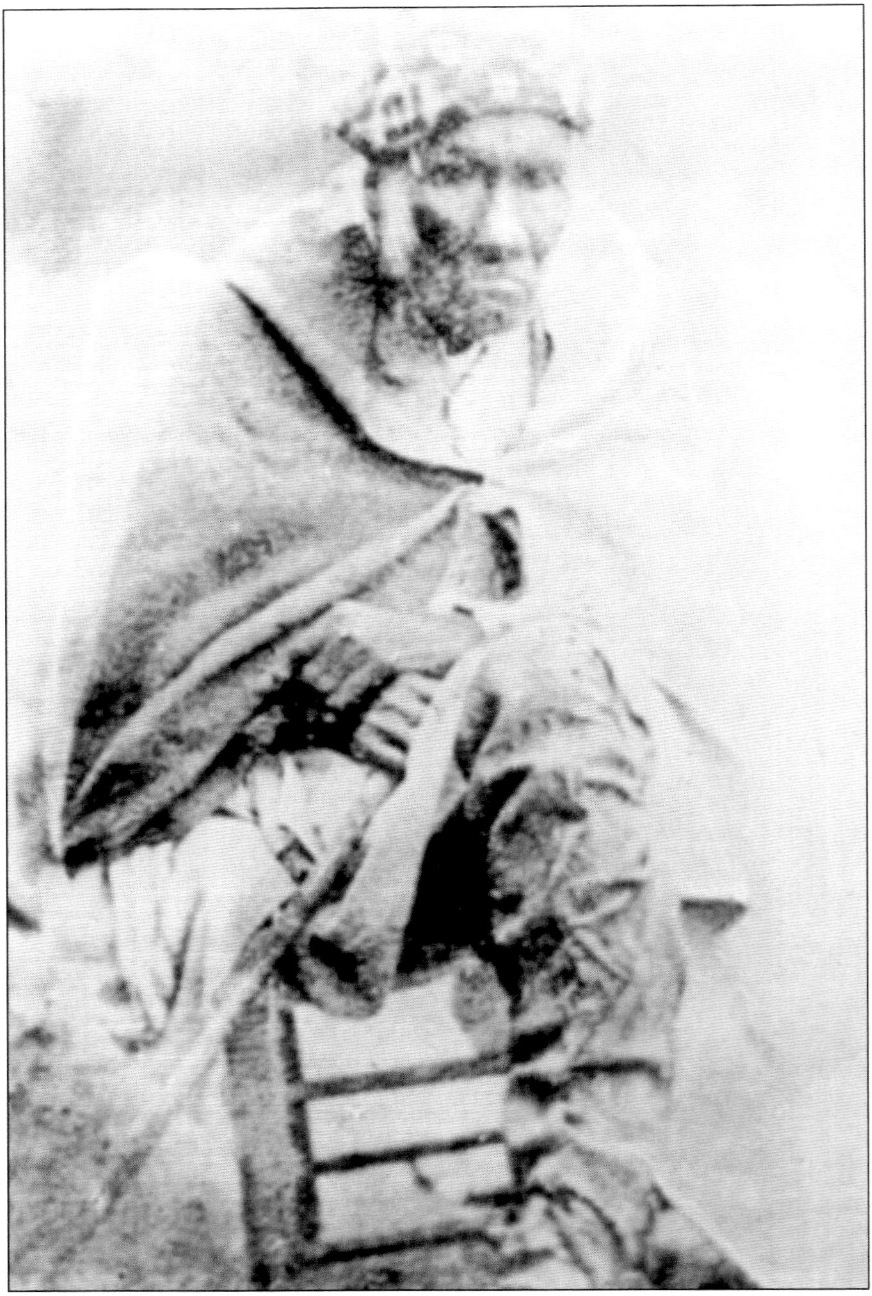

Chief Junaluska (1775–1858), a leader of the Eastern Band of the Cherokee, lived in the western region of North Carolina. He became an ally of the colonists during the Creek War and saved the life of Andrew Jackson in the Battle of Horseshoe Bend. He is credited with personally taking actions during battle that turned the tide of the conflict to the American advantage. The victory at Horseshoe Bend essentially ended the Creek War. On August 9, 1814, the Muscogee Nation was forced to sign the Treaty of Fort Jackson, which ceded 23 million acres of Creek land to the US government. Even allies had to cede land because Jackson held them responsible for allowing the Red Sticks to revolt. Chief Junaluska responded, "If I had known that Jackson would drive us from our homes, I would have killed him at Horseshoe."

Sam Houston (1793–1863) was severely wounded during the Battle of Horseshoe Bend in 1814 when an arrow pierced his upper thigh. He ordered a nearby comrade to pull it out, but the wound never fully healed. He was permanently scarred and plagued with pain for the rest of his life. His courage was brought to the attention of Andrew Jackson, who later became Houston's mentor and surrogate father.

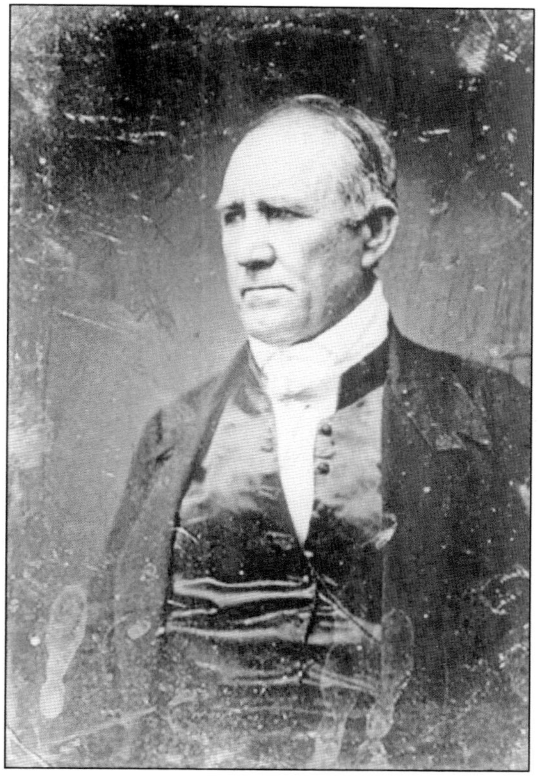

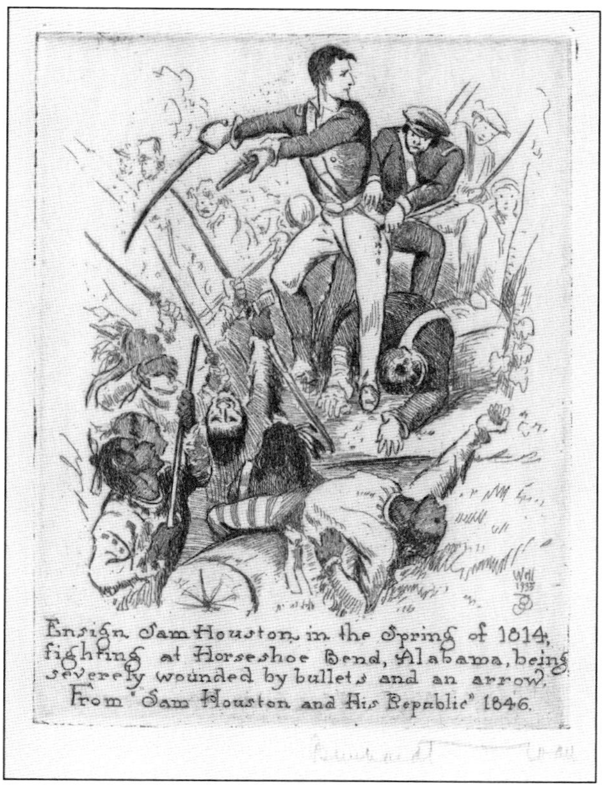

This early-20th-century engraving by Bernhardt Wall is based on the 1814 lead drawing Houston chose as an illustration for the book *Sam Houston and His Republic*, written by Charles Edward Lester and published in 1846.

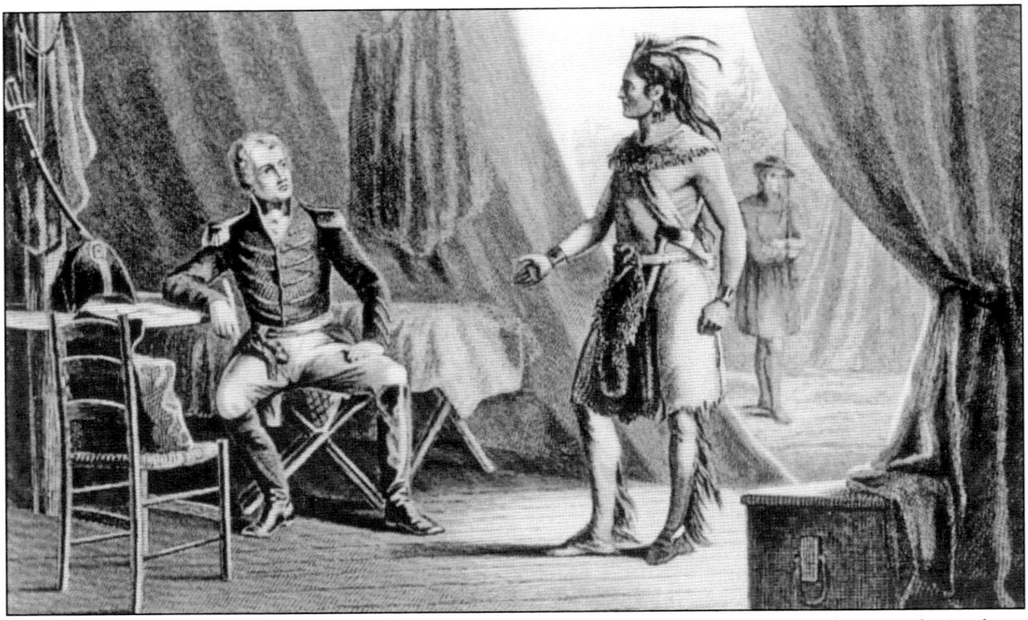

This engraving by J.R. Chapin shows William Weatherford (c. 1780–1824) speaking with Andrew Jackson in his tent after the Battle of Horseshoe Bend. The original caption read, "Interview Between Gen. Jackson & Weatherford." Reportedly, Jackson was so impressed with Weatherford's boldness that he let him go. However, their treaty, the Treaty of Fort Jackson, secured land that largely defined the territory of the future state of Alabama.

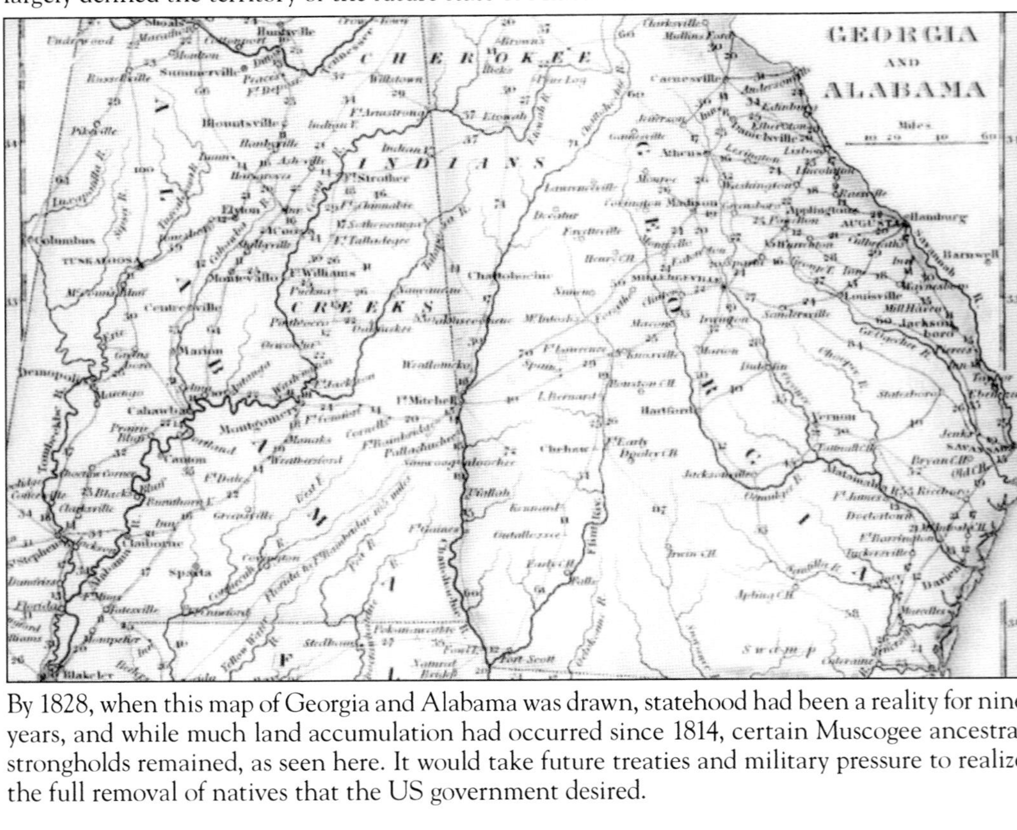

By 1828, when this map of Georgia and Alabama was drawn, statehood had been a reality for nine years, and while much land accumulation had occurred since 1814, certain Muscogee ancestral strongholds remained, as seen here. It would take future treaties and military pressure to realize the full removal of natives that the US government desired.

Gen. Thomas Simpson Woodward (1794–1859) was a commander of the US militia and cavalry during the Creek Indian wars, often serving under the direct leadership of Gen. Andrew Jackson. He laid out the city of Tuskegee in 1833 when commissioned to form a seat of government in Macon County, and built the first home on the ridge where Tuskegee was established. After the home was partially destroyed by fire, it was rebuilt by William Campbell.

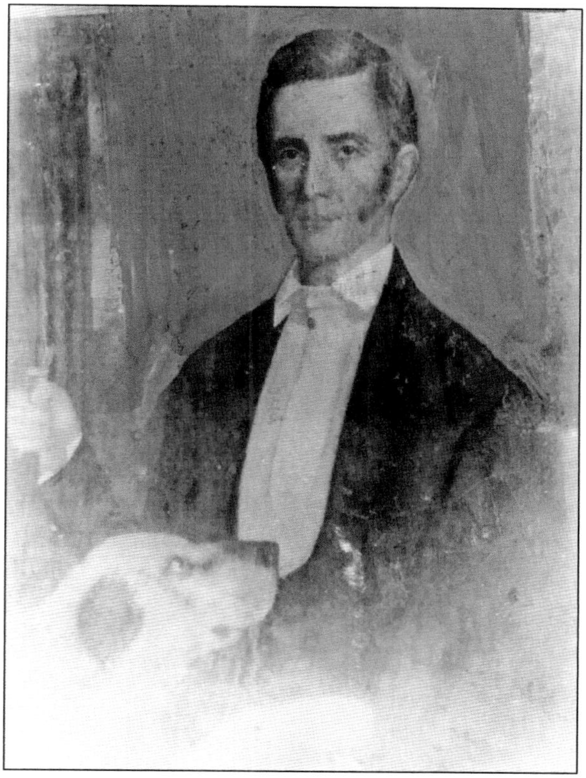

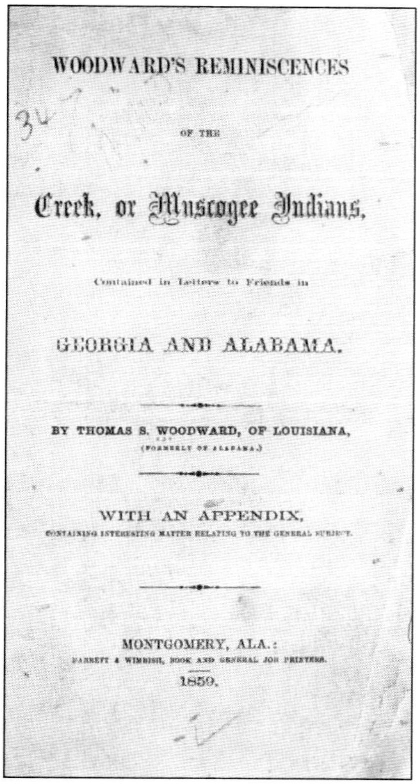

WOODWARD'S REMINISCENCES

OF THE

Creek, or Muscogee Indians,

Contained in Letters to Friends in

GEORGIA AND ALABAMA.

BY THOMAS S. WOODWARD, OF LOUISIANA,

(FORMERLY OF ALABAMA.)

WITH AN APPENDIX,

CONTAINING INTERESTING MATTER RELATING TO THE GENERAL SUBJECT.

MONTGOMERY, ALA.:

BARRETT & WIMBISH, BOOK AND GENERAL JOB PRINTERS.

1859.

In 1859, Woodward wrote a small account of his experiences with Native Americans called *Woodward's Reminiscences of the Creek, Muscogee Indians: Contained in Letters to Friends in Georgia and Alabama.* Woodward wrote from firsthand experiences, having grown up on the frontier among Indians and then having fought against Indian forces during the Creek wars.

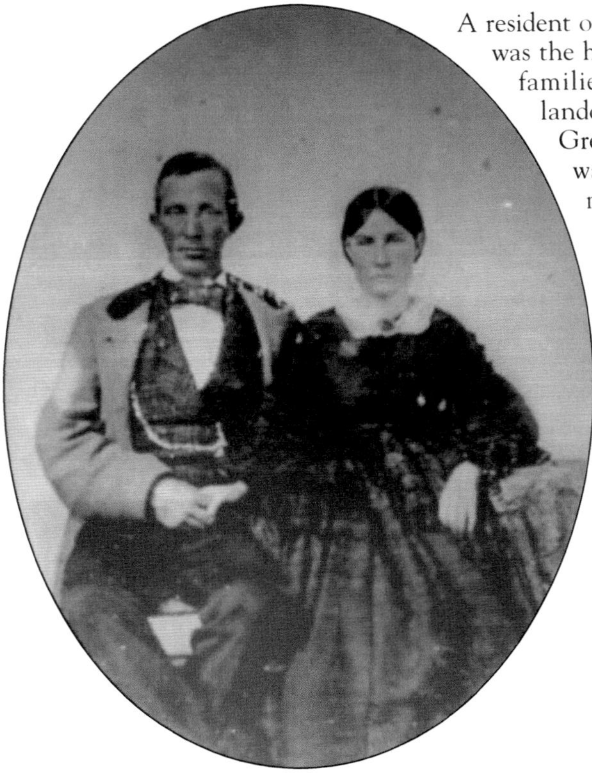

A resident of Tuskegee by 1850, William Varner Sr. was the head of one of the oldest and wealthiest families in Macon County. A planter and landowner, he built the historic plantation Grey Columns. His son Robert R. Varner was a building contractor, farmer, and merchant who owned most of the land surrounding Tuskegee Institute's original 100-acre campus. He gave Booker T. Washington brickworks and sold the institute and employees nearby land for buildings and homes. Robert's son William Varner Jr. served as the mayor of Tuskegee, as a state representative, and as a probate judge. (Courtesy of the Alabama Department of Archives and History.)

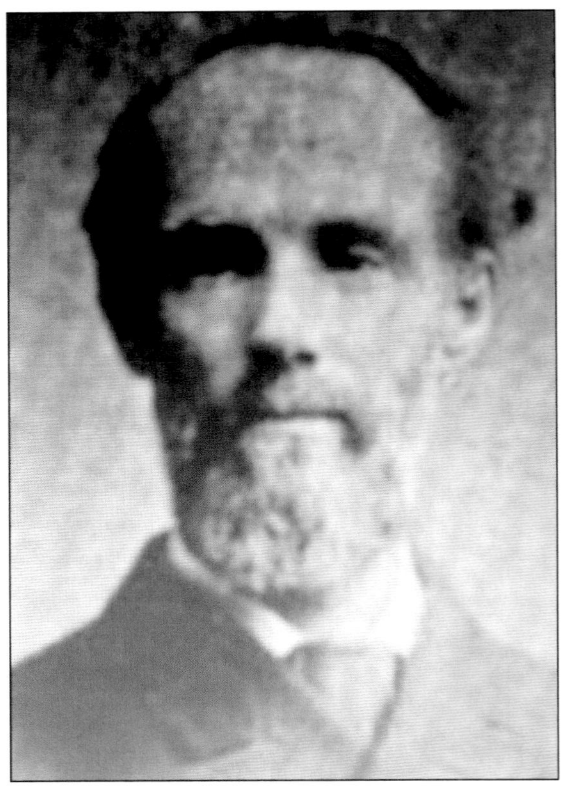

Col. James Edward Cobb, born in 1835, was a practicing lawyer when he joined the Confederate army in 1861. Captured and held at Gettysburg until the end of the war, he settled in Tuskegee, where he practiced law and became a circuit judge (1874–1886) and then a US congressman (1887–1895).

Charles Winston Thompson (1860–1904) was the son of William P. Thompson, the mayor of Tuskegee and the sheriff of Macon County. Charles worked for his father and sold his business when his father died to open the Bank of Tuskegee. He was the superintendent of education for Macon County from 1886 to 1888 and was appointed lieutenant governor by Gov. Joseph F. Johnston. Thompson was then elected to Congress twice, dying during his second term.

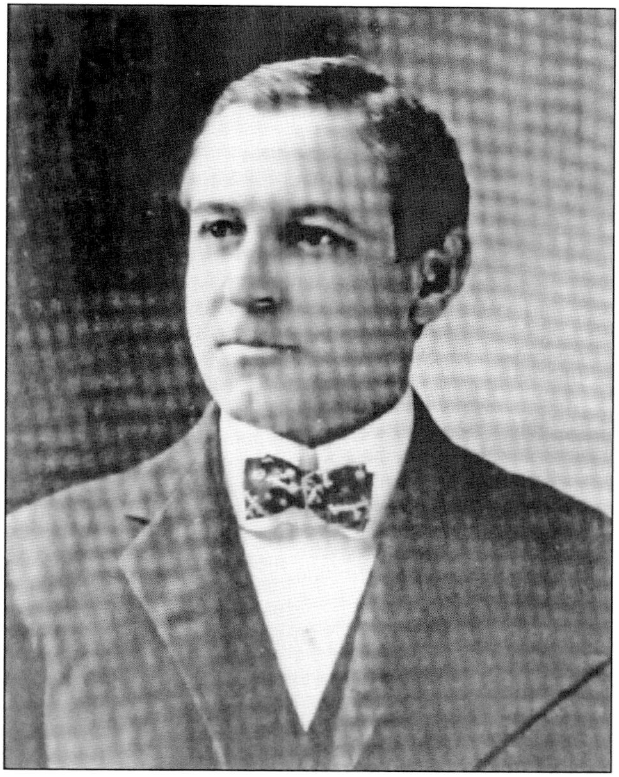

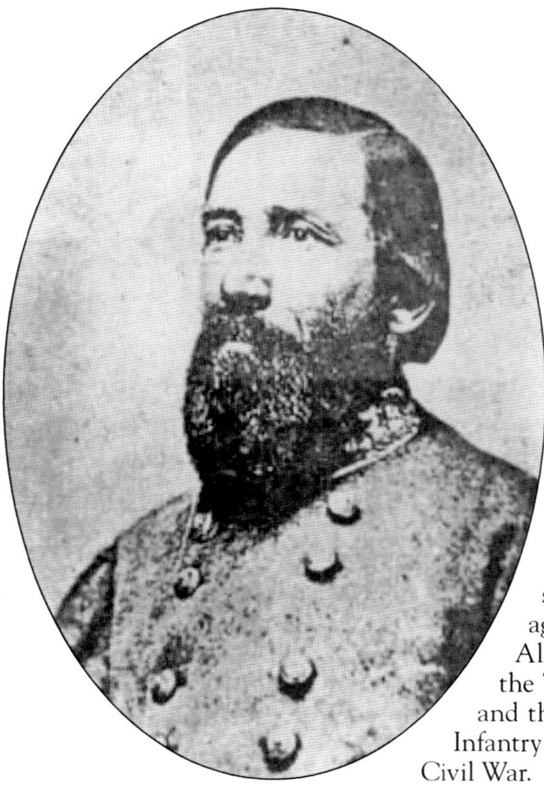

Gen. Cullen Battle was a local lawyer who set up a practice in Tuskegee in 1852 at the age of 23 but spent most of his life in politics. Also a planter, he became the commander of the Tuskegee Light Infantry of the Confederacy and then lieutenant colonel of the 3rd Alabama Infantry Regiment. He later became a colonel in the Civil War.

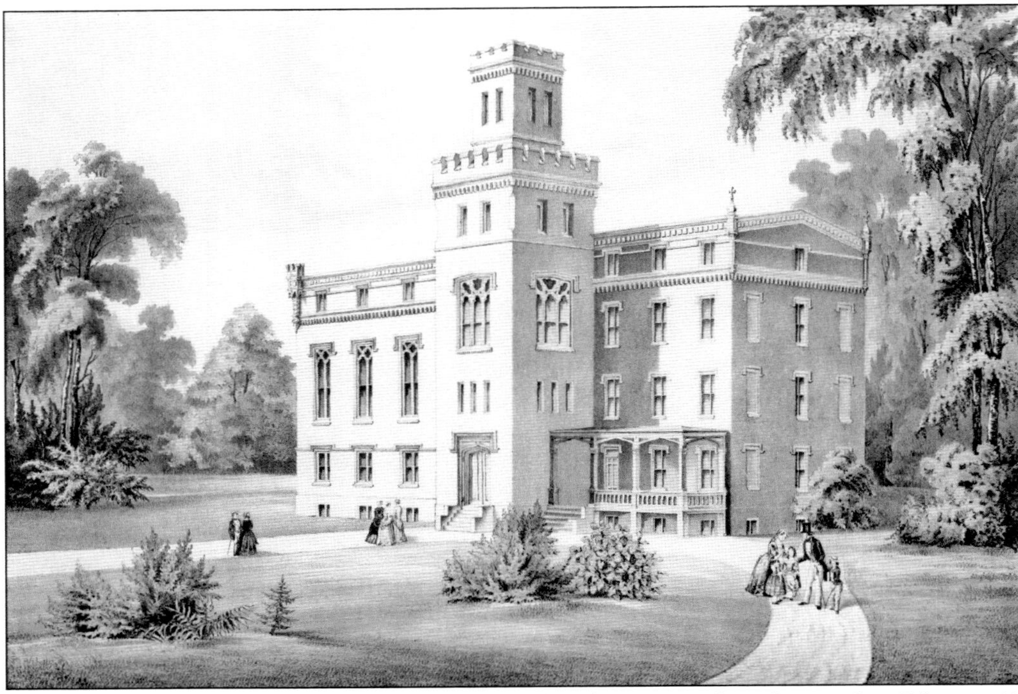

Tuskegee Female College was chartered by the state legislature in 1854 and opened on February 11, 1856. Rev. A.A. Lipscomb was the president until 1859, around the time Peter S. Du Val created this illustration. The name was changed to Alabama Conference Female College in 1872 when the Methodist Church purchased the property. In 1909, the college relocated to Montgomery and became the Women's College of Alabama. Since 1935, it has been known as Huntingdon College. (Courtesy of the Library of Congress.)

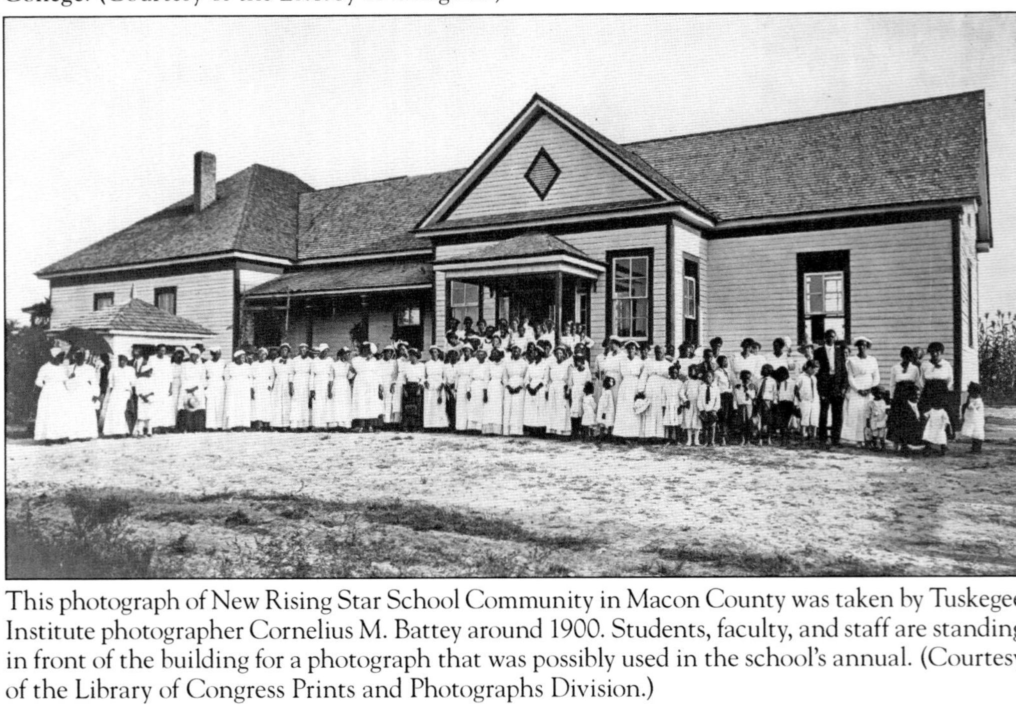

This photograph of New Rising Star School Community in Macon County was taken by Tuskegee Institute photographer Cornelius M. Battey around 1900. Students, faculty, and staff are standing in front of the building for a photograph that was possibly used in the school's annual. (Courtesy of the Library of Congress Prints and Photographs Division.)

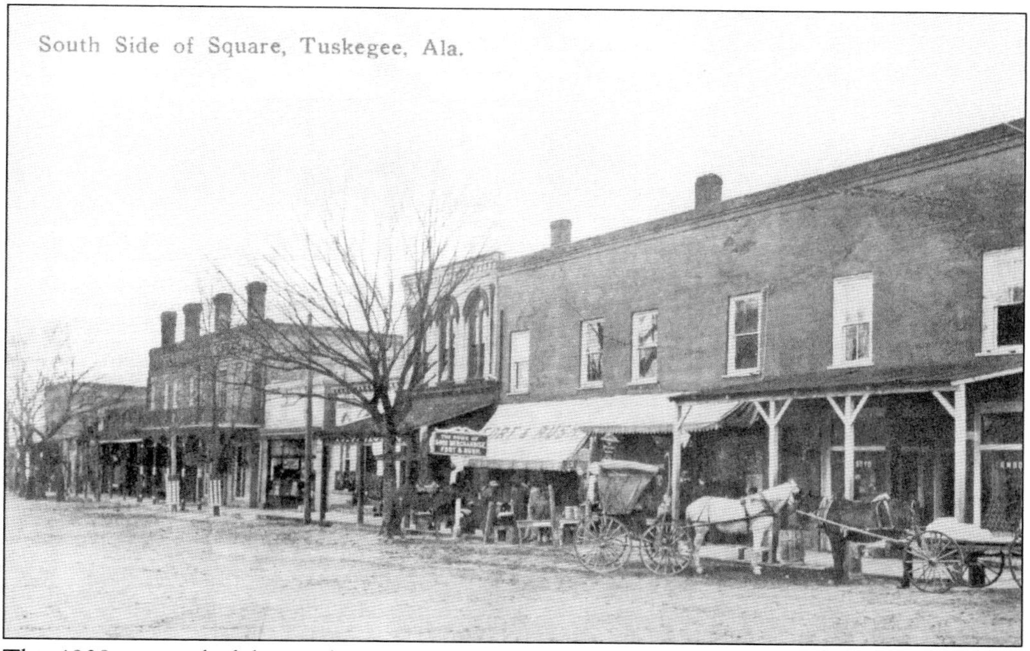

This 1908 postcard of the south side of the square in downtown Tuskegee reveals the architectural simplicity that defined the business district around 1900. Low, unadorned shops lined the streets, which converged in the direction of the courthouse fronting the town square. The square included a grassy yard of azaleas and a statue of an armed Confederate soldier looking northward.

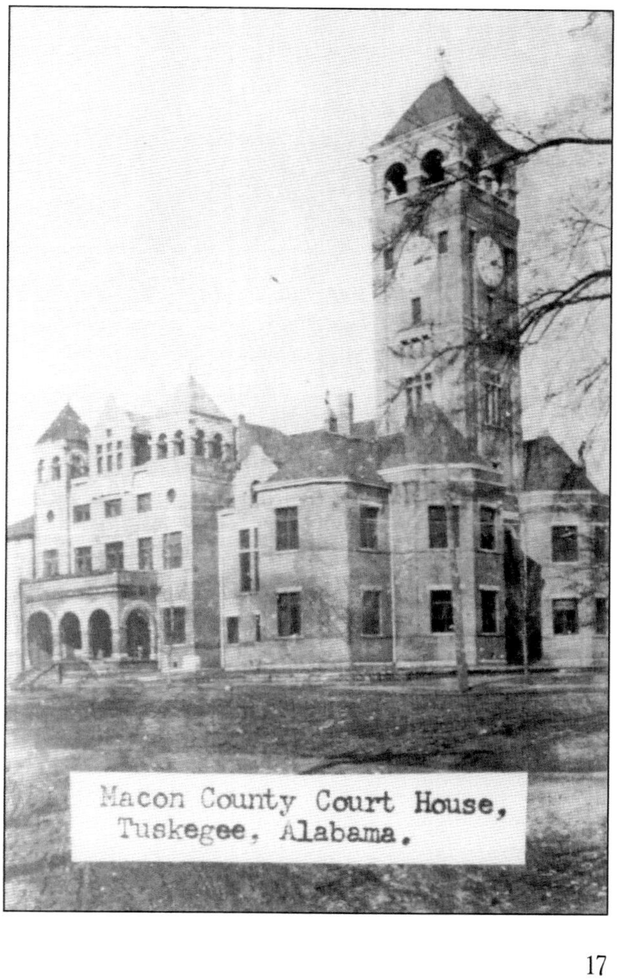

This postcard of downtown Tuskegee shows the Macon County Courthouse with its Victorian design, somewhat fortress-like elements, and yellow brick. The county was named for Sen. Nathaniel Macon and established on December 18, 1832, from land acquired after the final removal of Creek Indians on March 24, 1832. Its current boundaries were laid out in 1866.

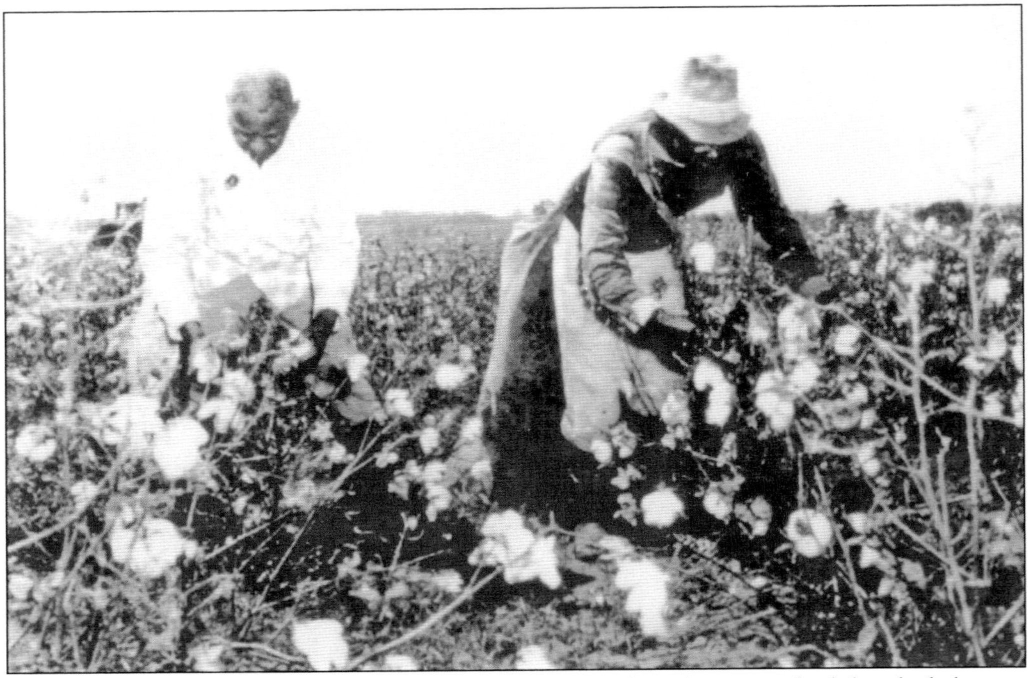

Macon County was developed for cotton plantation agriculture because it had the ideal climate, soil, and terrain for cotton. Cotton remained an important product in the county even after emancipation. This 1939 photograph, captioned "Cotton Pickers," was taken by Prentice Herman Polk of two unidentified tenant farmers. (Courtesy of the estate of P.H. Polk.)

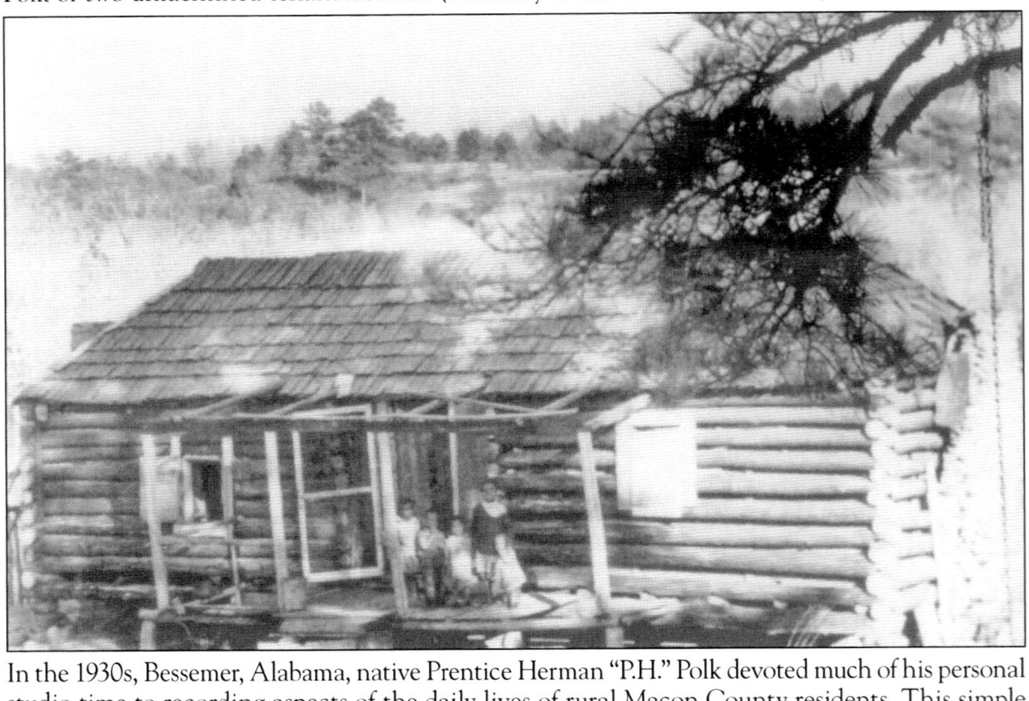

In the 1930s, Bessemer, Alabama, native Prentice Herman "P.H." Polk devoted much of his personal studio time to recording aspects of the daily lives of rural Macon County residents. This simple image of a cabin with figures is one of the 1932 photographs that were a part of his photo essay. (Courtesy of the estate of P.H. Polk.)

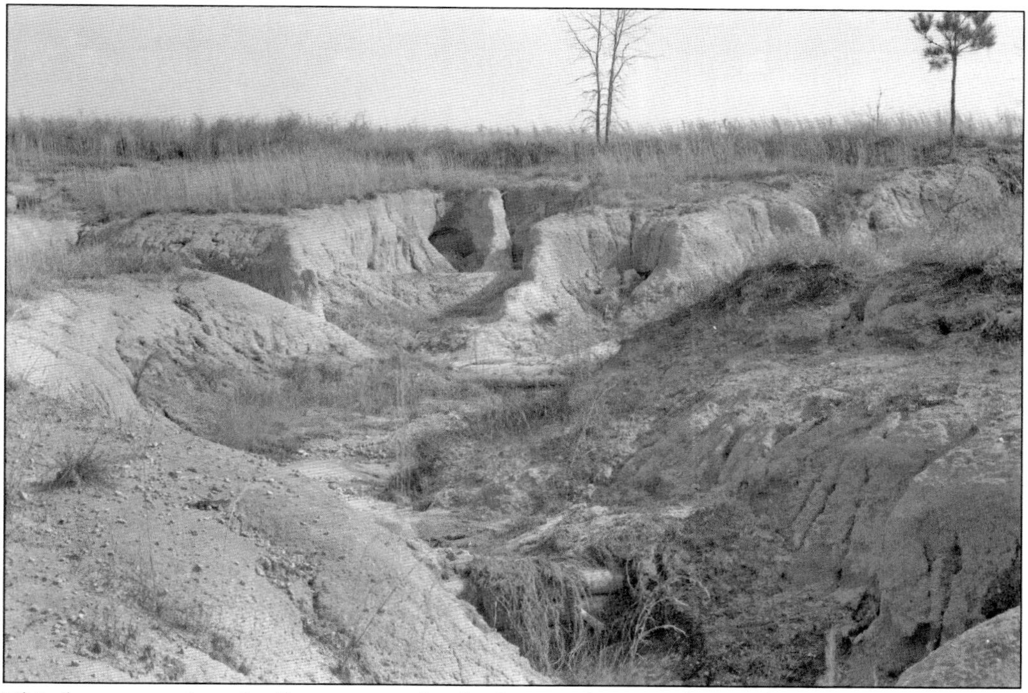

This documentation of gully erosion, taken by famous photographer Arthur Rothstein in 1937, is identified as "Gully Erosion by check dam, Tuskegee Project." Erosion was just one of numerous examples of severe damage to county land in the 1930s. (Courtesy of the Library of Congress Prints and Photographs Division.)

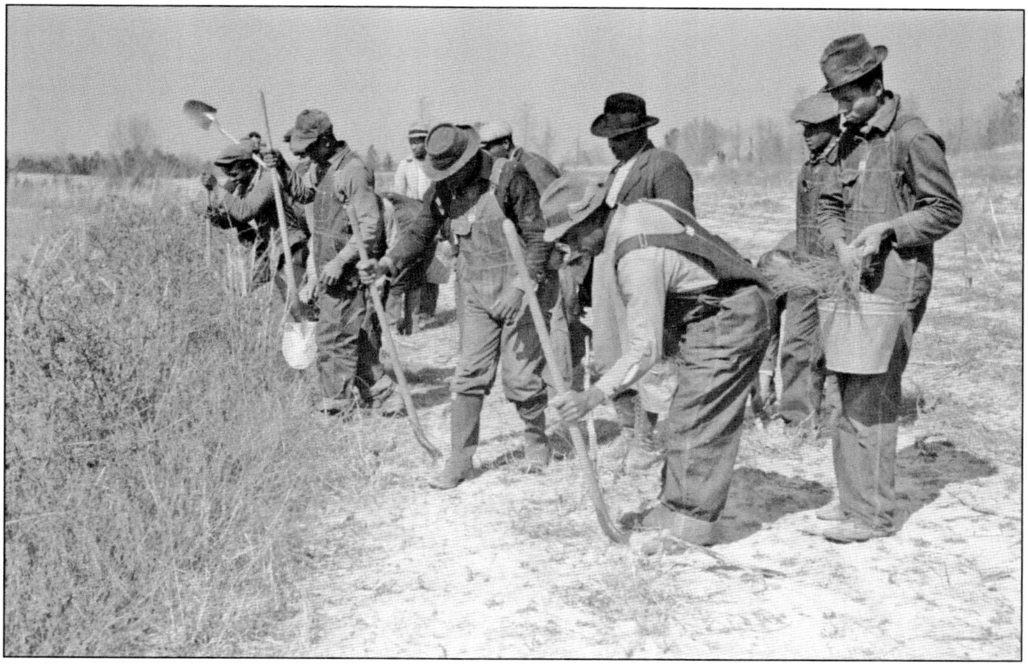

The Tuskegee Project, as one of its proactive measures, had labor crews like this one plant slash pine. The trees are fast growers and, being indigenous to the Southeast, can endure extreme humidity and moisture. (Courtesy of the Library of Congress Prints and Photographs Division.)

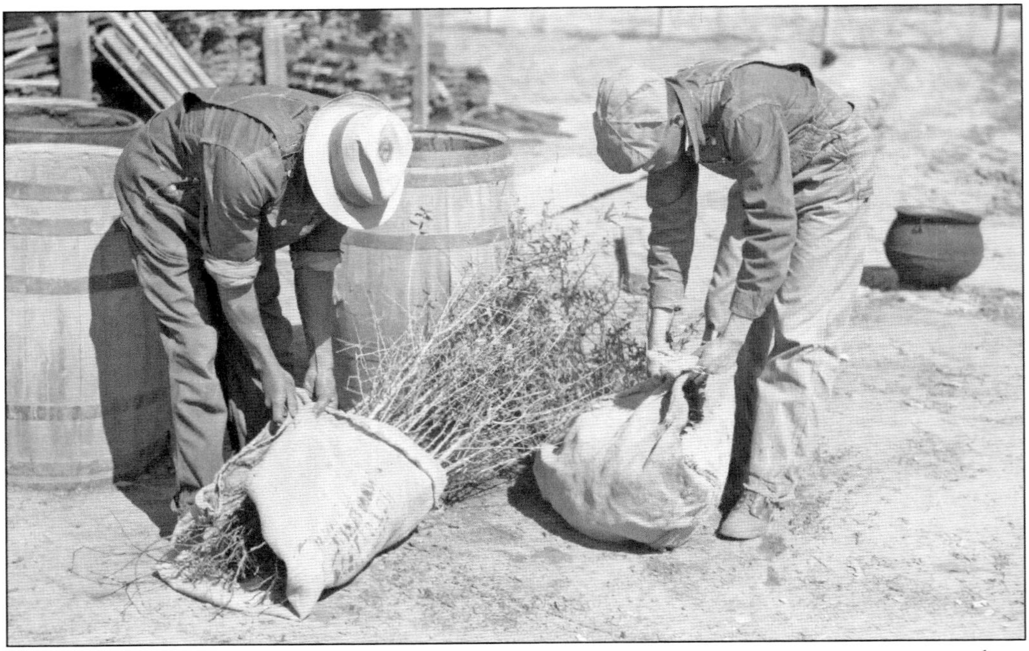

As this photograph indicates, saplings and small trees were introduced to jump-start growth in the more aggressive phase of reforestation in the damaged areas. The Tuskegee Project provided employment for some of the poorest in Macon County in a depressed economy and created a temporary interaction between scientists and farmers. (Courtesy of the Library of Congress Prints and Photographs Division.)

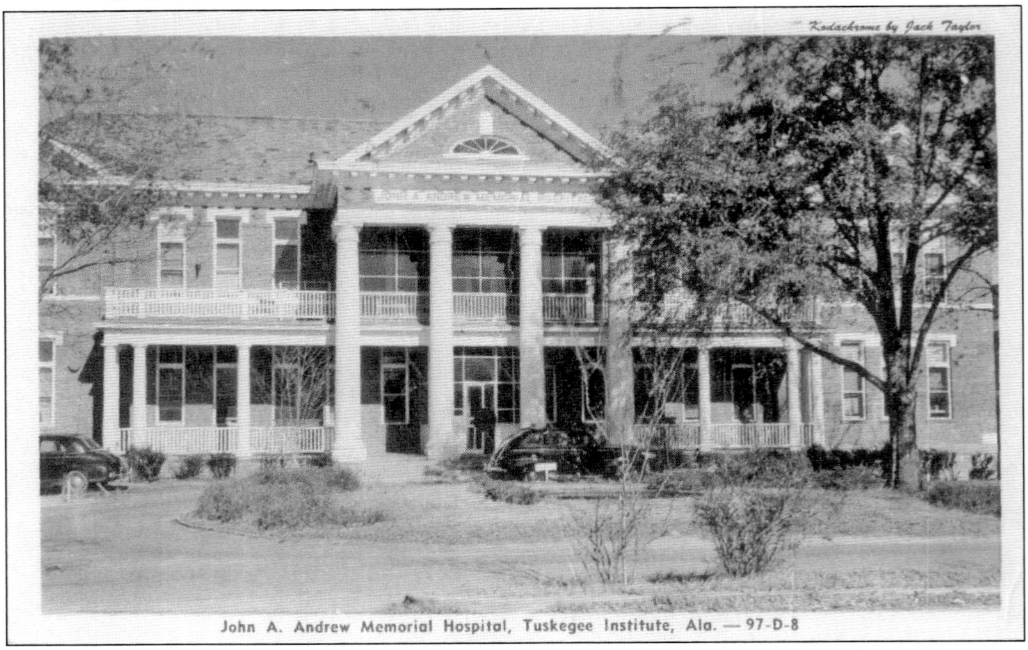

This is a postcard of the John A. Andrews Memorial Hospital, dedicated on February 21, 1913. The hospital was the gift of Elizabeth A. Mason of Boston in memory of her grandfather, the governor of Massachusetts during the Civil War. After additions in 1930 and 1946, the hospital contained 165 beds. The Infantile Paralysis Unit annex opened in 1941.

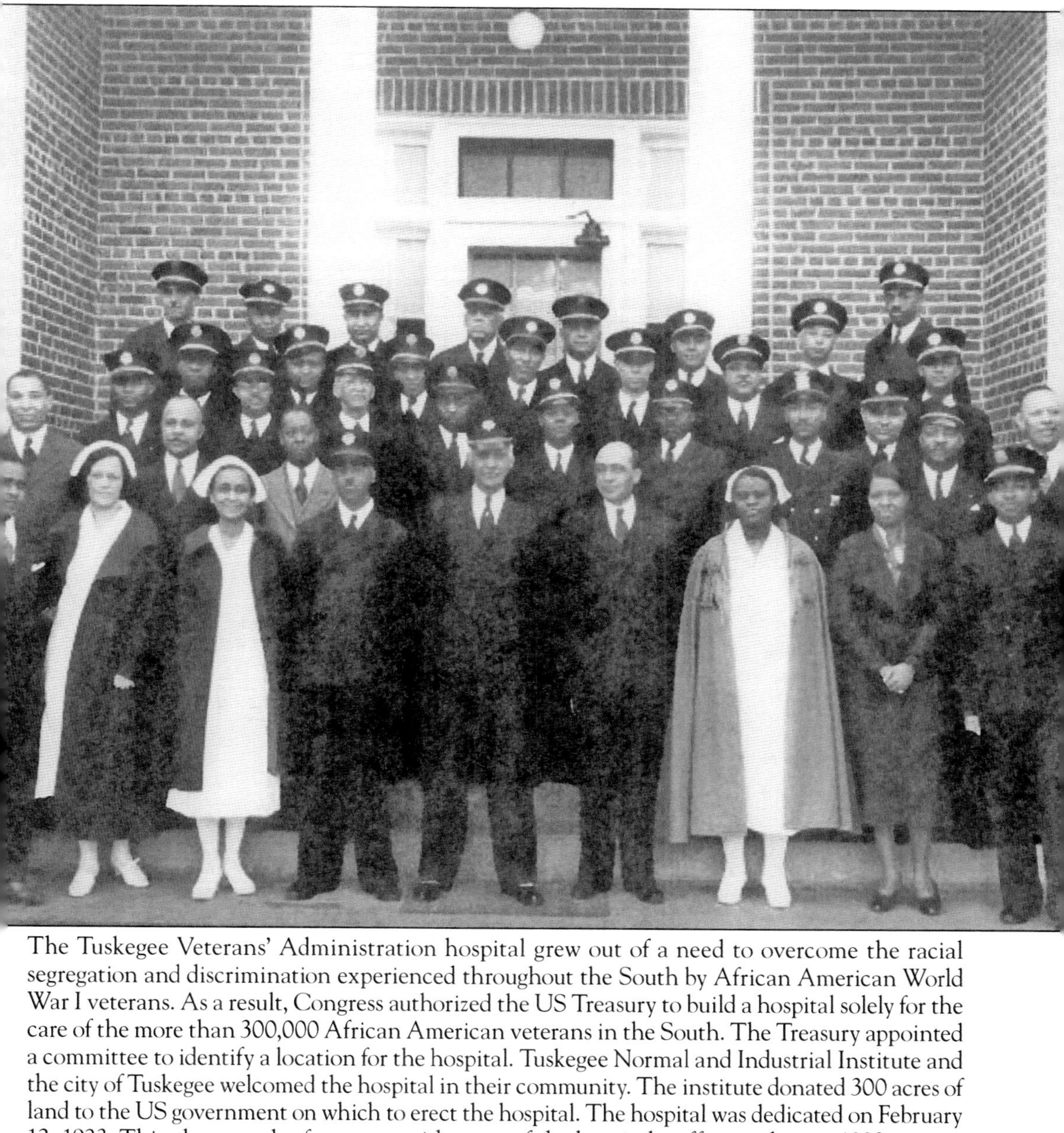

The Tuskegee Veterans' Administration hospital grew out of a need to overcome the racial segregation and discrimination experienced throughout the South by African American World War I veterans. As a result, Congress authorized the US Treasury to build a hospital solely for the care of the more than 300,000 African American veterans in the South. The Treasury appointed a committee to identify a location for the hospital. Tuskegee Normal and Industrial Institute and the city of Tuskegee welcomed the hospital in their community. The institute donated 300 acres of land to the US government on which to erect the hospital. The hospital was dedicated on February 12, 1923. This photograph of veterans with some of the hospital staff was taken in 1923.

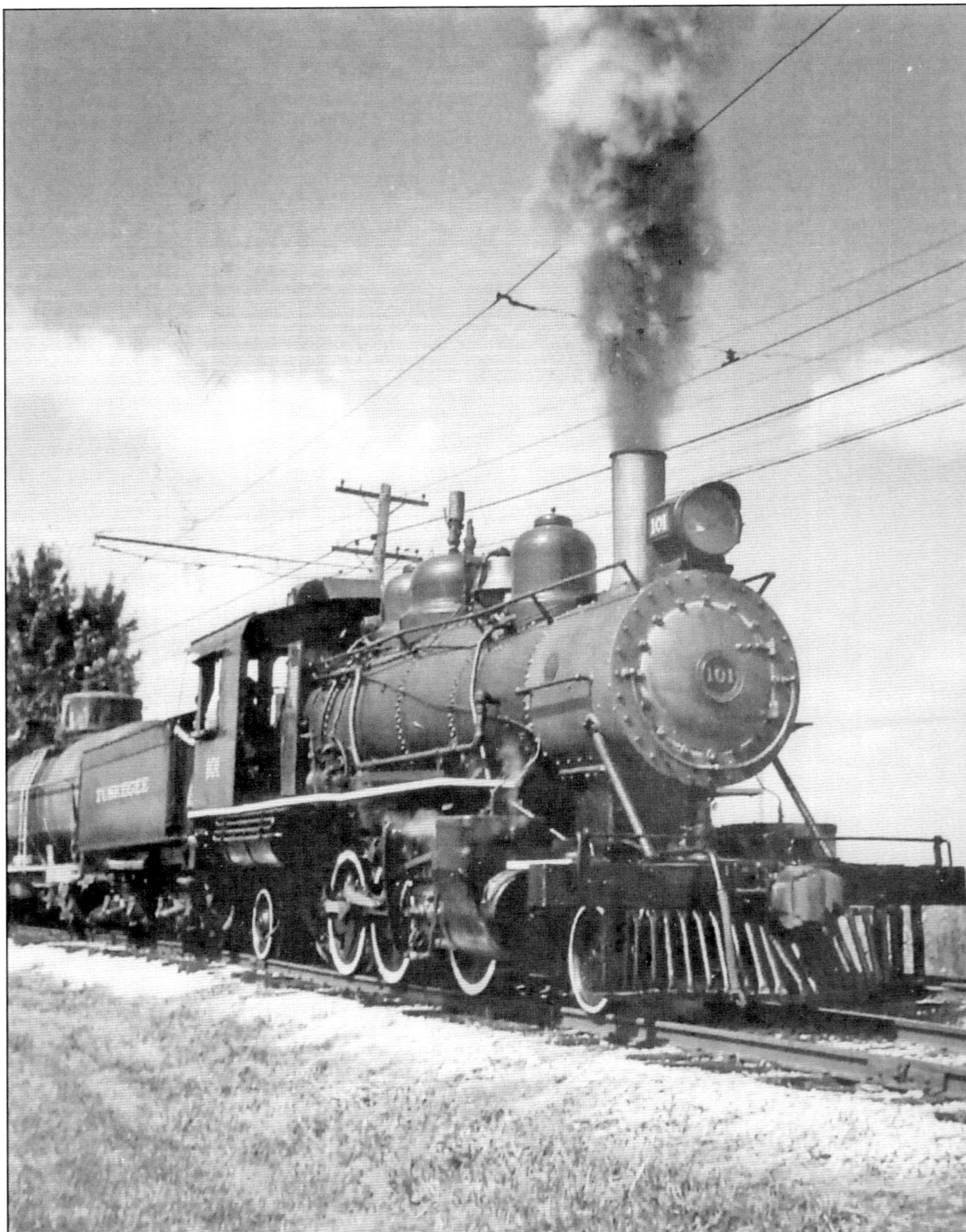

The Tuskegee Railroad Company was organized under the name of E.T. Varner & Co., with George W. Campbell, who conceived it, remaining a principal in partnership with president Edward T. Varner, Mrs. Lou V. Alexander, and general manager William H. Wright. The line ran nearly six miles from Tuskegee to Chehaw on the Western Railway of the Alabama. Organized in February 1860, it was reorganized in April 1870 after a public sale. Operations were suspended during the Civil War because the rolling stock (all vehicles including locomotives, rail cars, coaches, and passenger cars) was sold in 1863. The conclusion of the war brought the rapid return of the railroad and the profits it generated.

Two

Tuskegee Houses

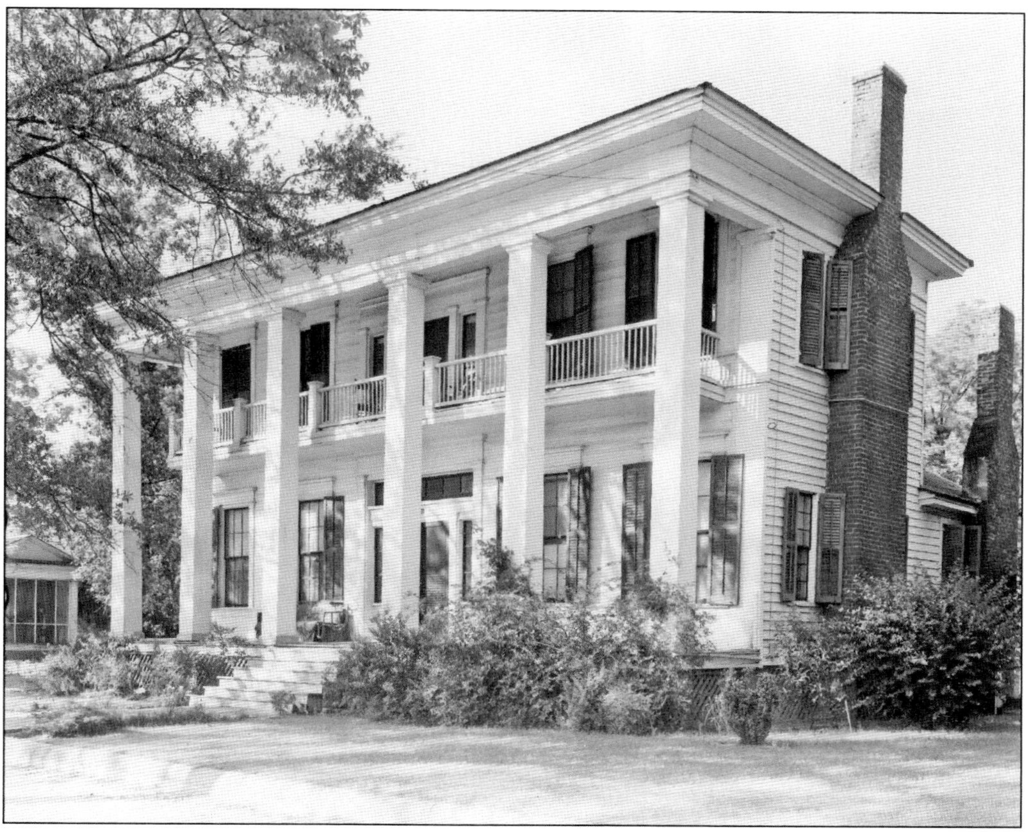

Tuskegee was a town situated on a heavily forested ridge with rows of Greek Revival houses lining its long, shaded streets. Like the Wheat House, seen here in the 1930s, the stately houses were designed in sharp contrast to the architectural simplicity that defined the buildings downtown. (Courtesy of the Library of Congress Historic American Buildings Survey.)

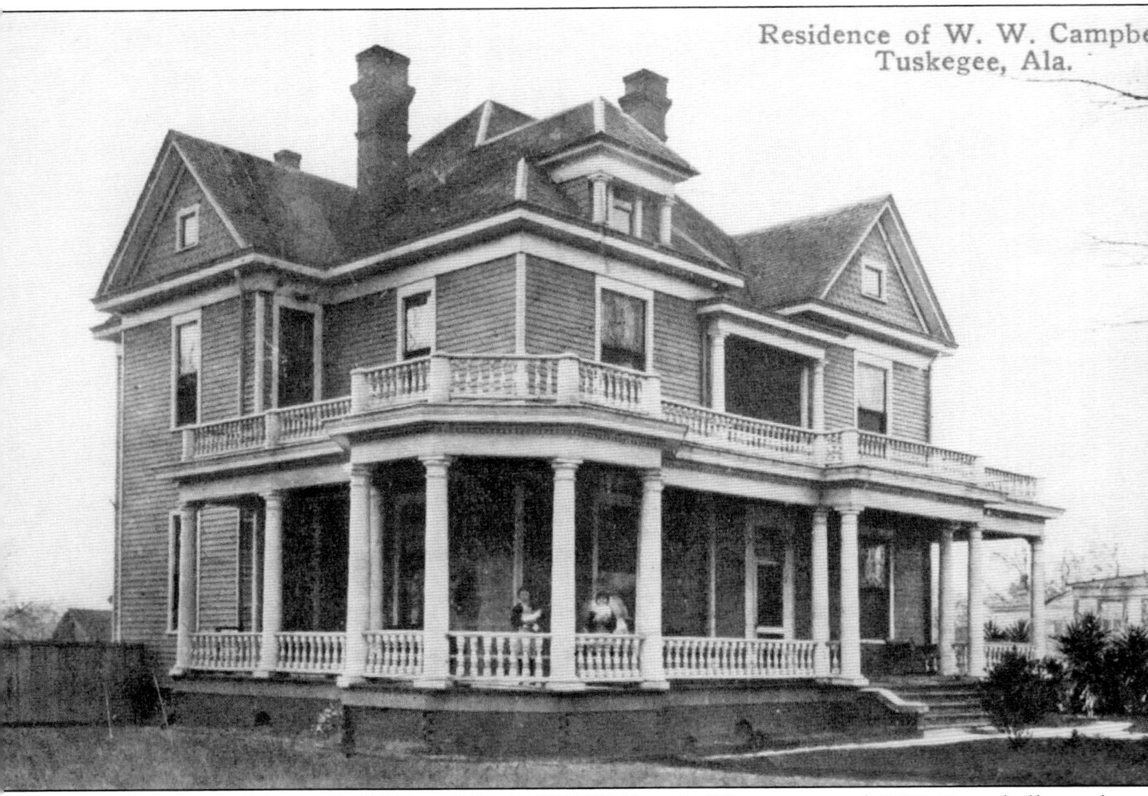

This postcard shows the William Wright "W.W." Campbell house around 1900. Campbell was the son of prominent merchant George Washington Campbell and Eliza Jane Wright Campbell. W.W. Campbell was successful in his own right but also continued his father's legacy in the mercantile business and as a supporter of Tuskegee Normal and Industrial Institute. Also like his father, he served as president of the board of trustees at the institute, leading the board's strong backing of Pres. Robert Moton's efforts to have the veterans' hospital staffed by African Americans.

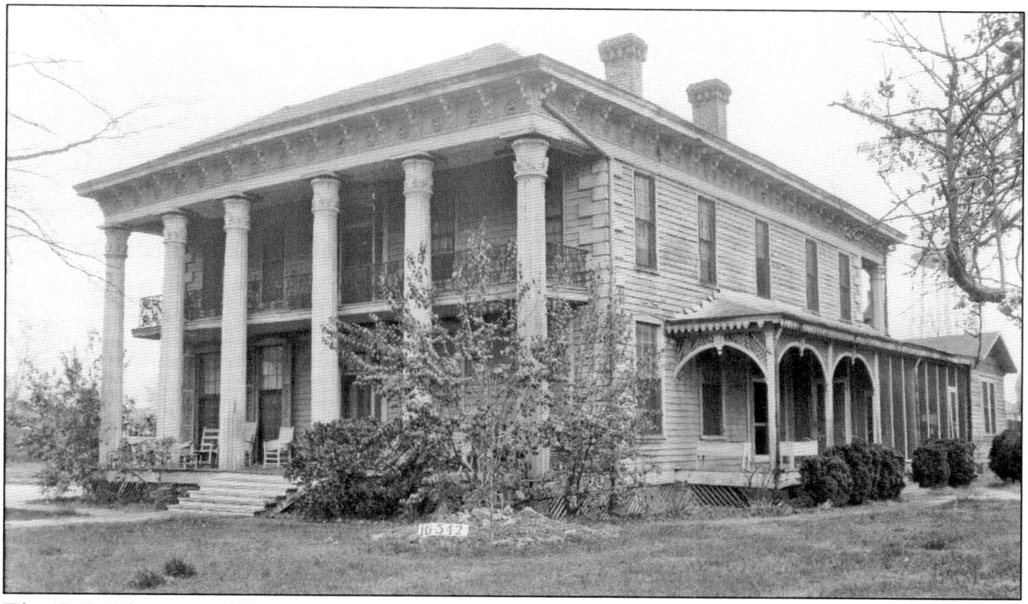

The G.C. Thompson House, at 302 E. Main Street, was built around 1850 by Peter Coffee Harris, who lived there for three years. Through the years, the house was owned by Judge Thomas S. Tate, M.B. Swanson, W.P. Thompson, Congressman Charles W. Thompson, and G. Cleveland Thompson. When Pres. William McKinley visited Tuskegee Institute in 1898, Booker T. Washington arranged for him to reside at Congressman Thompson's home. On December 16, 1898, President McKinley addressed the citizens of Tuskegee from Thompson's veranda. (Courtesy of the Library of Congress Historic American Buildings Survey.)

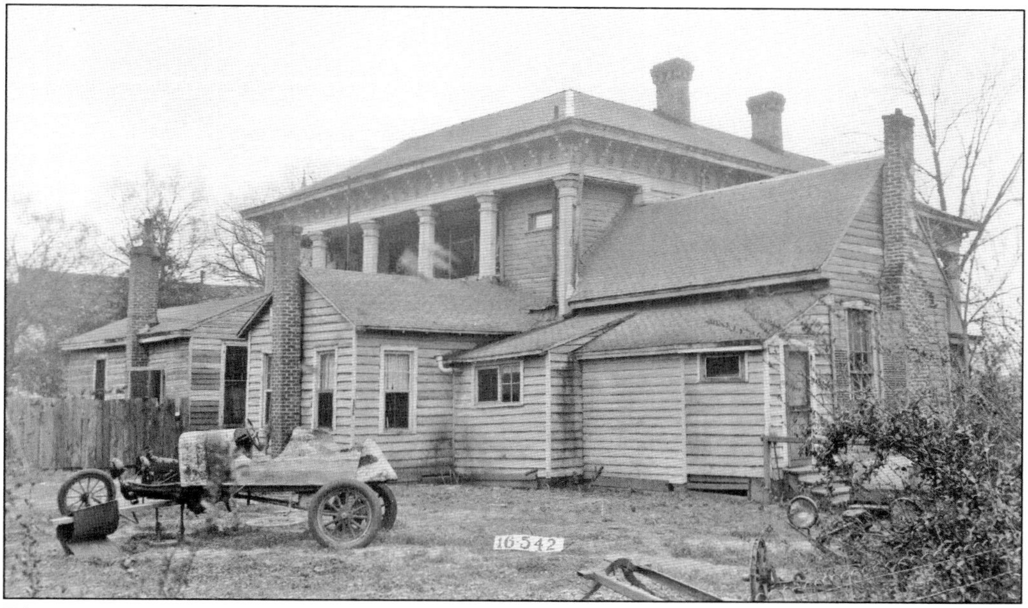

This rear view of the Thompson house was taken in 1935. A few of the distinguishing elements in the design of the house are its two-story wooden structure, the soft slants in its rear roofs, and its round columns, which are fluted with carved wooden capitals modeled after those at Edfu, Egypt, and Pergamon, Asia Minor. (Courtesy of the Library of Congress Historic American Buildings Survey.)

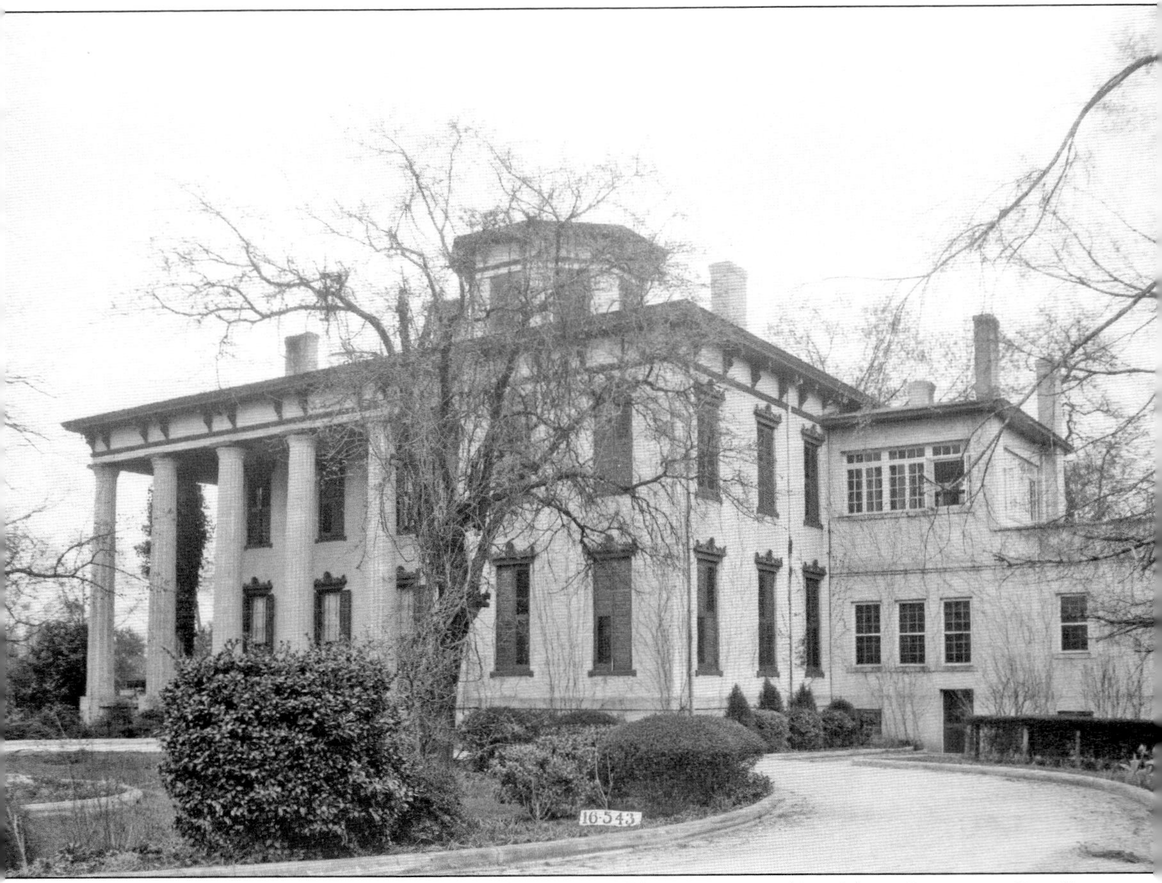

Grey Columns, the Varner-Alexander house on Old Montgomery Road (now Interstate Road), was considered the town's architectural masterpiece. Constructed from 1854 to 1857 by pioneer settler William Varner Sr., who arrived in 1850, the mansion's design replicated the Greek Parthenon, emphasizing the preferred architectural style of the more elaborate homes in the county. Grey Columns, the focal point of one of Varner's plantations, avoided destruction during a Civil War raid when the lead Union commander recognized Varner as a classmate from Harvard and ordered troops off the grounds. The two spent the remainder of the afternoon renewing their acquaintance. The house is also associated with E.R. Alexander. This photograph of Grey Columns was taken on March 8, 1935. (Courtesy of the Library of Congress Prints and Photographs Division.)

In the 1920s, extensive alterations were made to Grey Columns following a fire, including a new kitchen wing to the rear and bathrooms adjacent to the second-floor front stair hall and south bedroom. In the 1950s, bathrooms were restored in the west parlor closets and the west bedroom. In 1974, the National Park Service acquired Grey Columns as part of the Tuskegee Institute National Historic Site. (Courtesy of the Library of Congress Historic American Buildings Survey.)

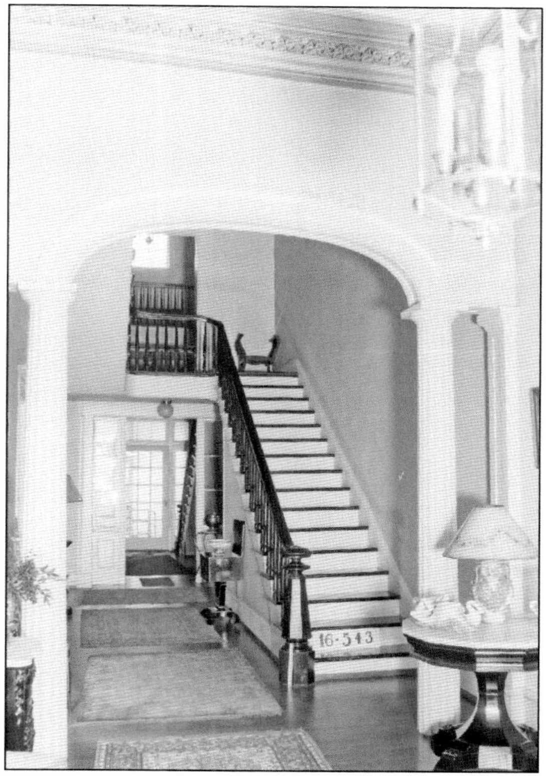

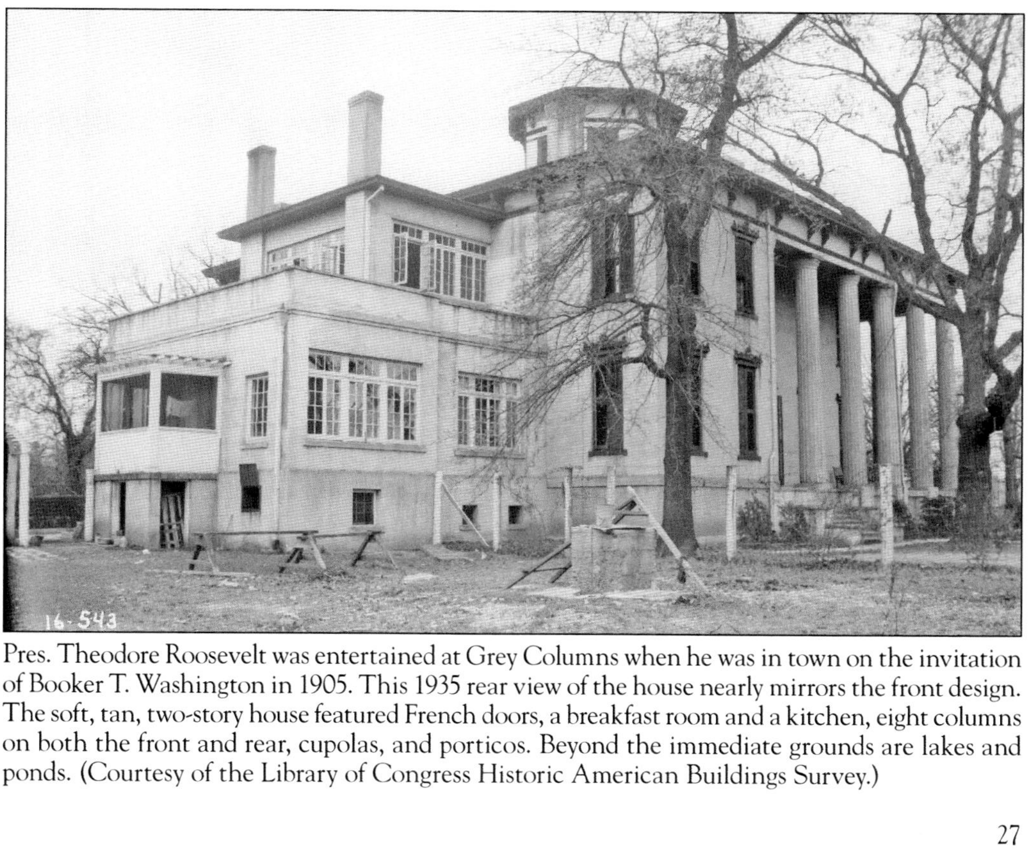

Pres. Theodore Roosevelt was entertained at Grey Columns when he was in town on the invitation of Booker T. Washington in 1905. This 1935 rear view of the house nearly mirrors the front design. The soft, tan, two-story house featured French doors, a breakfast room and a kitchen, eight columns on both the front and rear, cupolas, and porticos. Beyond the immediate grounds are lakes and ponds. (Courtesy of the Library of Congress Historic American Buildings Survey.)

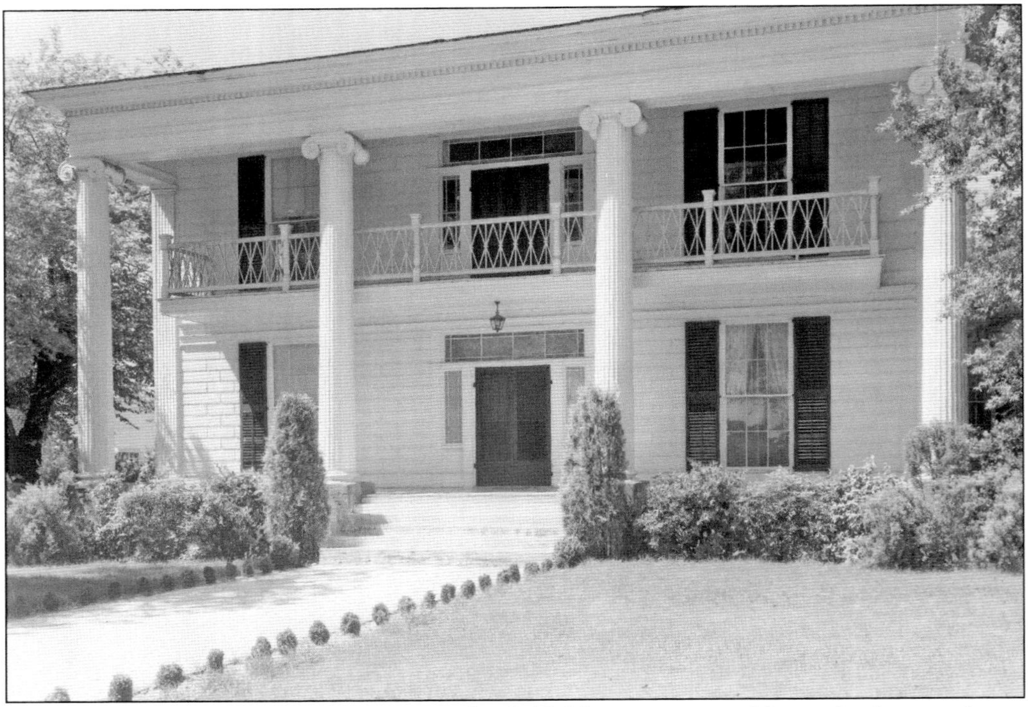

Built around 1855 at 504 East Main Street, the Cobb House was named for its third owner, James Edward Cobb. It was originally designed by architect James Daniel for William Foster. William Edmunds, the second owner, sold it to Cobb in 1874. Upon his death in 1903, ownership transferred to his grandson Edward C. Laslie. Daniel incorporated Ionic features, including the four widely spaced columns across the front portico. (Courtesy of the Library of Congress Historic American Buildings Survey.)

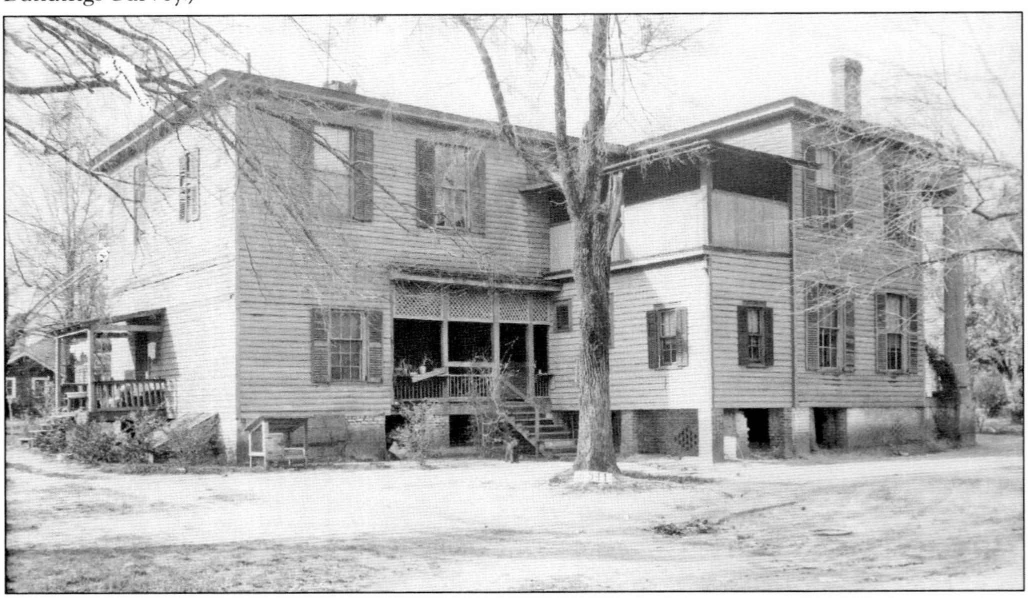

This rear view of the Cobb House in 1935 reveals features that are less ornate that the front, with its four large columns and their ornate tops. The roof is relatively flat, and the side and back entrances are easily visible. (Courtesy of the Library of Congress Historic American Buildings Survey.)

The Alexander Hurt Whatley house, also known as the judge William H. Hurt house, was built in 1845. It sits very far off the road two miles east of Tuskegee on Old Columbus Highway. The plantation house, seen here in 1935, is a two-story masonry construction and features six large, round masonry columns with wooden balustrades between them. (Courtesy of the Library of Congress Historic American Buildings Survey.)

This octagonal structure in the rear of the house was Hurt's office. Hurt (1846–c. 1900) joined Company C of the 15th Alabama Infantry at age 15 in 1861, fighting in Winchester, Port Republic, Richmond, Cross Keys, Manassas, Harper's Ferry, Sharpsburg, Fredericksburg, and Gettysburg. He was captured on July 2, 1863, and held in Fort Delaware until June 1865. Upon his return, he became the Macon County tax collector and then a probate judge. (Courtesy of the Library of Congress Historic American Buildings Survey.)

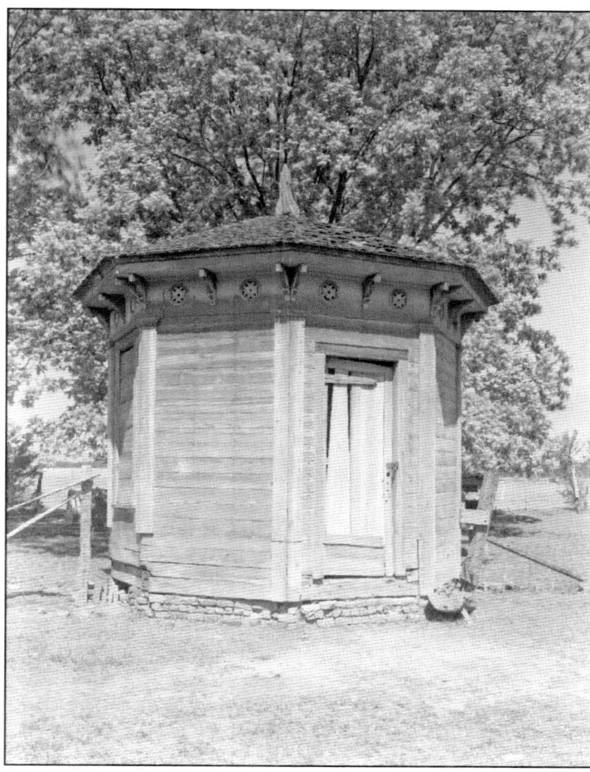

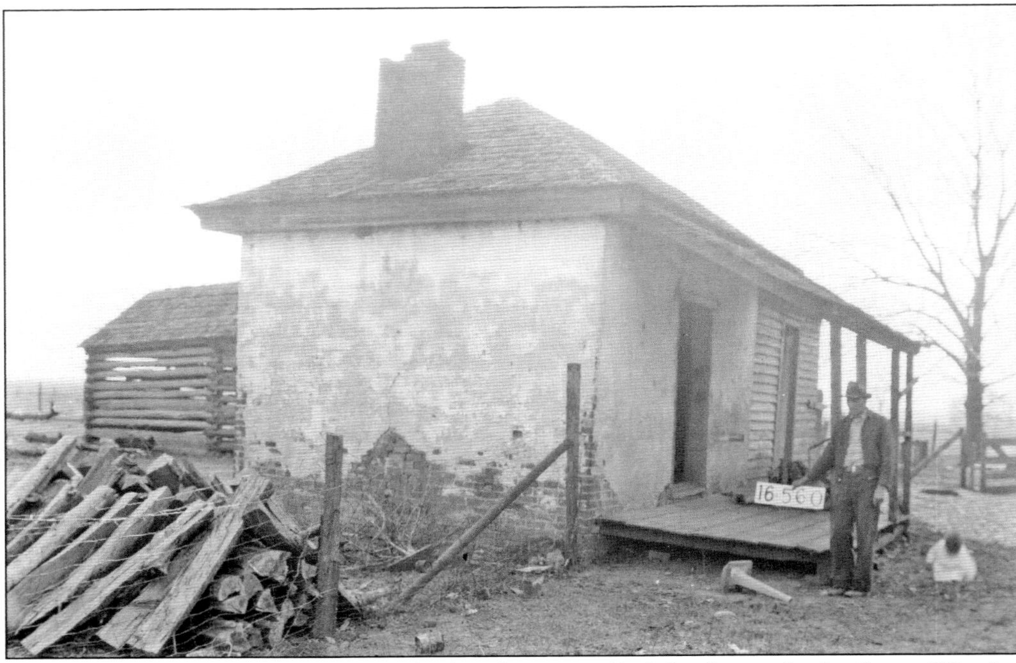

This is a former slave house on the Whatley plantation. Built by slaves of judge Lewis Whatley, interior repairs were done in 1889 when the plantation was owned by Judge William H. Hurt. The walls are 18 inches thick and comprised of bricks made by slaves. (Courtesy of the Library of Congress Historic American Buildings Survey.)

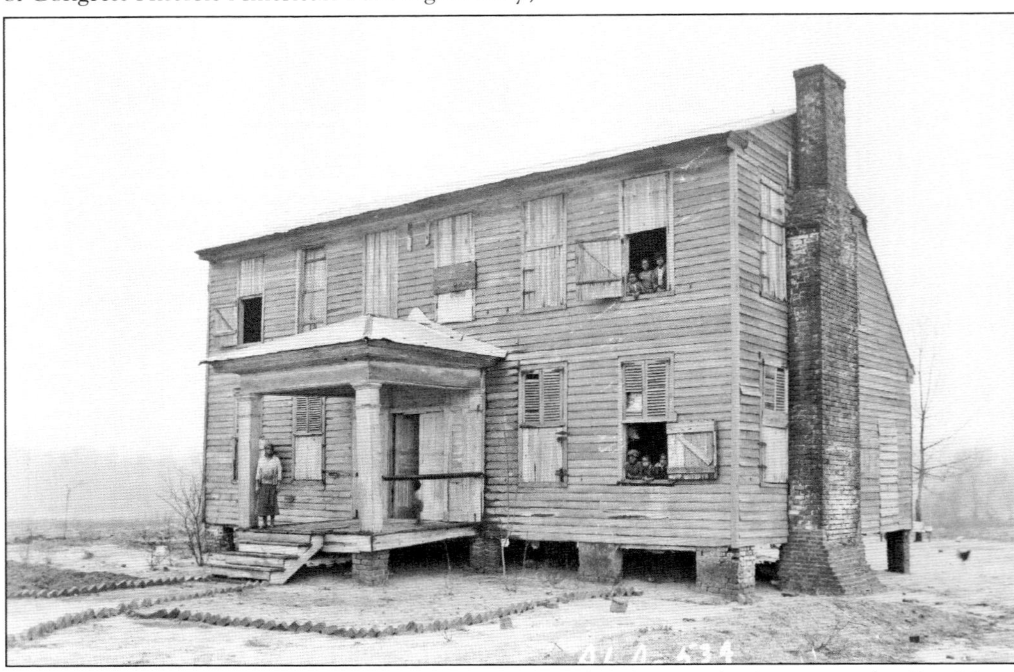

The Frame plantation house, built on Route 26 around 1850, was also known as the Cox House and Stagecoach Inn when it was used as a tavern. Notable features include the clearly exposed single chimney on one side of the structure, narrow entryways, and an unadorned exterior. (Courtesy of the Library of Congress Historic American Buildings Survey.)

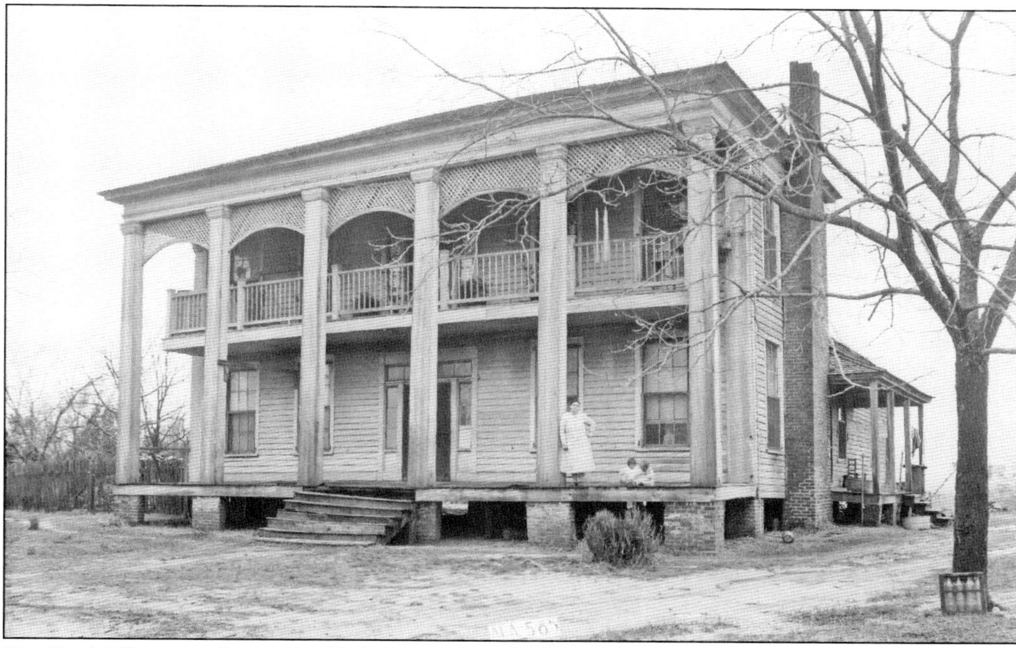

The Rush-Thornton house, on Highway 29, has also been known as the Thornton house, the Rush house, and the Rev. Lewis Flourney Dowdell house. It was built around 1840. Reverend Dowdell (1830–1902) was the pastor of Seale United Methodist Church in 1885. He was born in Harris County, Georgia, and settled in Alabama in the 1840s. He married Arcadia Esther Mitchell of Lafayette, Alabama, in 1852. The photograph above was taken in 1939 by Frances Benjamin Johnston. The unidentified woman standing on the front porch gives a sense of the height of each floor. Both the front and rear (below) views provide some indication of the expanse of the spacious home. The photograph below was taken in March 1935. (Both courtesy of the Library of Congress Historic American Buildings Survey.)

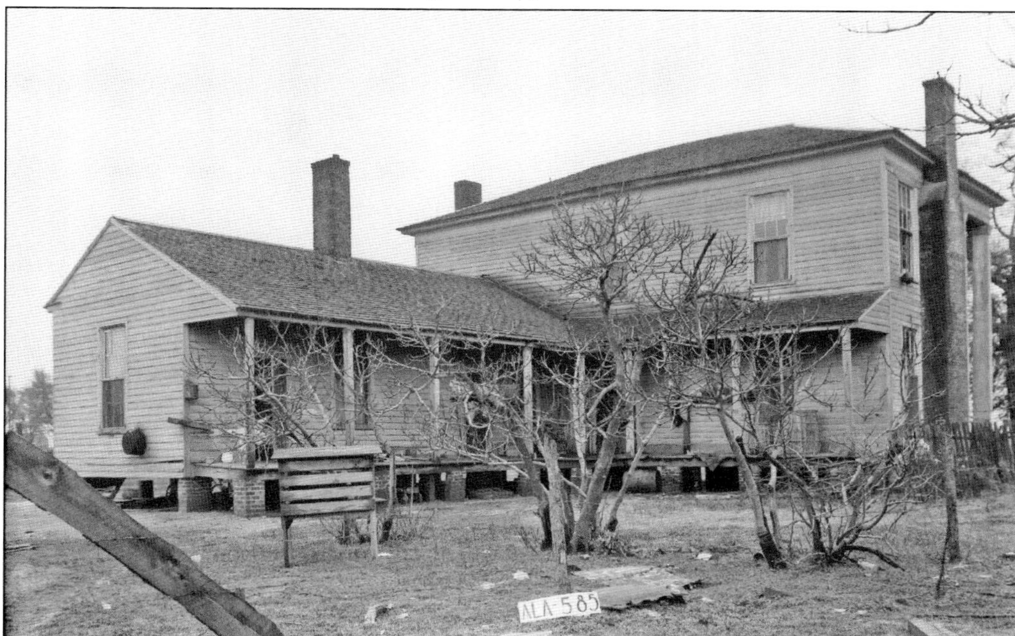

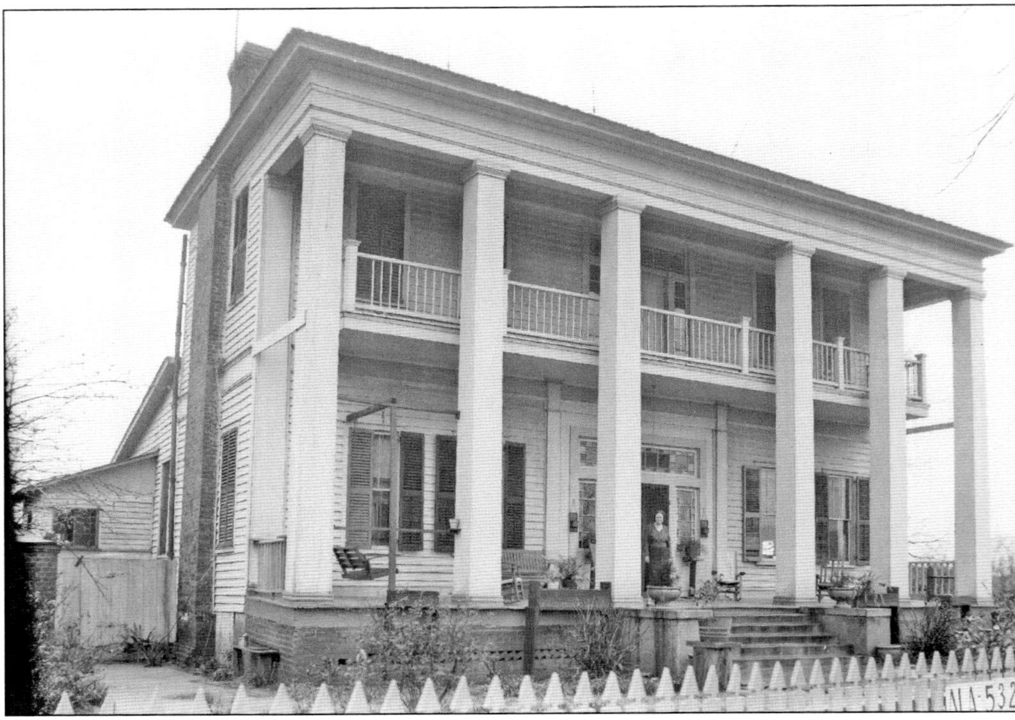

The G.Y. Lamar house, also known as the Johnston-Abercombie-Lamar house and the Dr. J.M. Vason house, was built on Routes 29 and 15. These two photographs of the front and back of the house were taken in 1933. (Both courtesy of the Library of Congress Historic American Buildings Survey.)

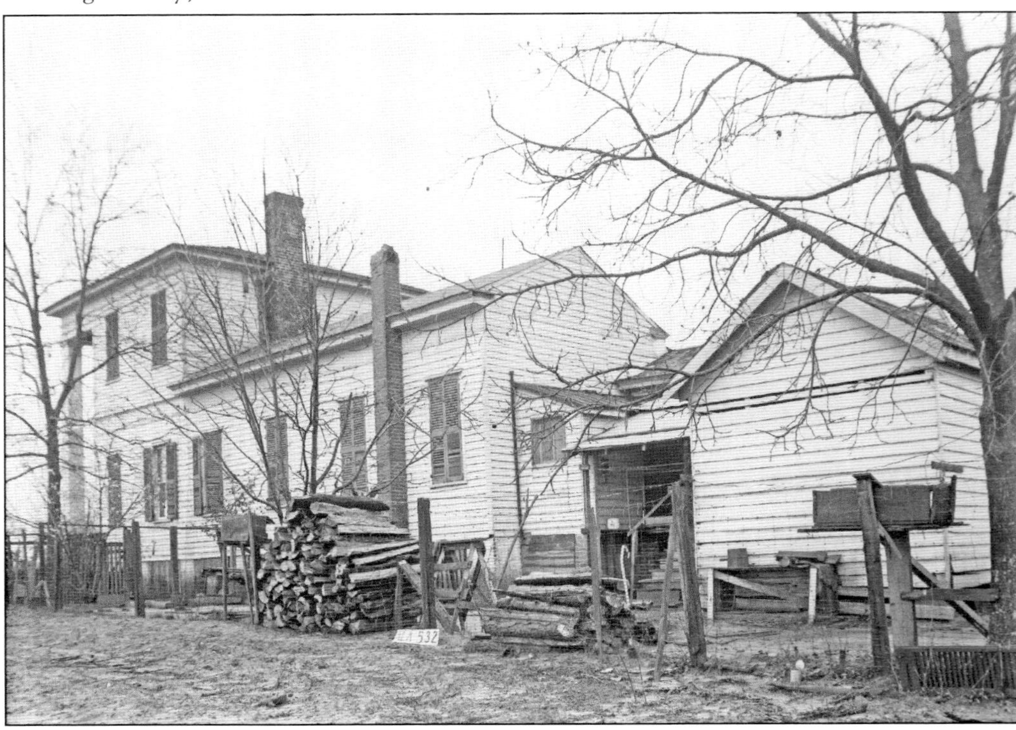

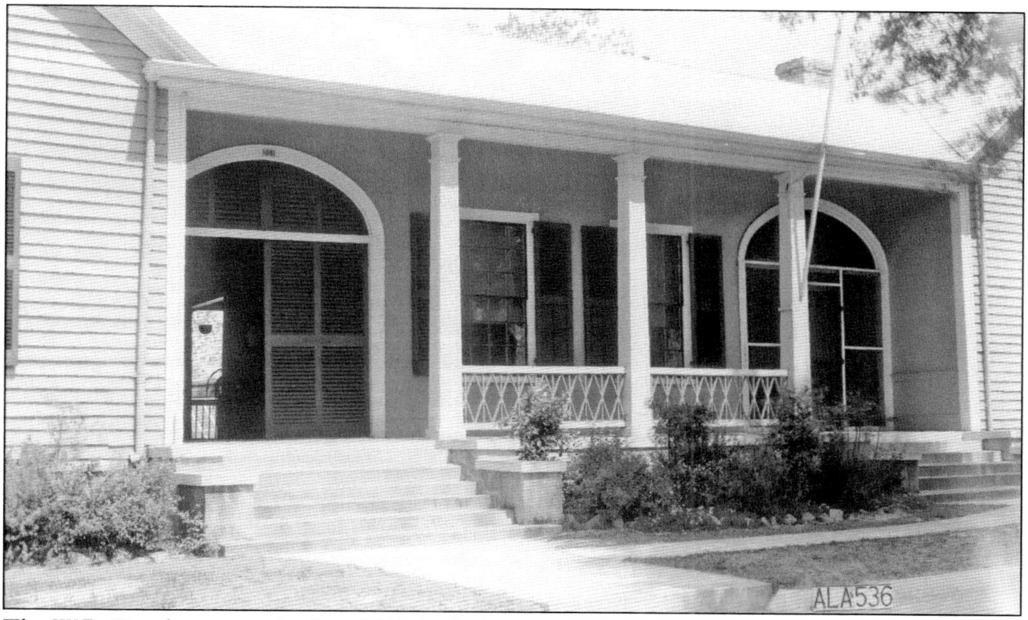

The W.B. Carr house was built at 301 Maple Street around 1850. This close-up of the single-story front elevation was taken on April 2, 1926. Frances Carr and Carribec Carr are also both likely former occupants. (Courtesy of the Library of Congress Historic American Buildings Survey.)

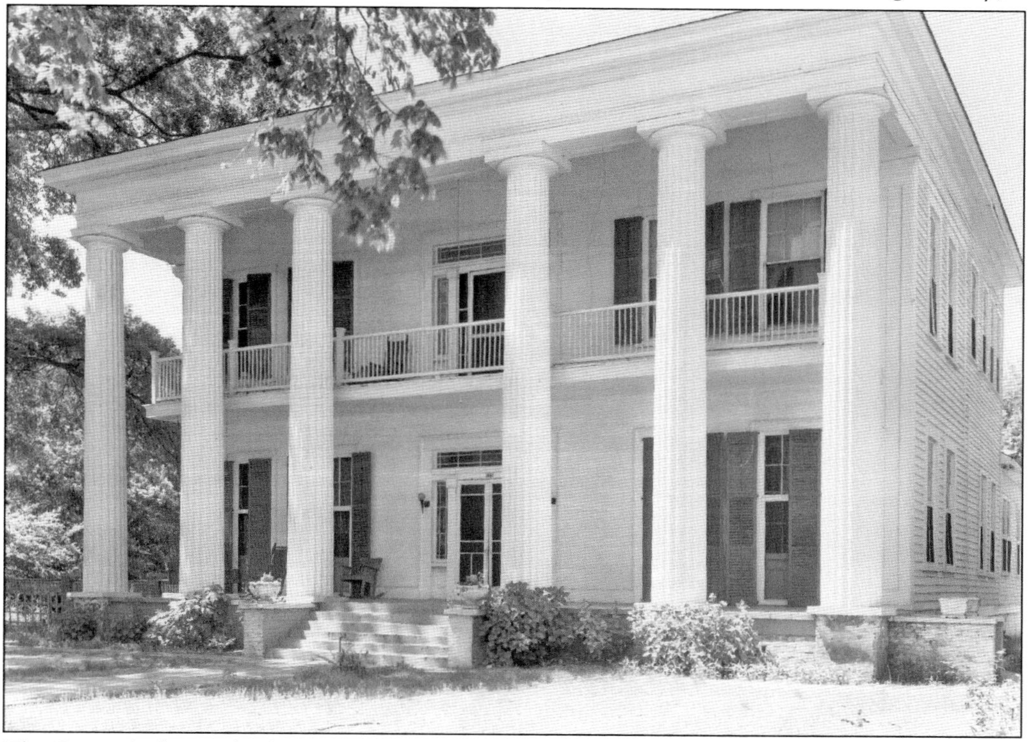

The Cartright house, built around 1850, is seen here in 1939 with its six columns across the front. It also had four columns at the side entrance. Some of its additional features include a wrought-iron balcony railing and nearly floor-to-ceiling second-story windows. (Courtesy of the Library of Congress Historic American Buildings Survey.)

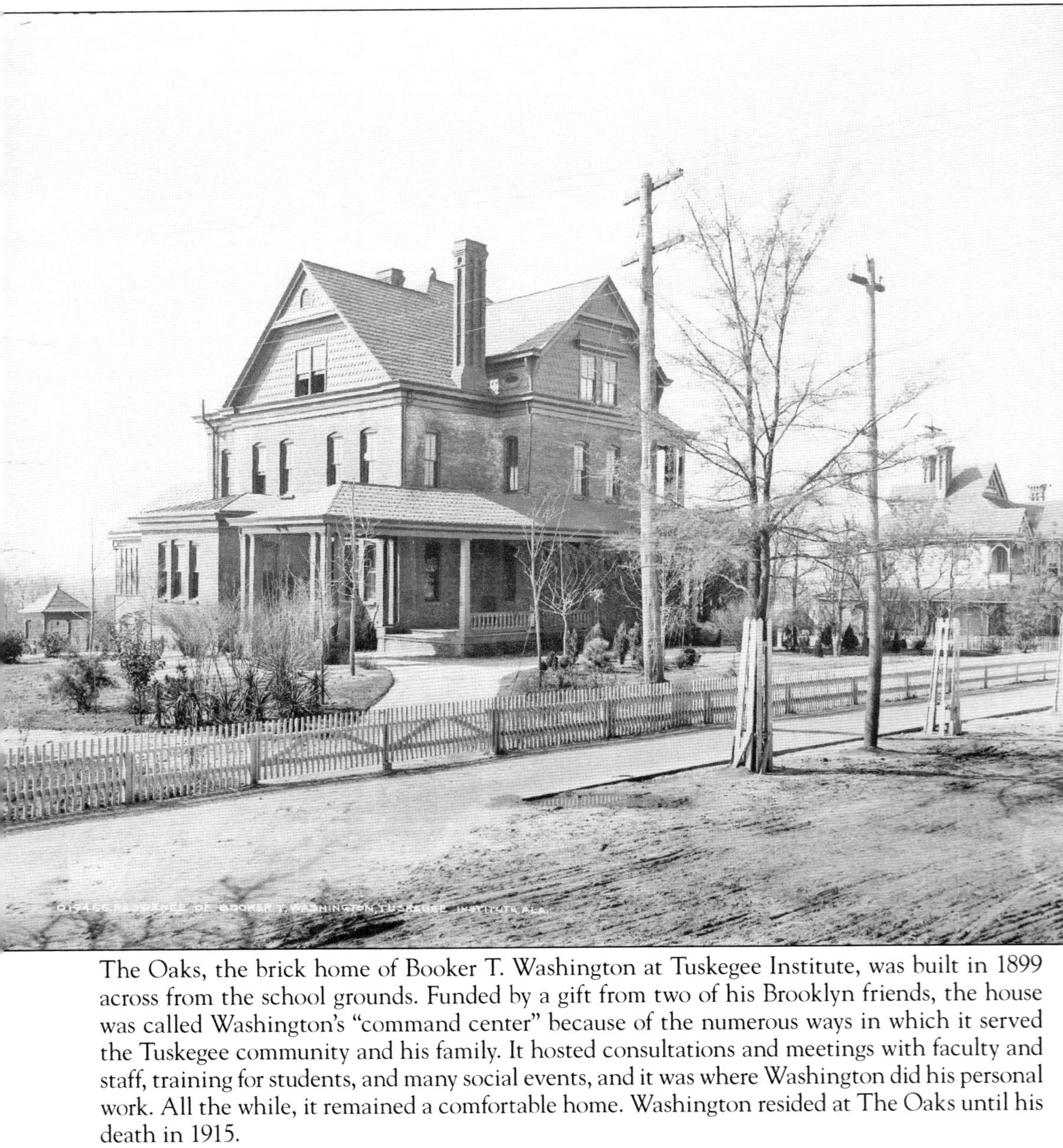

The Oaks, the brick home of Booker T. Washington at Tuskegee Institute, was built in 1899 across from the school grounds. Funded by a gift from two of his Brooklyn friends, the house was called Washington's "command center" because of the numerous ways in which it served the Tuskegee community and his family. It hosted consultations and meetings with faculty and staff, training for students, and many social events, and it was where Washington did his personal work. All the while, it remained a comfortable home. Washington resided at The Oaks until his death in 1915.

Three

Tuskegee University

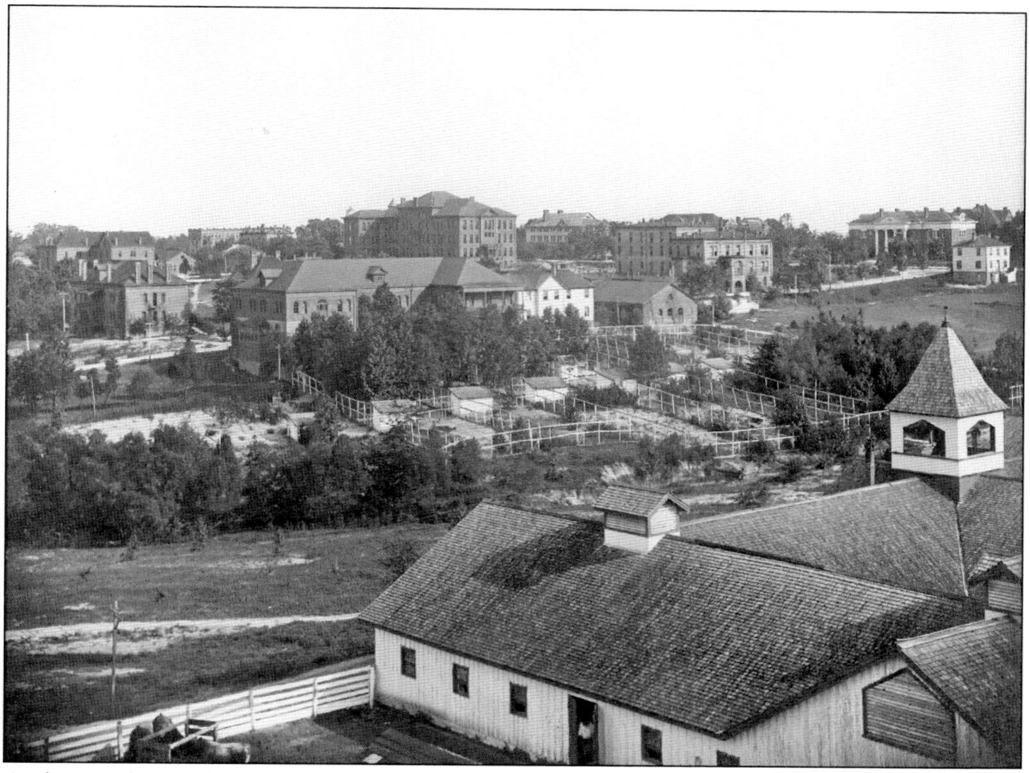

Arthur Bedou took this bird's-eye view of Tuskegee's campus in 1907. It was one of several landscapes and formal portraits taken by him that year. Bedou was hired to travel and record Booker T. Washington at various events for five years before working as an onsite photographer at the institute from late 1913 until 1917.

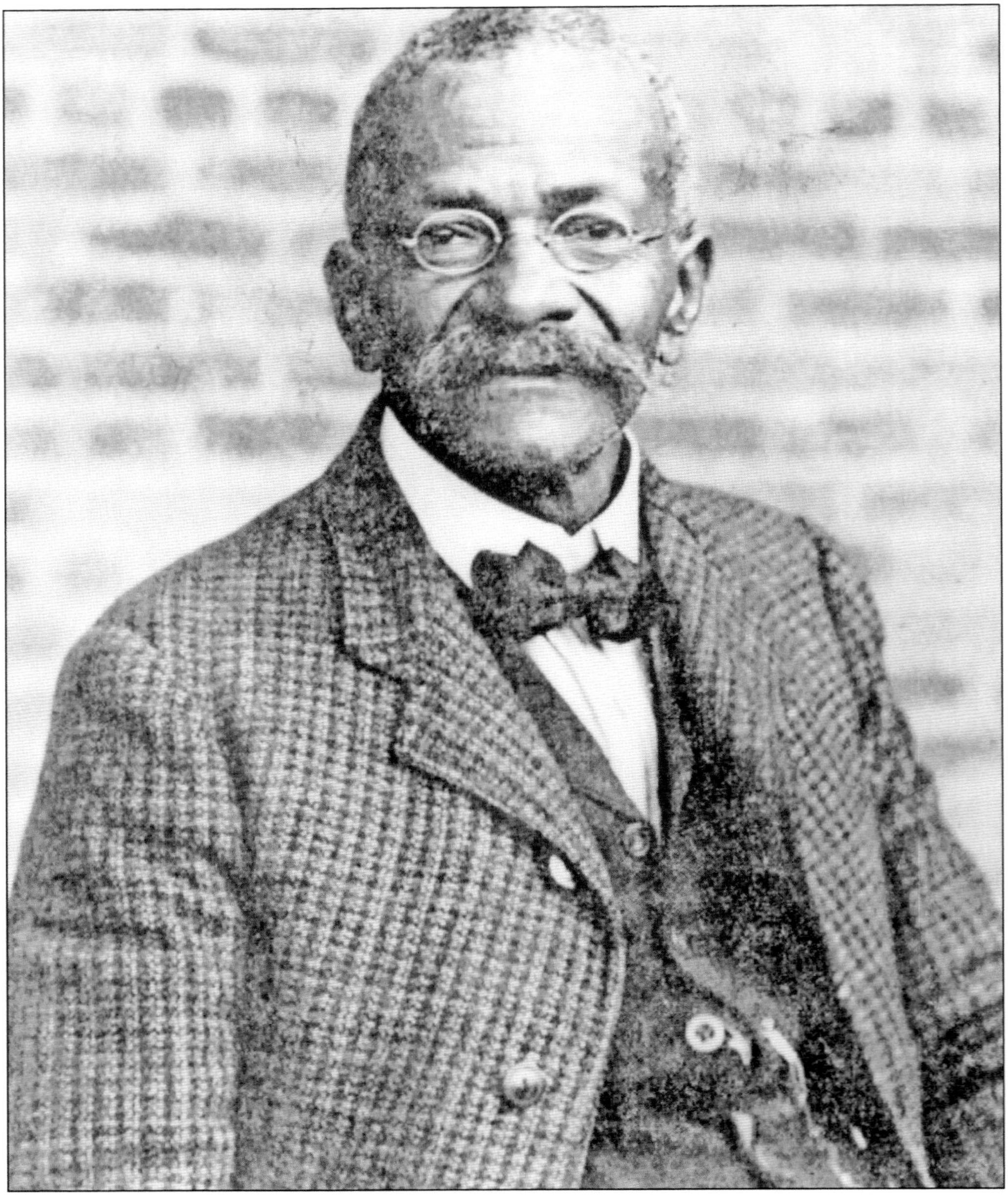

Lewis Adams (1842–1905), a former slave who could read, write, and speak several languages, collaborated with former slave owner George W. Campbell to establish a school for African Americans in Tuskegee. On July 4, 1881, Tuskegee Normal School for Colored Teachers opened, with Booker T. Washington as its principal. Adams, a tinsmith, harness-maker, shoemaker, Prince Hall freemason, and influential county resident, was approached by Wilbur F. Foster and Arthur L. Brooks about delivering black votes in their 1880 state campaigns. Adams, seen here around 1900, agreed on the condition that they would help secure a school for African Americans. Foster and Brooks won their seats and kept their promise, facilitating the passage of House Bill 165, which established "a Negro Normal School in Tuskegee." Adams, Thomas Dyer, and M.B. Swanson comprised the school's board. Adams served on the board until his death. (Courtesy of the Library of Congress.)

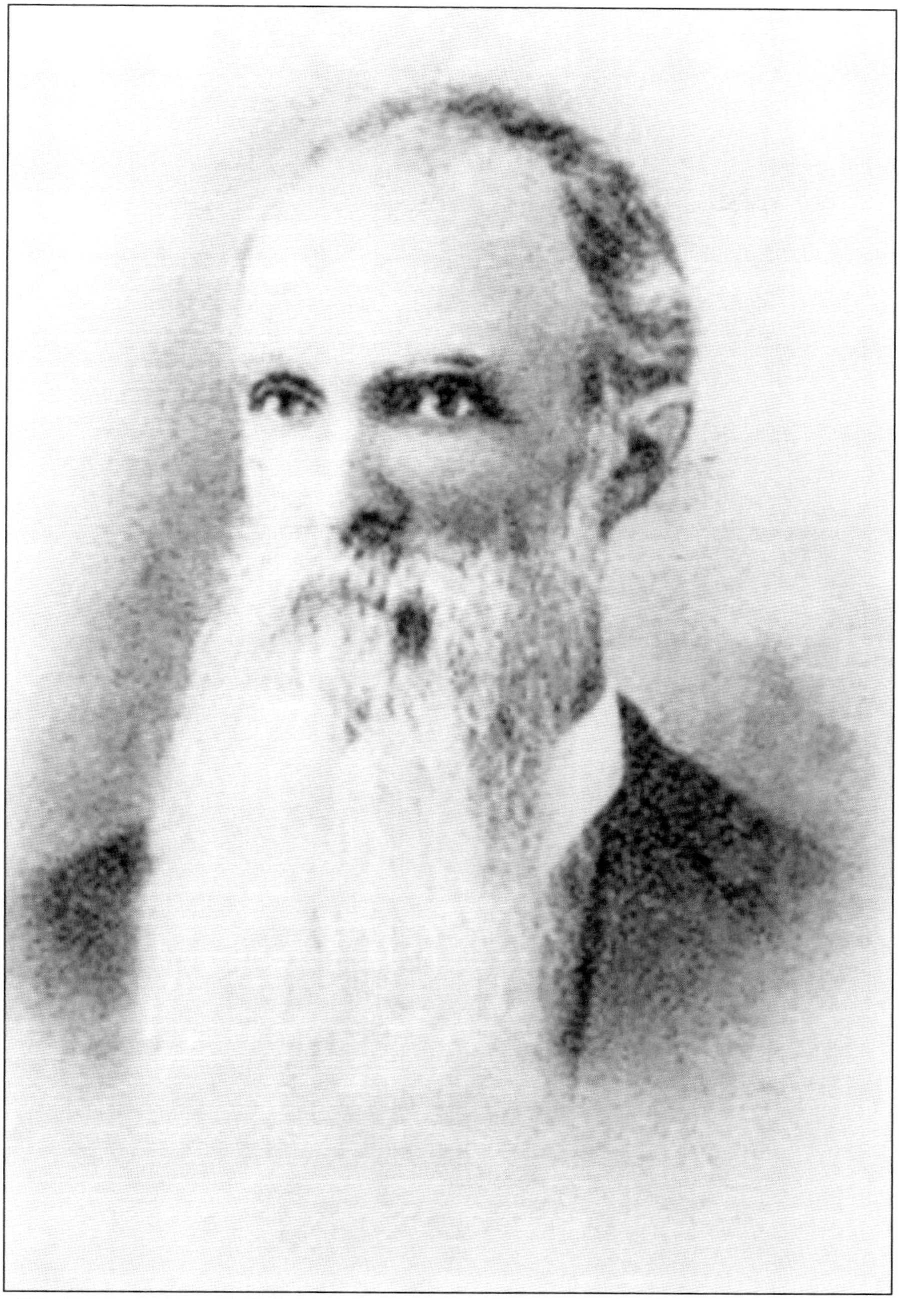

George Washington Campbell (1828–1905) was the senior partner of Campbell & Wright, the oldest firm in the state, established in 1852. In 1871, his firm and E.T. Varner constructed a railroad from Tuskegee to Chehaw. Campbell also owned an insurance brokerage and, in 1882, founded the only bank in Macon County. He assisted Lewis Adams with building the groundwork for Tuskegee Normal School and was one of its earliest trustees, assuming the role in 1881 after the sudden death of Thomas Dyer. He advised Booker T. Washington on financial matters during his 24 years of affiliation with the school and served as board president until his death in 1905. Campbell, who grew up in Tuskegee, and Eliza Jane Wright, a native of Lincoln County, Georgia, were married in December 1851. He is seen here in the late 1800s.

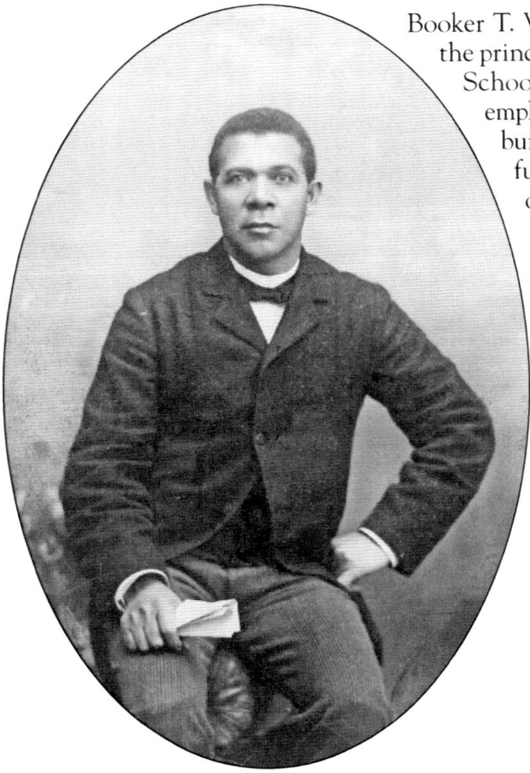

Booker T. Washington, seen here around 1880, became the principal of the newly established Tuskegee Normal School for Colored Teachers in 1881. Washington emphasized developing industrial skills and character building. He proved to be proficient at educating, fundraising, building, and lobbying in all areas on behalf of the institute.

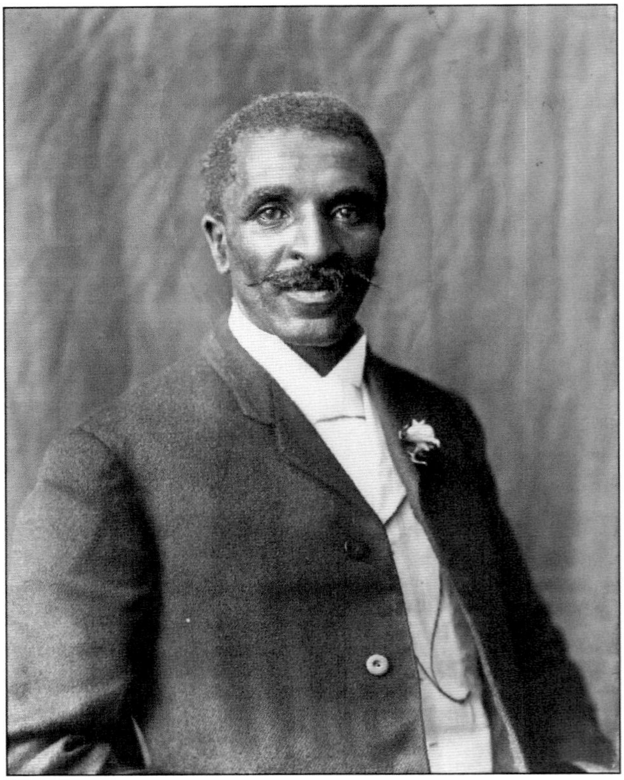

George Washington Carver (1864–1943) was born a slave on a Missouri plantation but became one of the most renowned scientists and inventors of his time. He excelled as a teacher and researcher at Tuskegee, developing 100 products from the peanut and many others from various additional crops, and becoming an innovator of farming and land use methods. Frances Benjamin Johnston took this photograph of Carver in 1906.

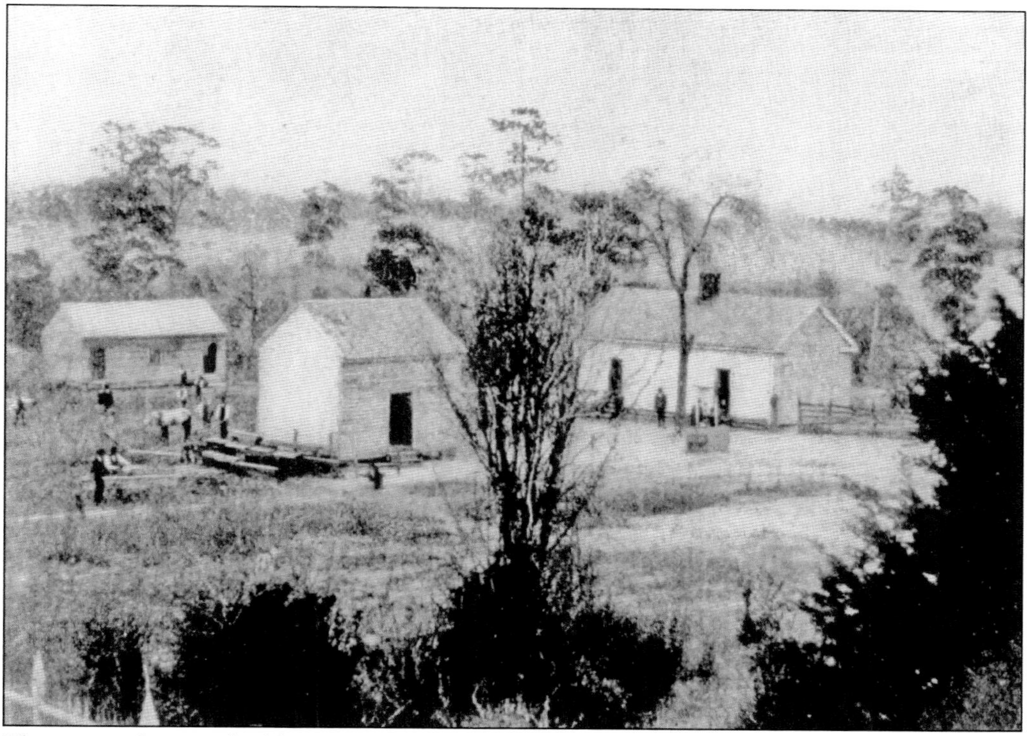

There were three outbuildings on the Bowen plantation when Washington secured resources to purchase the property as the site of the institute. The first classes were held in a shanty until improvements could be made.

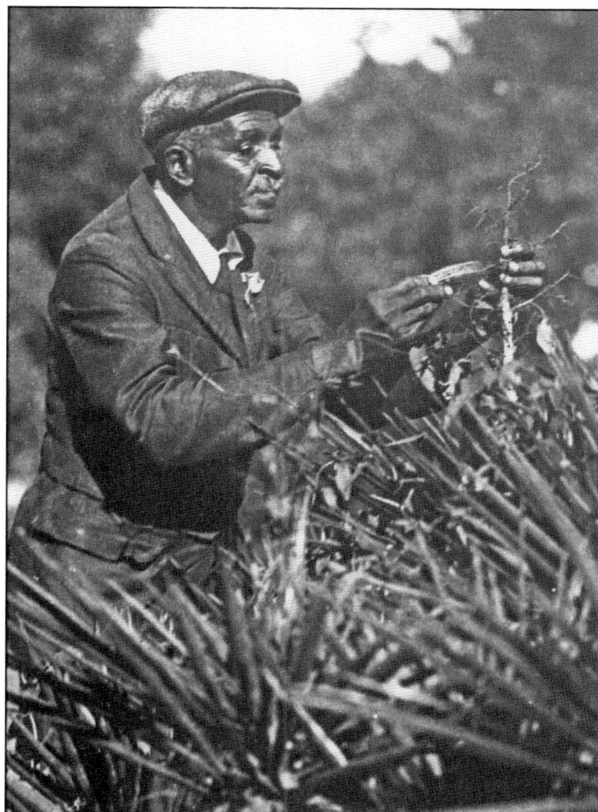

Washington initiated the annual Negro Conference in 1892, a one-day meeting when black farmers came to the institute to discuss their problems and receive advice from faculty. George Washington Carver frequently traveled to rural areas to give scientific demonstrations, a practice that became institutionalized as the Farmer's College on Wheels and was also known as the Jesup Agricultural Wagon. In 1906, the program evolved into a regional black farm extension service of Tuskegee Institute. Carver is seen here in the field in 1931. (Courtesy of the estate of P.H. Polk.)

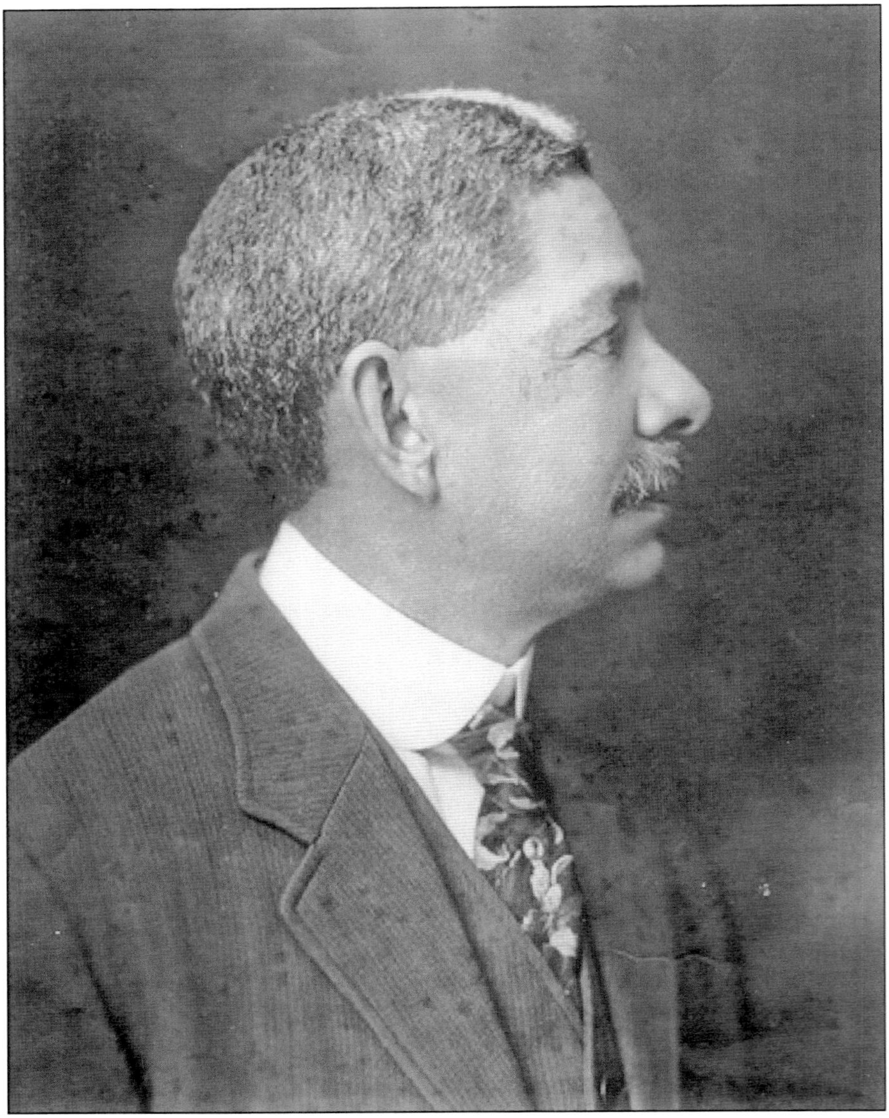

Robert Robinson Taylor (1868–1942) was the first academically trained African American architect and the first black graduate of the Massachusetts Institute of Technology. He was recruited by Booker T. Washington while he was still a student, but he designed several private and public buildings in Cleveland after graduating in 1892 before arriving at Tuskegee in November. Back in Cleveland from 1899 to 1902, he worked on his own and as a draughtsman for the Charles W. Hopkinson architectural firm. Other than those years, Taylor's career was spent at Tuskegee, as he returned to be the director of industries before becoming the vice principal in 1925. His buildings included the Science (Thrasher) Hall (1893), the chapel (1895–1898), The Oaks (1899), Huntington Hall (1900), the four Emery dormitories (1900), Dorothy Hall (1901), the institute's Carnegie library (1901), the Administration Building (1902–1903), Rockefeller Hall (1903), Douglass Hall (1904), the Collis P. Huntington Memorial Building (1904–1905), Tantum Hall (1907), the Milbank Agriculture Building (1909), Tompkins Hall (1910), White Hall (1910), John A. Andrew Memorial Hospital (1913), the laundry (1915, now the Carver Museum), James Hall (1921), Logan Hall (1921), Sage Hall (1927), the Wilcox Trade Buildings (1928), the Armstrong Science Building (1932), and the Hollis Burke Frissell Library (1932).

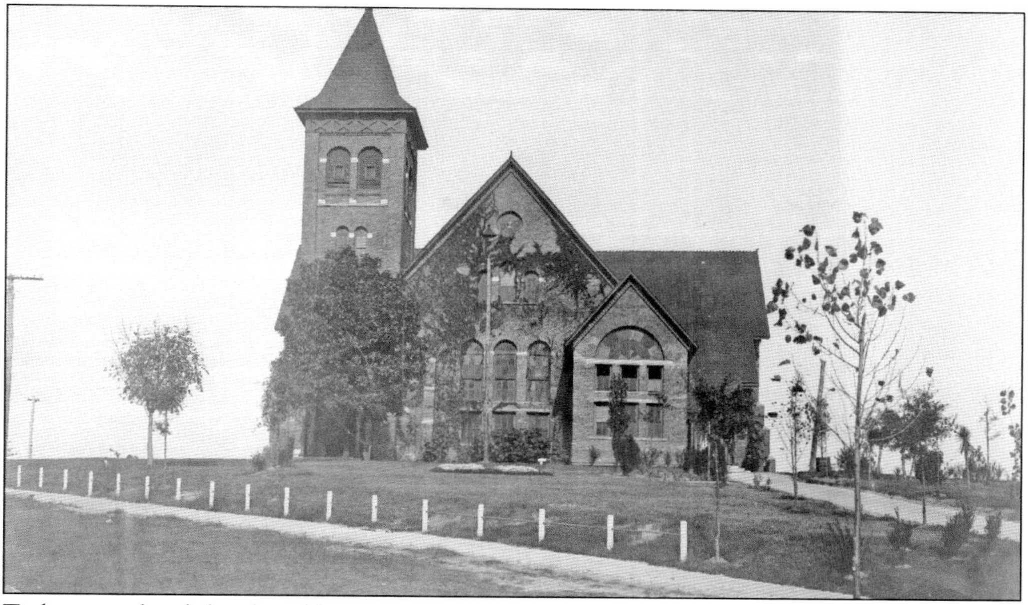

Taylor considered the chapel his masterpiece. Washington called it the most imposing building on campus. Institute supporter Max Bennett Thrasher felt that it epitomized the school's mission. Built by students and funded by New York philanthropist Helen Phelps Stokes, it was the first electric building in the county. Pres. William McKinley spoke there during his visit in 1899, devotional services were held there, and the annual Negro Conference convened there.

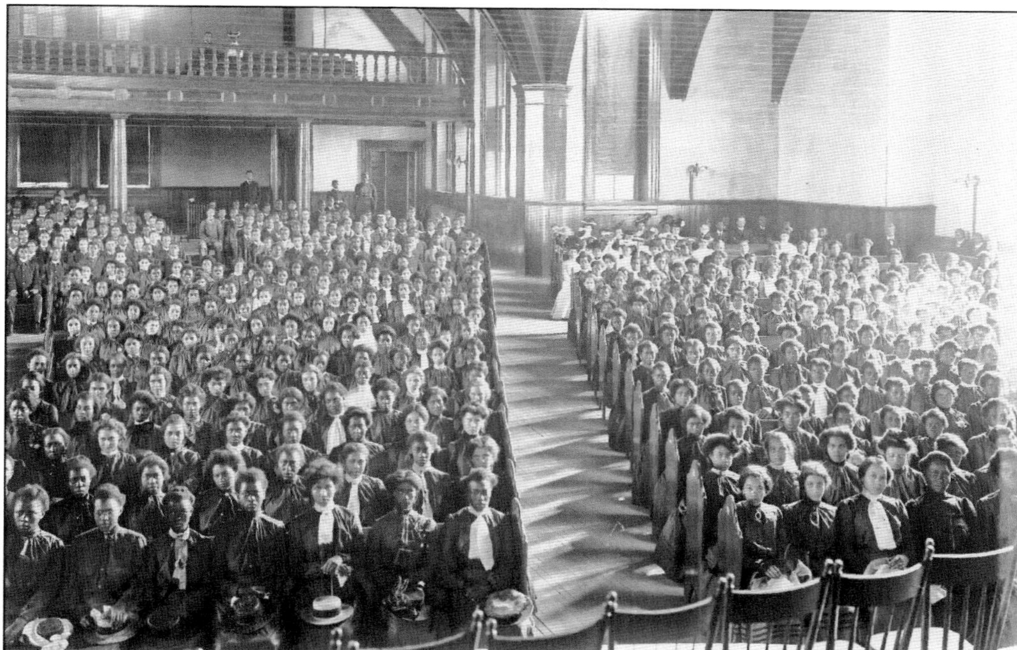

This 1902 Frances Benjamin Johnston photograph shows female students in the forefront of an assembly and male students seated in the rear sections of the chapel. The chapel was a brick structure with stone trimmings in the configuration of a cross. The building was 154 feet long through the nave and choir and 106 feet long through the transepts. The seating capacity of the auditorium was 2,400.

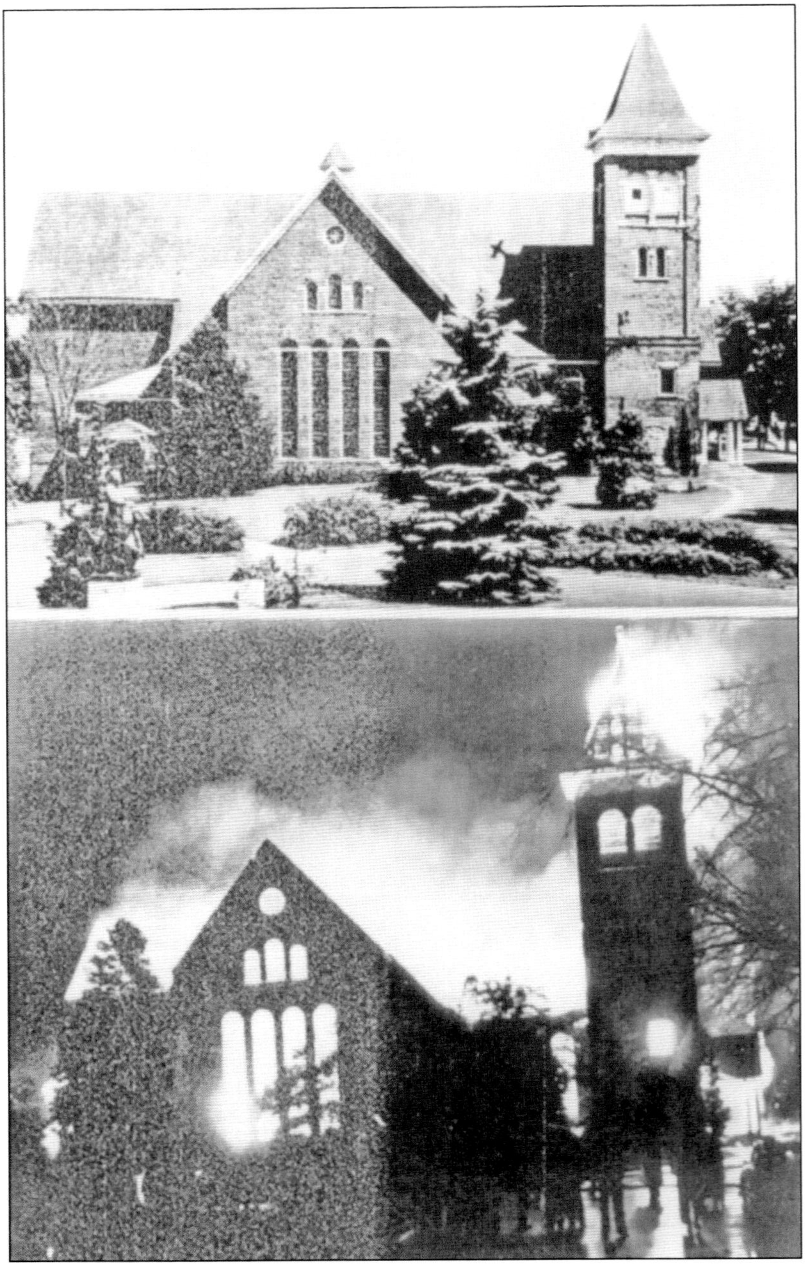

According to Max Bennett Thrasher in *Tuskegee: Its Story and Its Work*, "1,200,000 bricks were made by students in the school's brick yard and laid by the men in the brick-laying classes. The lumber was cut on the school's land and sawed in the saw mill on the grounds. The various wood-working classes did the work which came in their departments. The floor is oak; the rest of the finish is in yellow pine, and the use of this wood in the lofty arch of the ceiling gives a particularly rich effect. The pews were designed by one student, and another student designed the cornices. The tin and slate roofing was put on by students, and the steam heating and electric lighting apparatus was installed by them." On January 23, 1957, Tuskegee's beloved chapel was lost to a fire. The current chapel was built at the same site in 1967–1969. (Courtesy of the Manuscript, Archives, and Rare Book Library, Robert W. Woodruff Library, Emory University.)

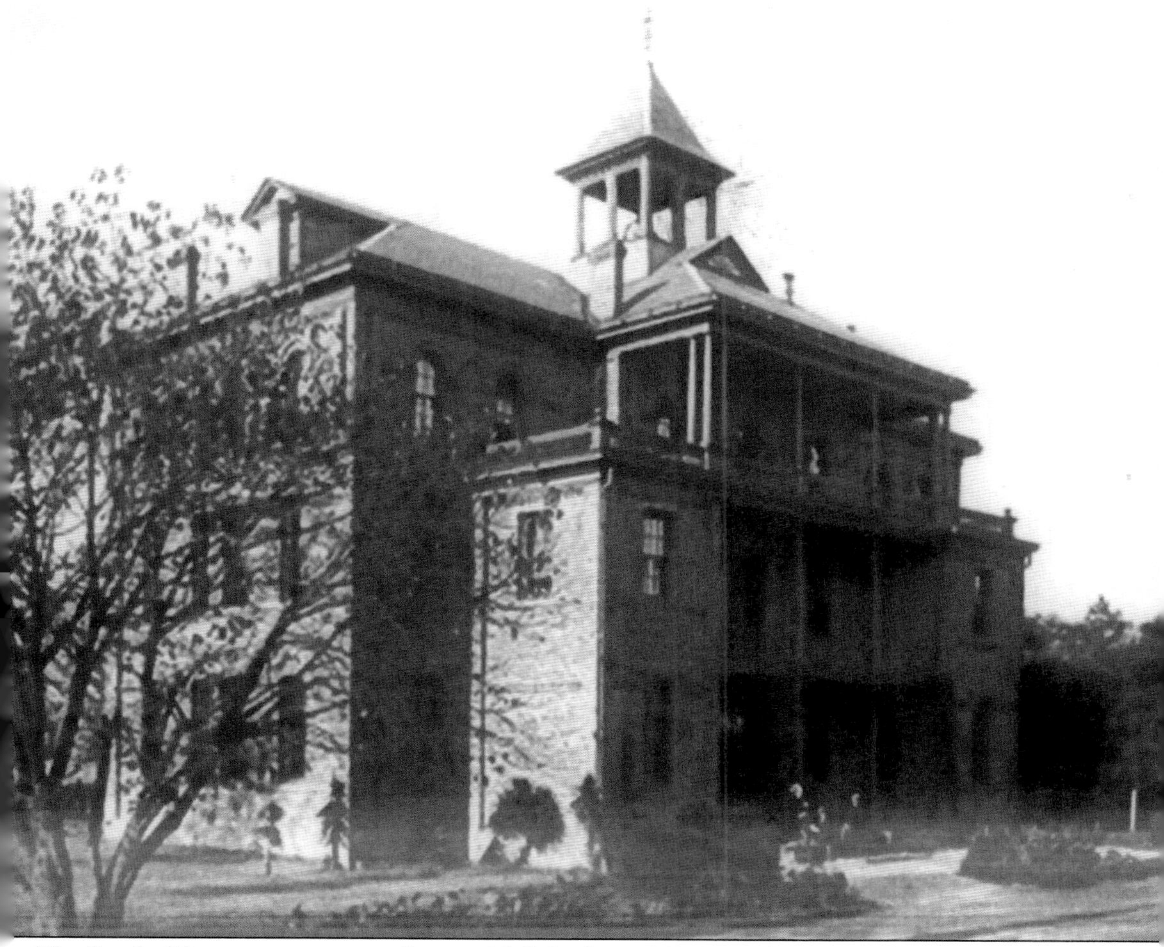

The first building on campus was Science Hall, built in 1893. It was later named Thrasher Hall after Washington's ally Max Bennett Thrasher. The three-story structure was made up of recitation rooms and laboratories on the first two stories and sleeping rooms for teachers and male students on the third floor. Constructed under Taylor's supervision by students, using bricks made also by students, the proportion and parts of the building's design were influenced by the architect's thesis completed at MIT the previous year.

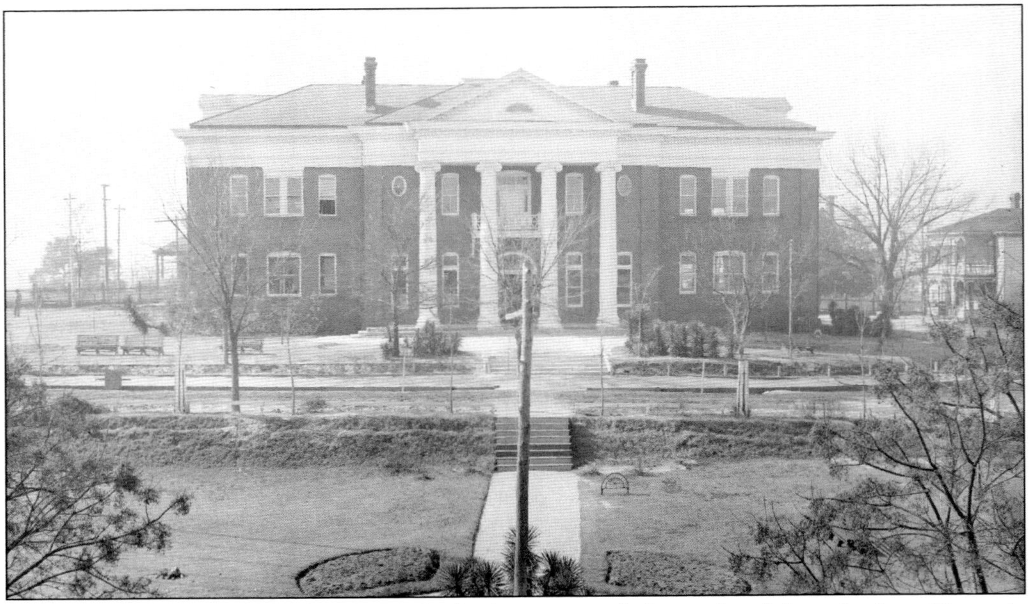

The Carnegie library at Tuskegee was built almost entirely by student labor. Andrew Carnegie donated $20,000 for the library, enough money to cover materials for furniture that was all made by students. The school constructed a Colonial-style brick building with four columns on the front to support a well-designed pediment that forms a porch and lends to the impressive overall appearance. This 1906 photograph shows the wings on each side of the central portion, which each measure 30 feet by 40 feet. Overall, the two-story building is 50 feet by 110 feet.

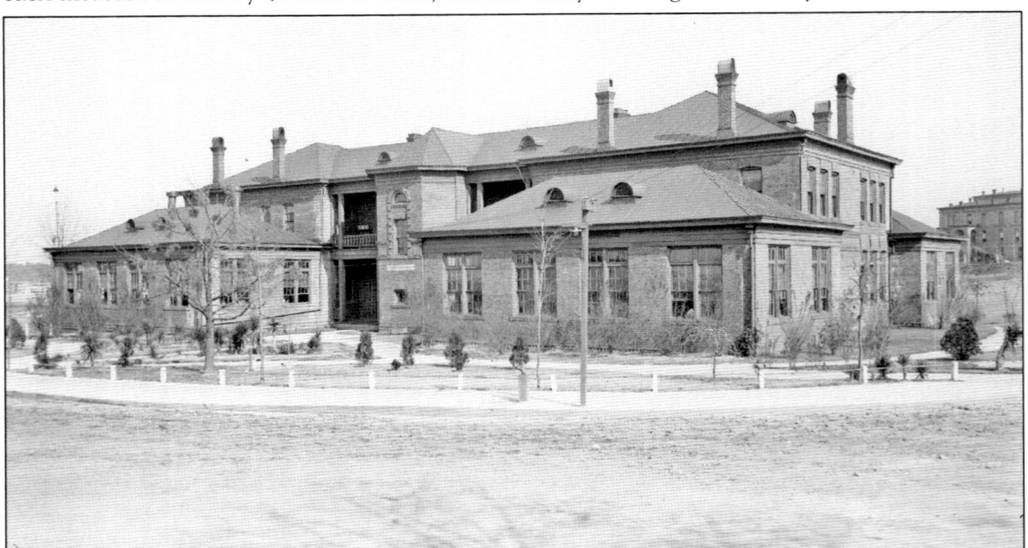

Dorothy Hall, also known as the girls' trades building, was built on the opposite side of the driveway from the boys' trades building. The hall, seen here in 1906, was needed to accommodate the girls' industrial department. Funds were provided by two female benefactors from New York who also underwrote the cost of the chapel and Phelps Hall. The rooms were designed to be large, airy, and well lit. Female students were taught sewing, dressmaking, millinery, laundering, cooking, housekeeping, mattress-making, upholstering, broom-making, and basketry. The building was stocked with equipment and accessories for teaching.

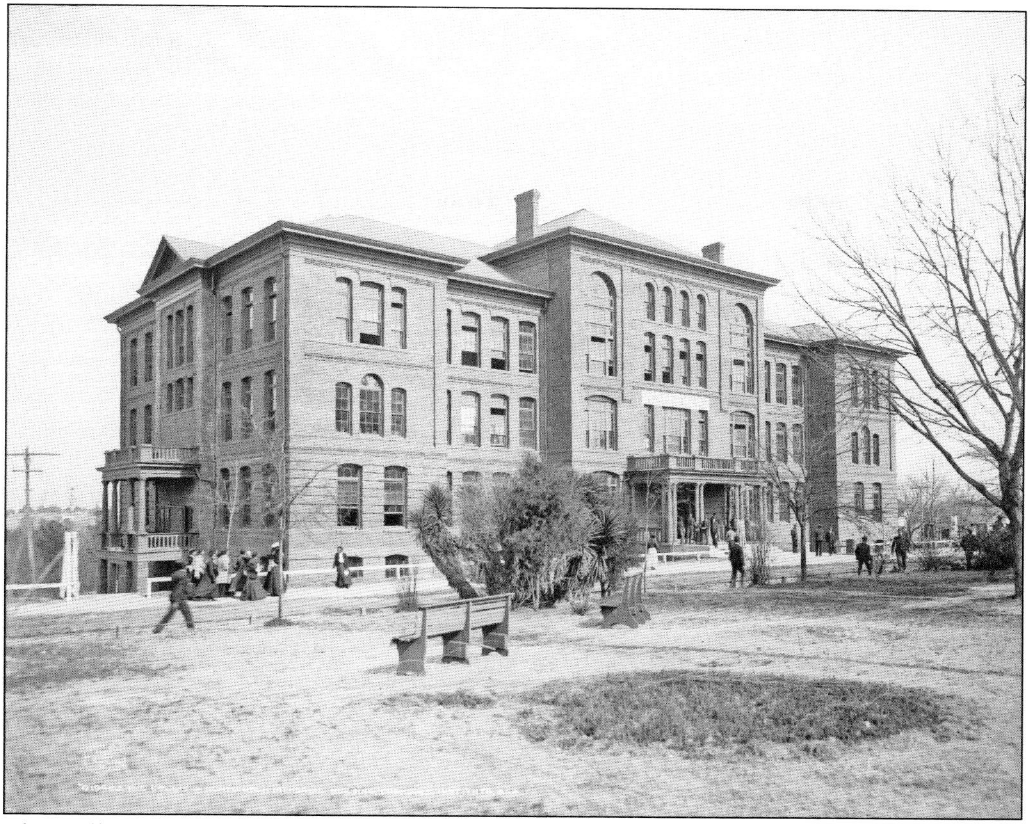

The Collis P. Huntington Memorial Building, an academic classroom building seen here one year after its completion, was financed with a gift from Arabella W. Huntington in memory of her husband.

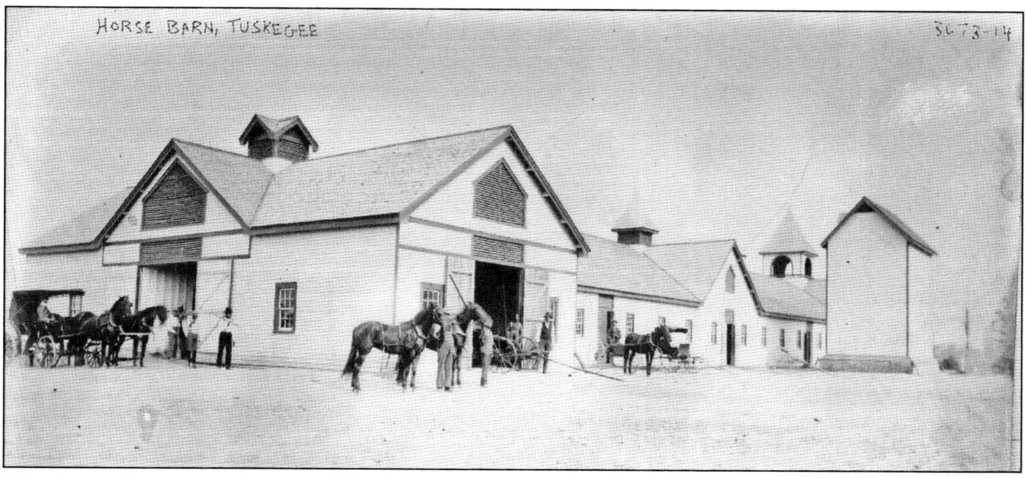

The horse barn was destroyed by fire in 1895. In 1900, Brooklyn donors provided funds to reconstruct the barn on a larger scale. However, the decision was made to forego a larger barn and build a number of smaller structures instead. A hennery, creamery, dairy barn, carriage house, tool house, piggery, silos, slaughterhouse, and barn for 47 thoroughbred horses were built. The barn is seen here around 1920. (Courtesy of the Manuscript, Archives, and Rare Book Library, Robert W. Woodruff Library, Emory University.)

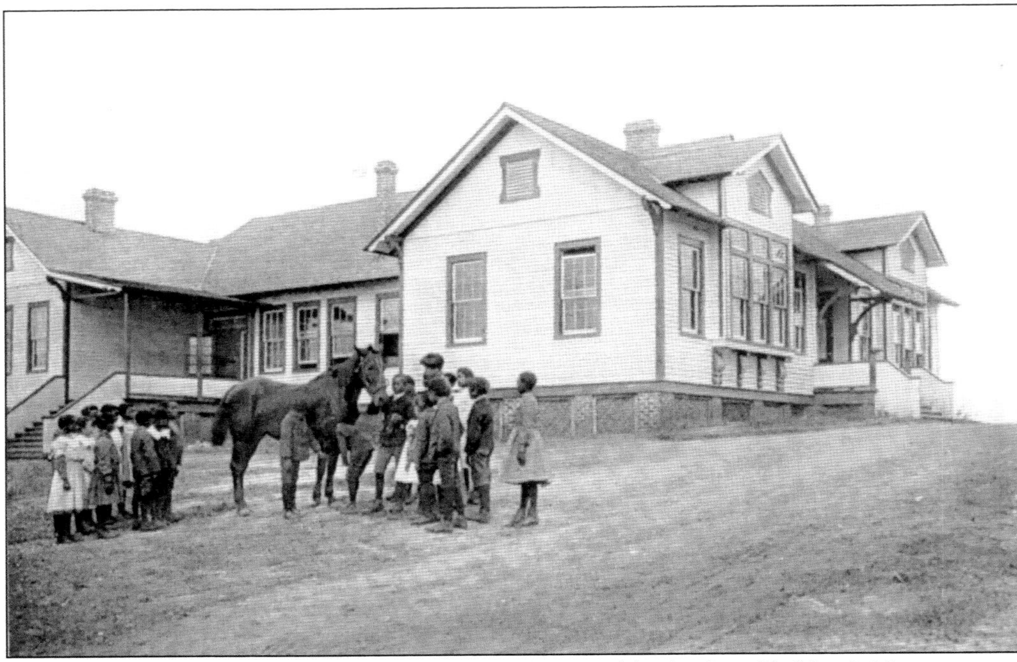

The second model school building, which was also possibly the first Children's House, is seen here in the 1890s. In 1901, the Children's House was built with $2,000 from Pauline Agassiz Shaw of Boston and $100 from institute graduates as a nucleus. A one-story frame building of good proportions, it was where primary education for the town was taught. It was the practice school for students at the institute who intended to teach. A kindergarten was also established.

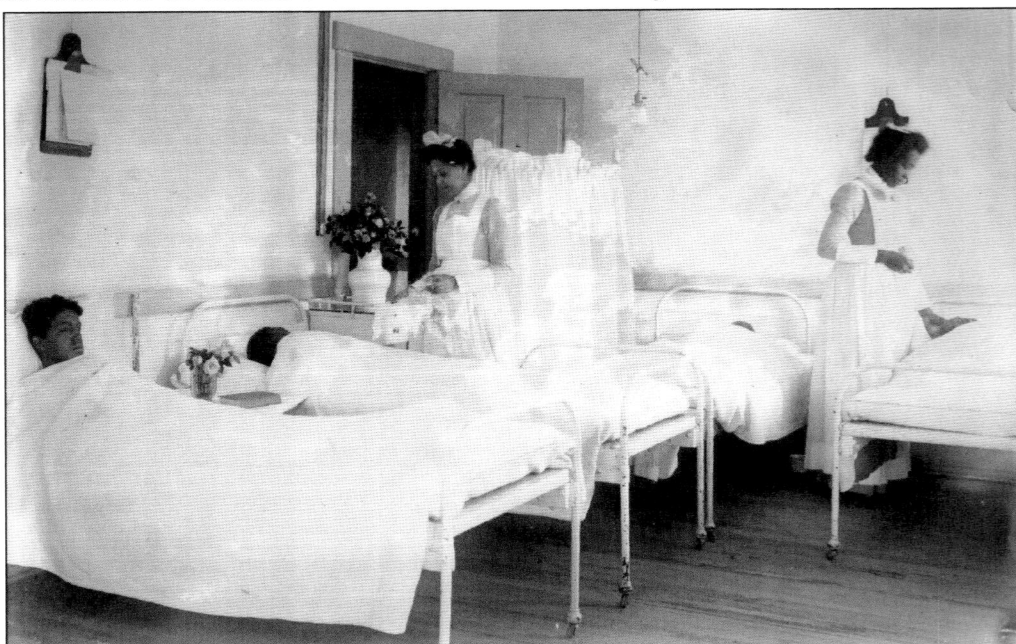

This photograph shows nurses and patients in one corner of the hospital ward at Tuskegee Institute around 1925. The hospital, opened in 1892 by Tuskegee Institute, was the first hospital for African Americans in Alabama.

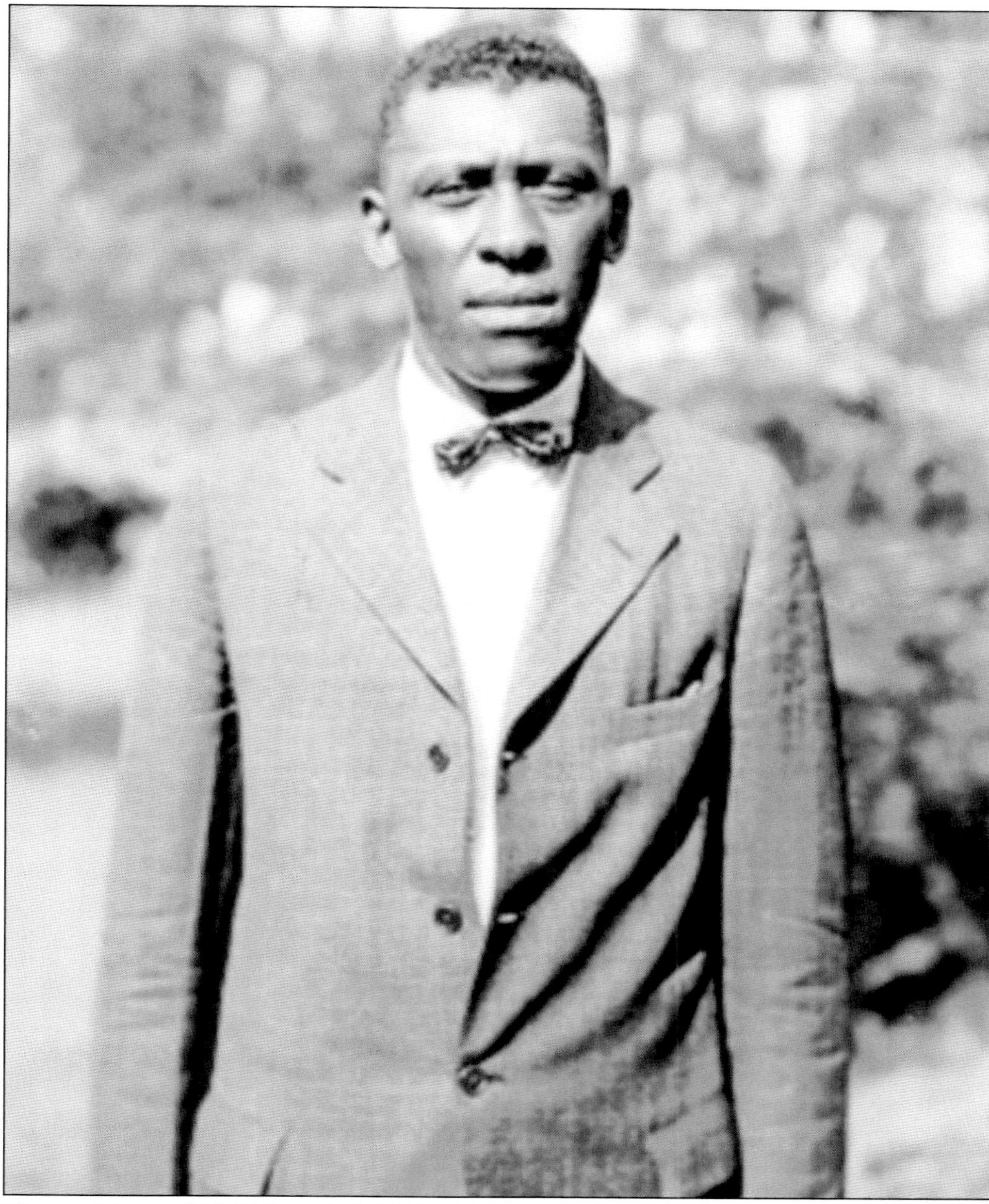

Thomas Monroe "T.M." Campbell (1883–1956) was the first African American demonstration agent with the US Department of Agriculture. He was recommended for the job by Booker T. Washington. Campbell ran away from home in 1899 to attend Tuskegee. It took him seven years to graduate, working odd jobs to pay for night classes that included study under George Washington Carver. The agent position allowed him to help farmers improve their lives and crop productivity on behalf of Tuskegee Institute and the Department of Agriculture. The wagonload of tools, plants, and livestock he traveled with was called the movable school, a name that remained when a truck was used and that inspired the title of his 1936 autobiography *The Movable School Goes to the Negro Farmer.* Campbell was later promoted to field agent, which allowed him to supervise comprehensive agricultural education programs among African American farmers in several southern states.

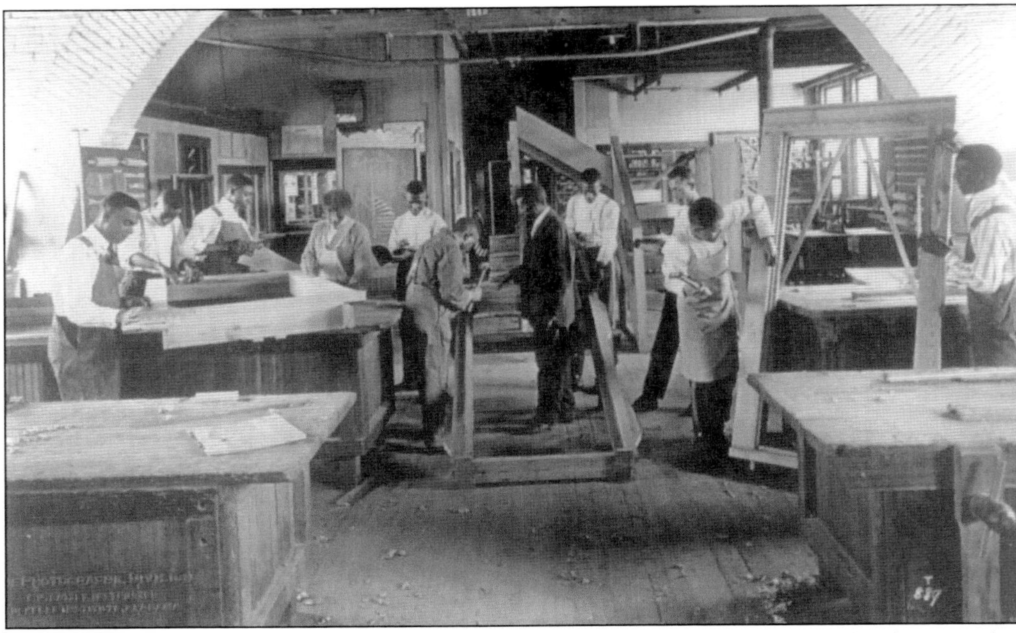

A carpentry class at the institute is seen here around 1920. The photograph was taken by Cornelius Marion "C.M." Battey, one of the most famous African American photographers in the country by 1900. Battey began Tuskegee's photography department in 1917 with financial assistance from George Eastman, the founder of the Eastman Kodak Company. Battey became Tuskegee's first official photographer and headed up the program until his death in 1927. Prentice Herman Polk, Ellie Lee Weems, and Elise Forrest Harleston were among the students in the program who went on to have successful careers. (Courtesy of the Library of Congress.)

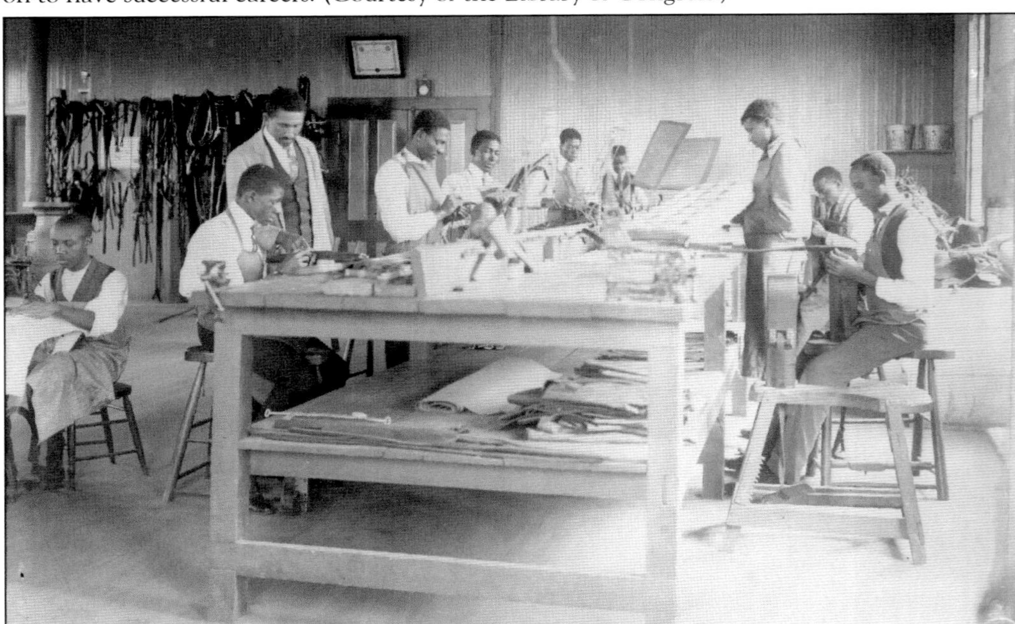

Male students are seen here with their instructor in an upholstery class around 1900. This field of study was popular with entering students because it was seen as a practical skill that could be useful in personal as well as professional life.

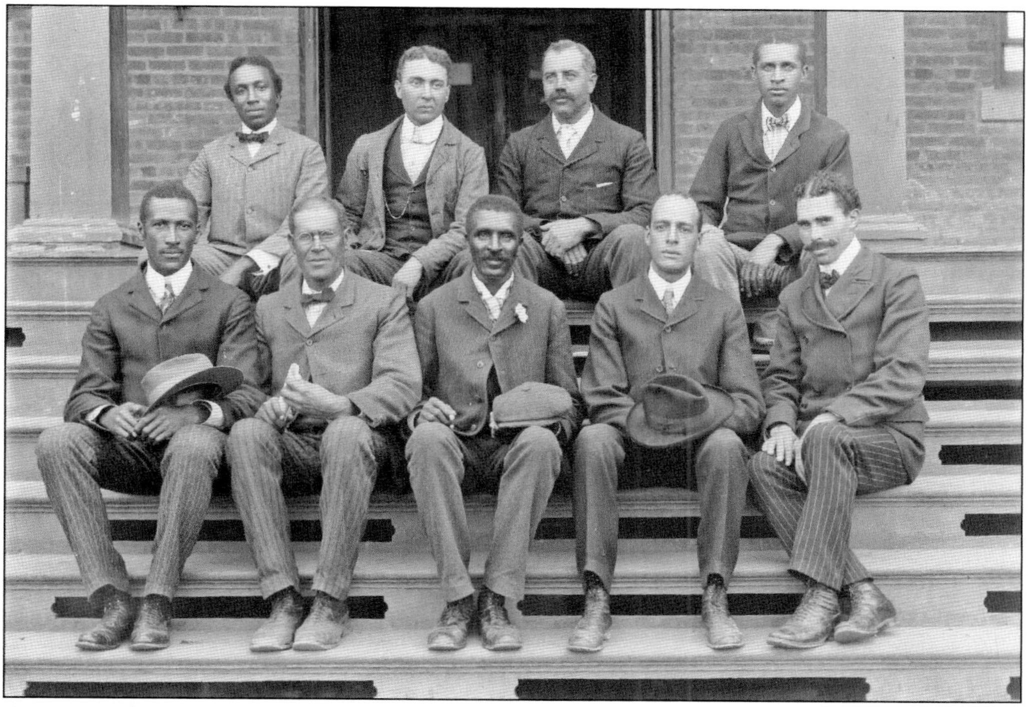

George Washington Carver (front center) is seen here with members of the faculty in 1902. Carver had been at the school for six years at the time. He was an automatic hit with students, but also had the regard and respect of fellow faculty members.

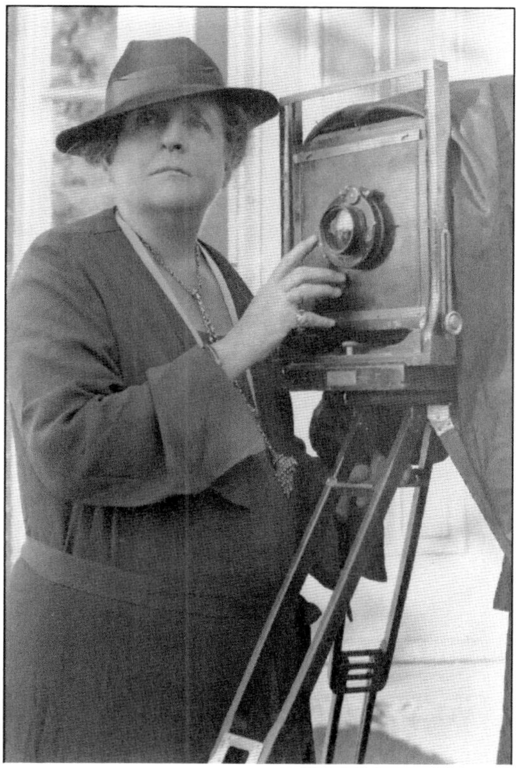

Frances Benjamin Johnston (1864–1952) was a prominent photojournalist and portrait photographer whose 60-year professional career included documentation of students at Tuskegee Institute in the early 1900s. Johnston is seen here in 1936 in front of the Arts Club in Washington, DC.

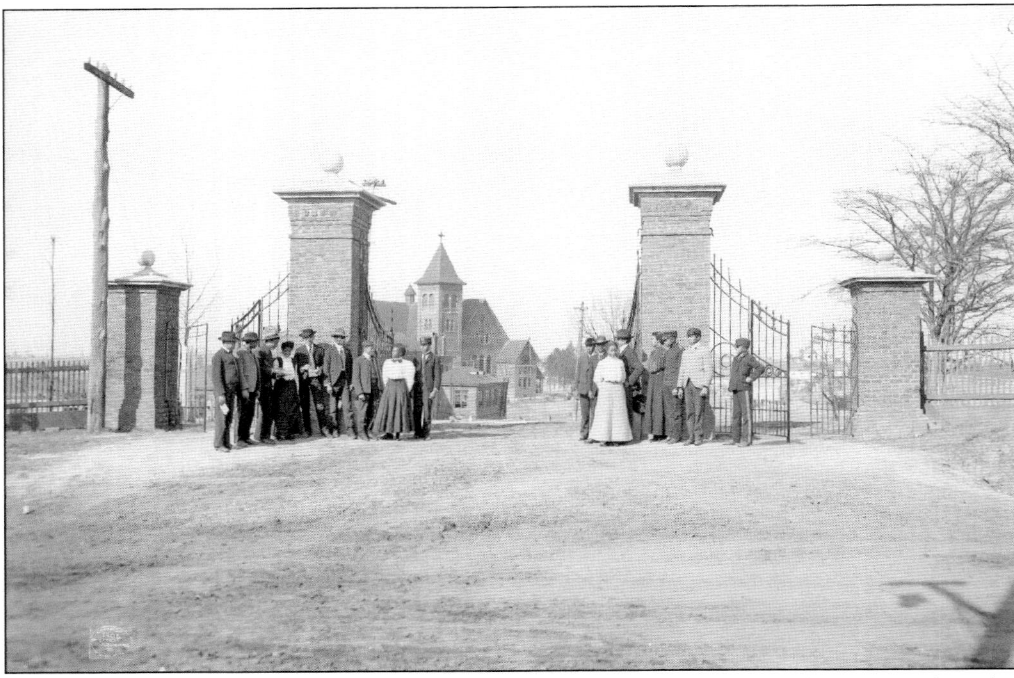

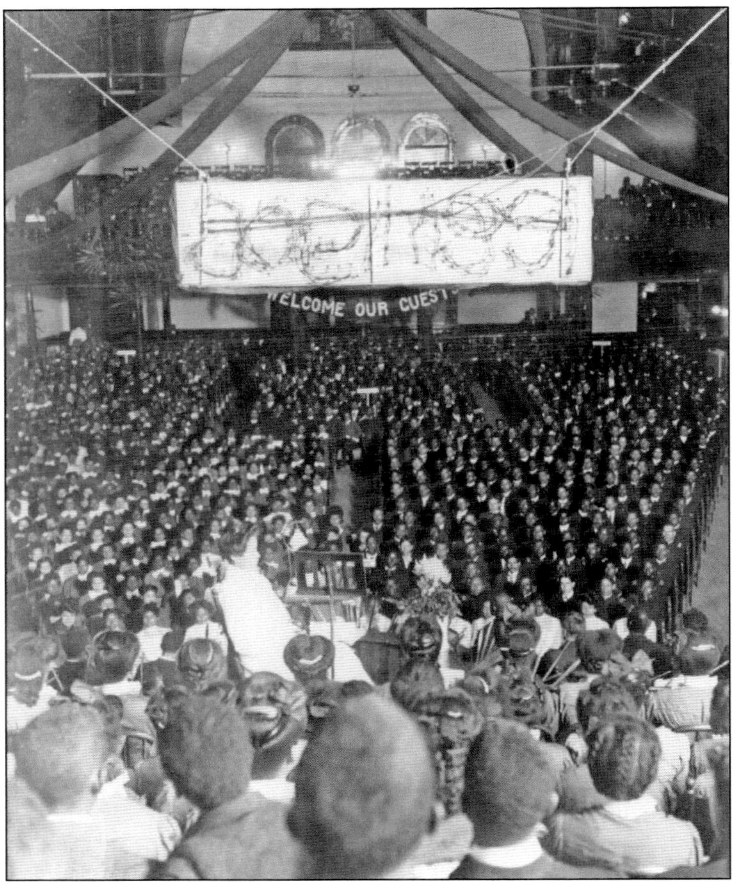

Students are gathered at the Lincoln gates during the 25th anniversary celebration in 1906. Acting as ambassadors, they wait for the arrival of guests.

Students, faculty, staff, and invited guests gathered in assembly for the 25th anniversary celebration. The view looks down from the top rear section of the chapel. More than 2,000 people were in attendance.

Cadets pose at attention while holding a flag in front of the *Lifting The Veil* statue near the entrance of the campus during the 25th anniversary parade.

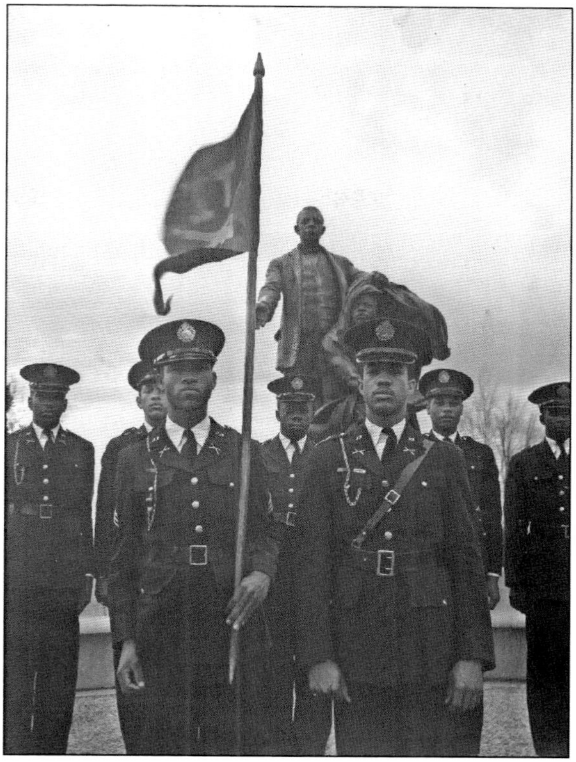

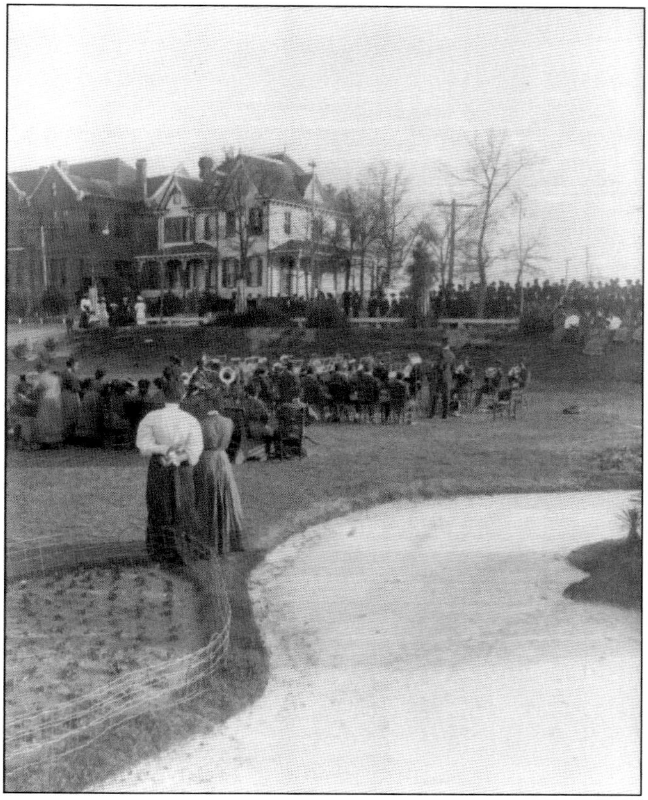

Faculty, students, staff, and guests attend a band concert on the lawn during Tuskegee's 25th anniversary celebration.

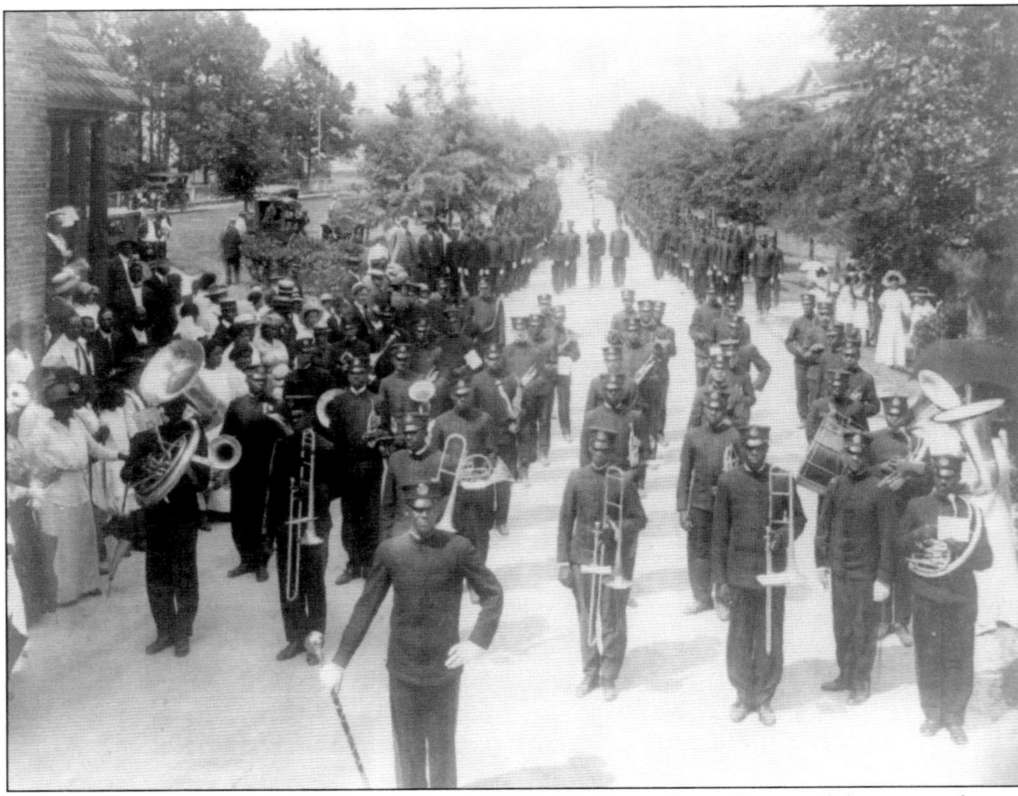

The inclusion of the corps of cadets in parades and other public celebrations became a popular part of public displays at the institute. Cadets are seen here marching in the 25th anniversary parade.

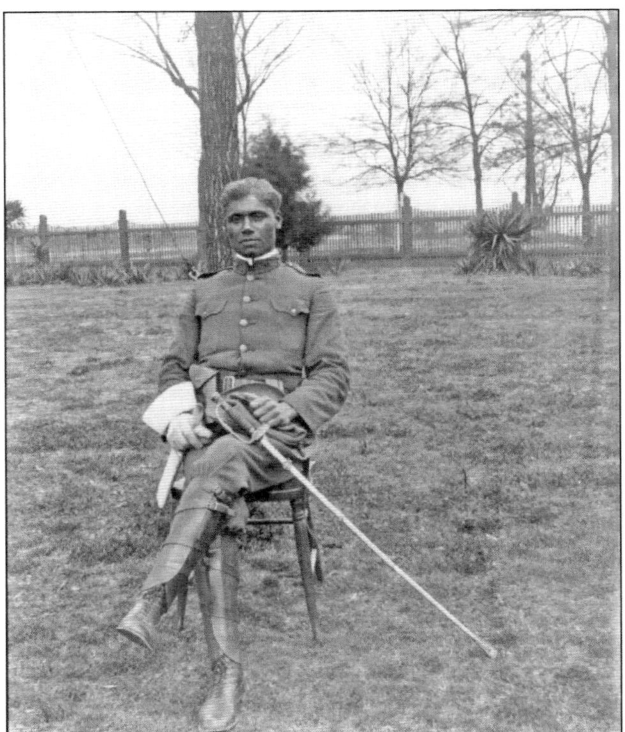

An unidentified cadet poses in a small chair on the lawn toward the conclusion of a full day of events during the institute's 25th anniversary celebration.

This portrait of Margaret Murray Washington (1861–1925) was taken by C.M. Battey, Tuskegee's official photographer, in 1917. Mrs. Washington, who married Booker T. Washington in 1893, becoming his third wife, was one of the founders of the National Association of Colored Women in 1896.

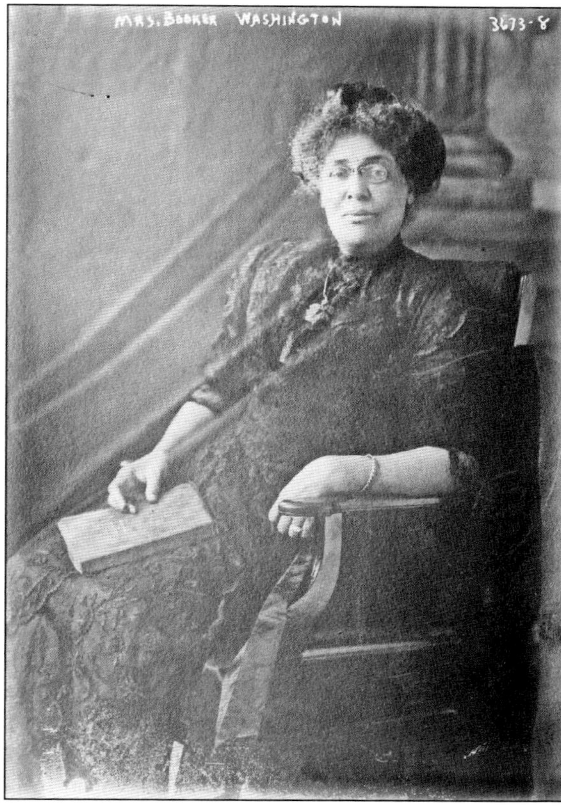

Booker T. Washington is seen here in a typical, classic working pose, seated at his desk in his office around 1905, when he was approaching his 25th year in leadership at the institute. Although he is more mature in years and experience in this photograph, when Washington first arrived in Tuskegee, he wore a moustache to appear older. This photograph was taken by Frances Benjamin Johnston.

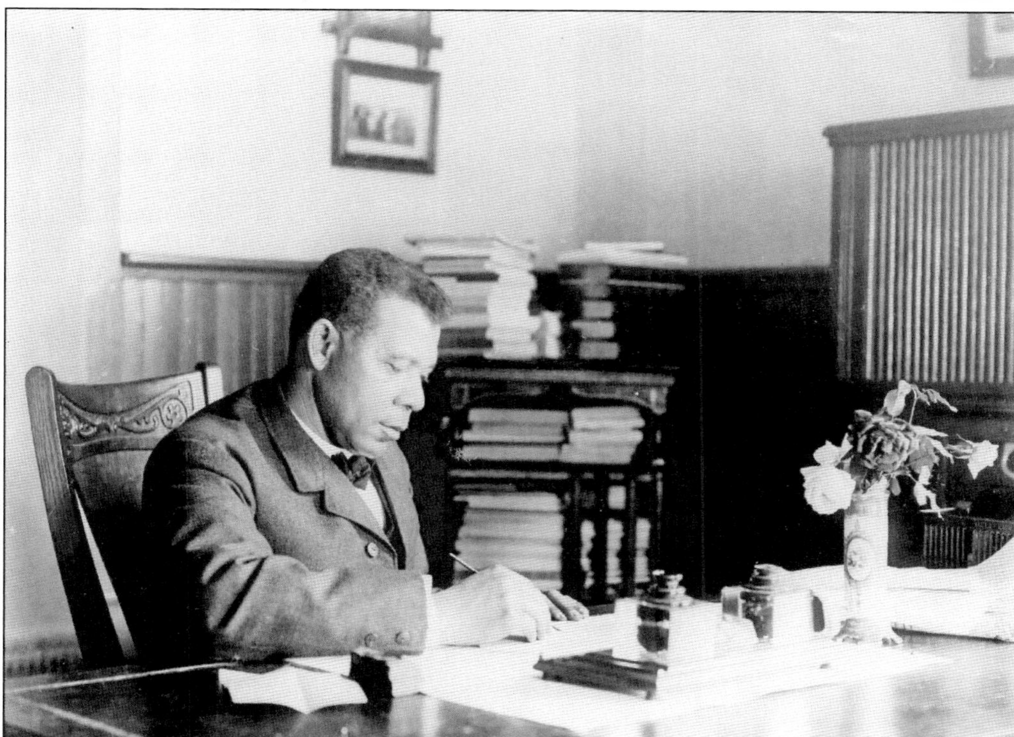

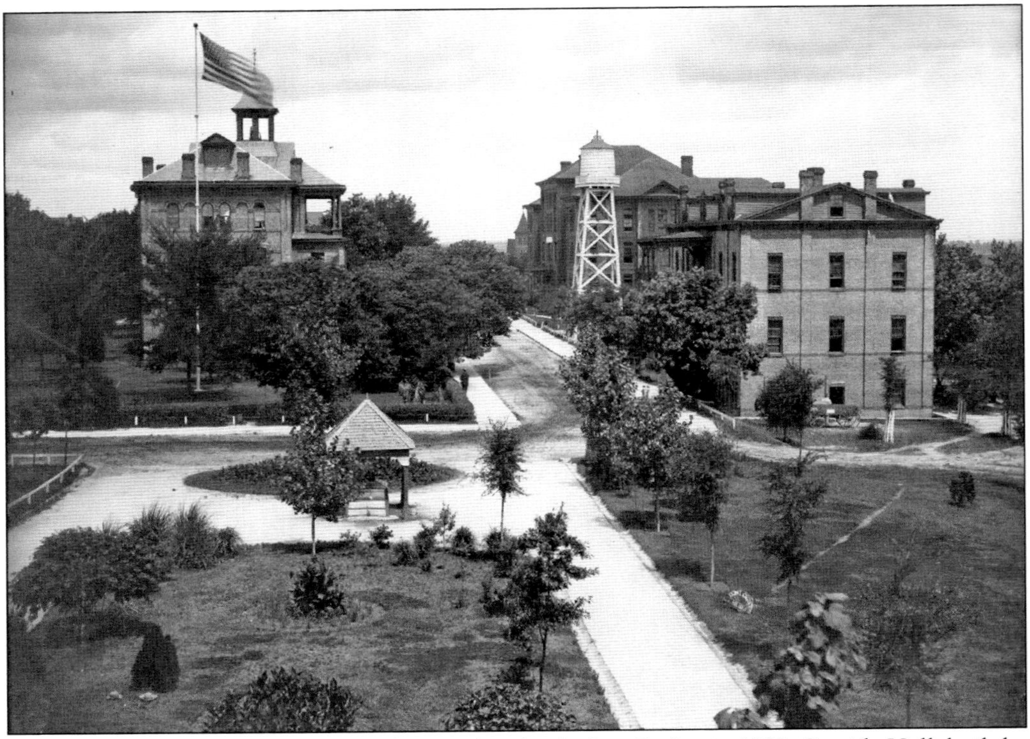

This photograph of Cassidy Hill Park was taken by Arthur Bedou in 1907. Cassidy Hall, built by students in 1892, was a three-story brick building at the east entrance to the grounds. It was used as a primary site for mechanical studies until 1900 when, through a gift from George F. Peabody of New York, it was converted into a male dormitory.

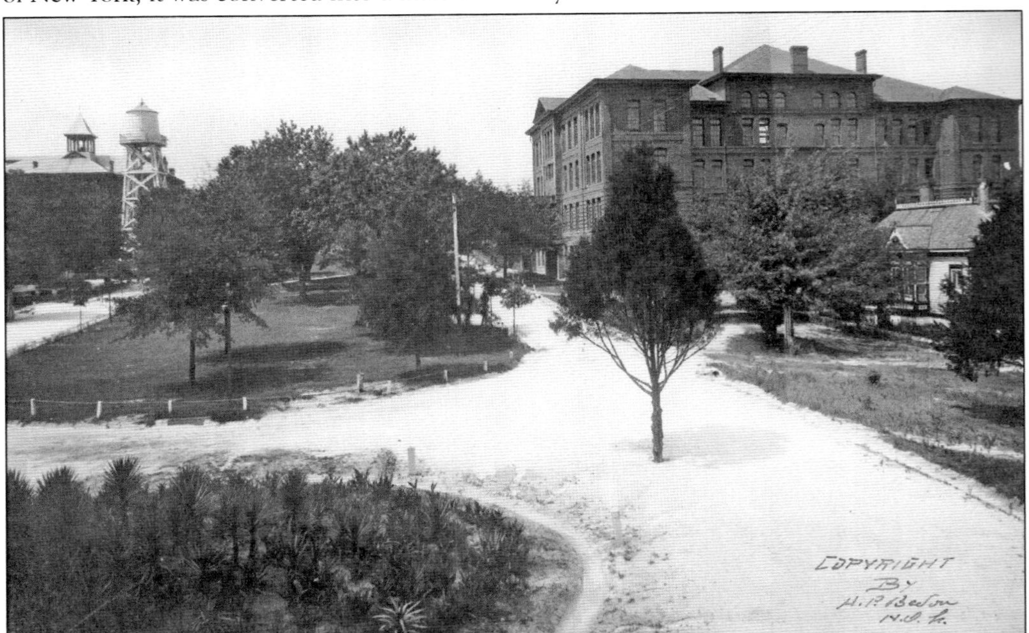

This view of Rockefeller Square was taken by Arthur Bedou in 1907. This was one of the locations on campus that was subject to heavy foot traffic at peak times during the day.

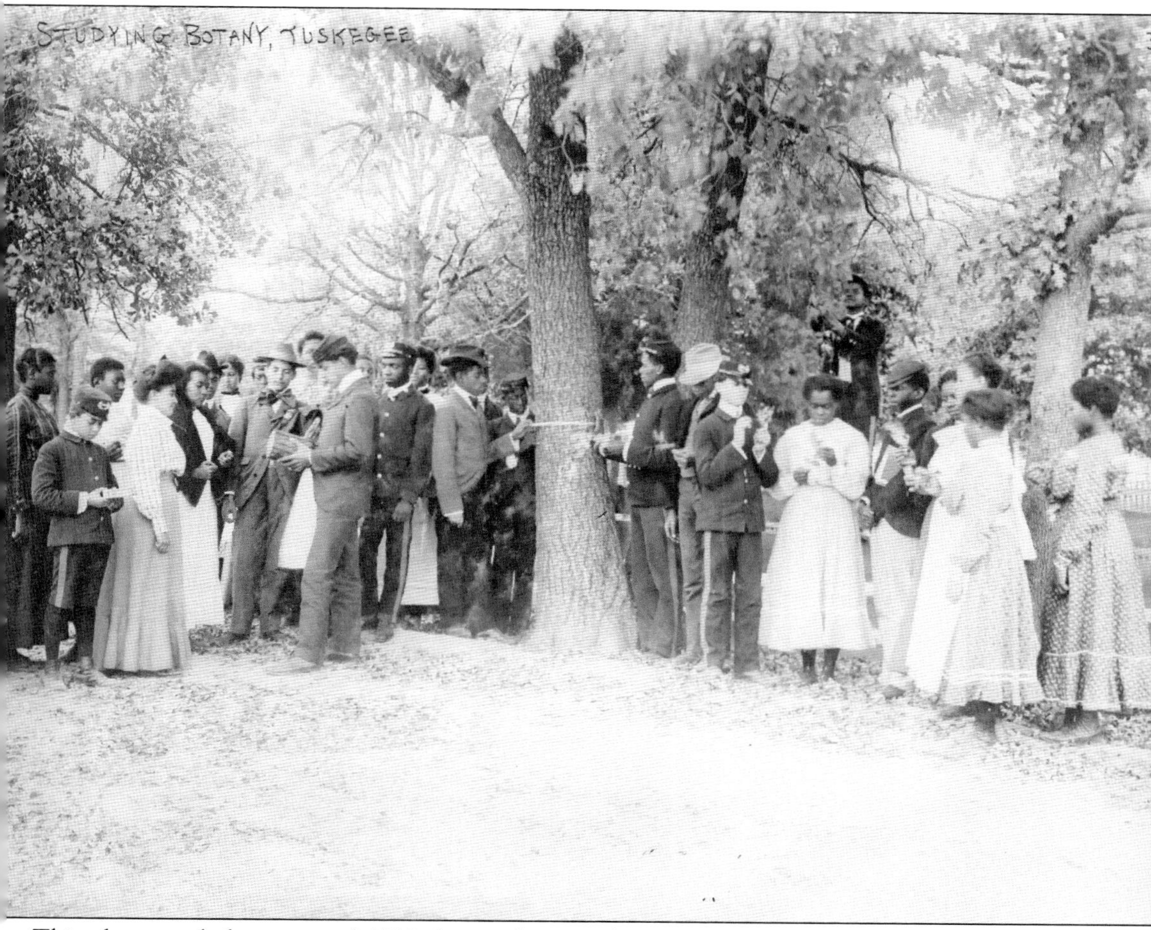

This photograph from around 1900 shows a botany class. Tuskegee taught almost 25 different trades, including plumbing, carpentry, masonry, shoe repair, and most other artisan skills that were useful to society. The largest enrollment was in the Department of Mechanical Industries, although an ample number of students were in the Department of Agriculture as well.

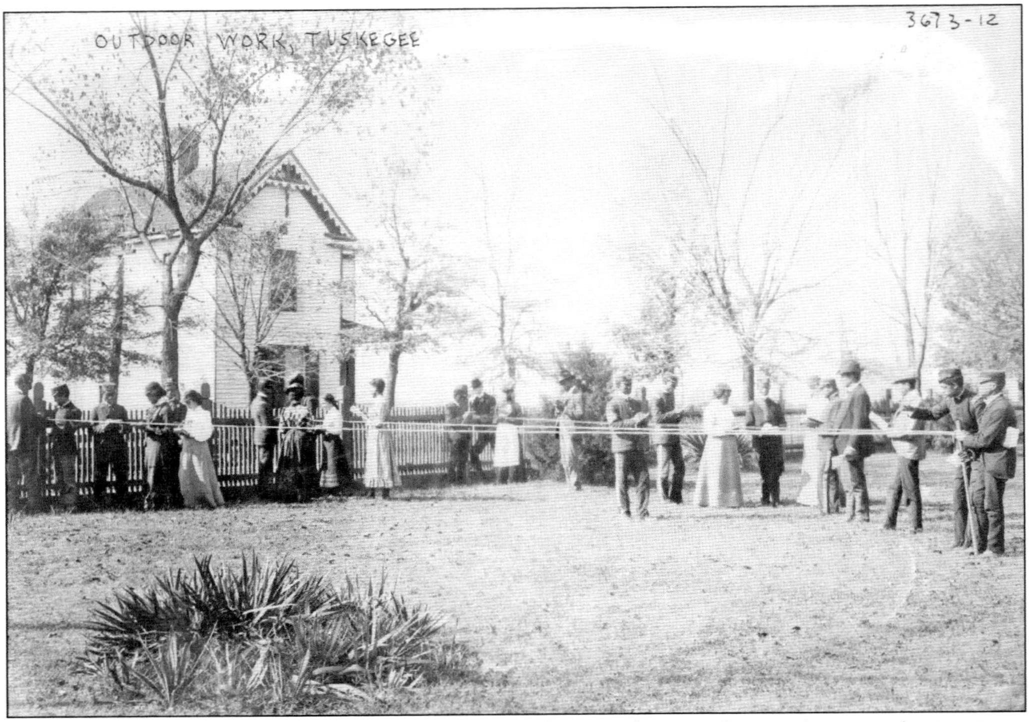

This orderly group of students is leisurely engaged in outdoor work on a lawn at the institute around 1920, taking measurements with an extended rope.

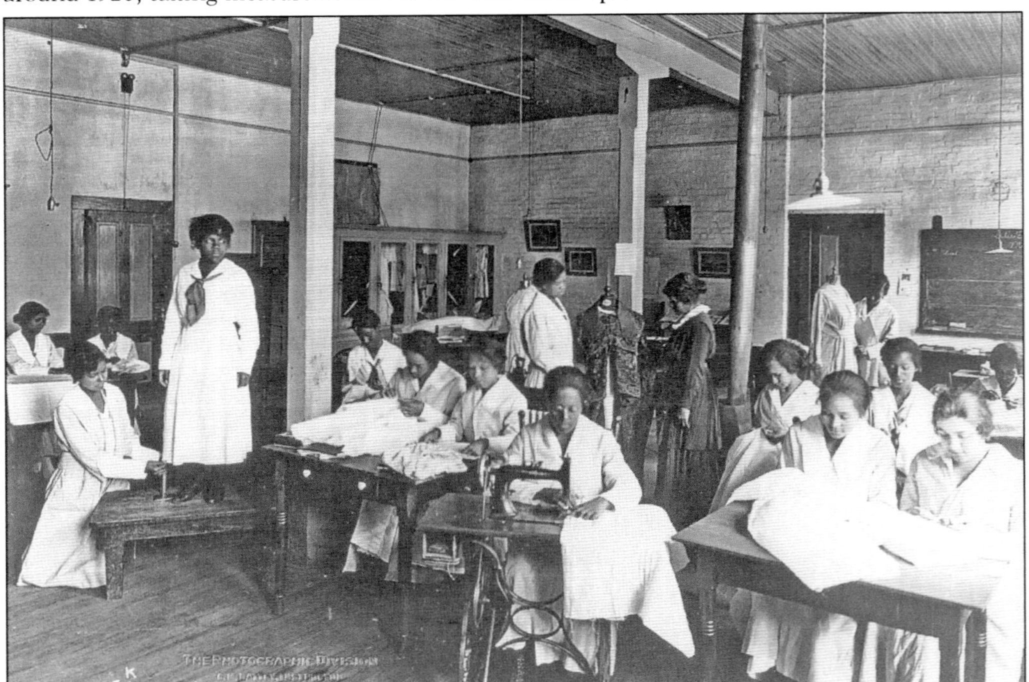

This large class of the dressmaking division spent the day, from 7:00 a.m. to 5:30 p.m., making blue uniform dresses, filling orders for tailor-made dresses in silk and cloth, measuring, drafting, cutting, and fitting. This postcard is from around 1890.

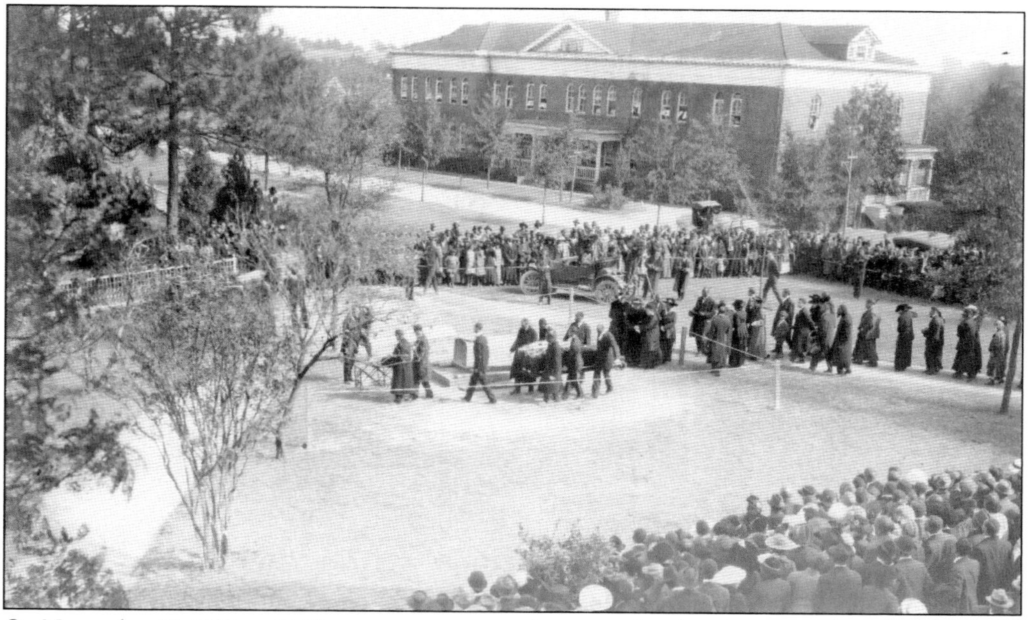

On November 17, 1915, at 10:20 a.m., a procession of trustees, faculty, alumni, visitors, honorary and active pallbearers, and students began to move slowly from The Oaks toward the chapel, carrying the body of Booker T. Washington. The long line moved to the sound of muffled drums, taking an expected amount of time to get to its conclusion. Inside, the chapel was packed to suffocation. Chaplains John W. Whittaker and Dean G.L. Imes of the Phelps Hall Bible School officiated.

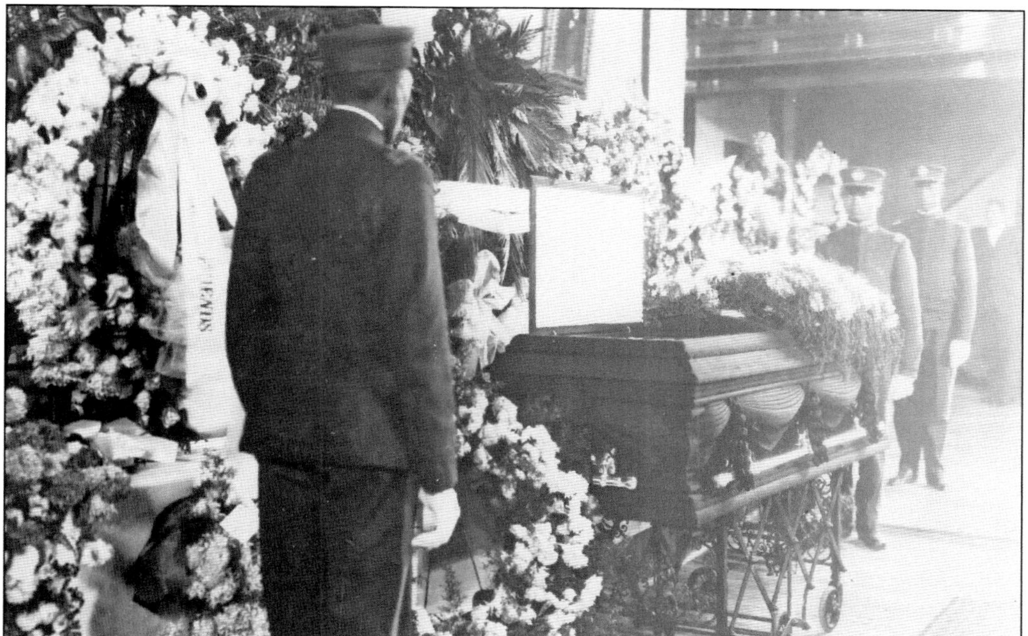

Booker T. Washington's body lay in state under the guard of 44 officers of the student battalions assigned to the chapel, changing watch every few minutes during the service. The program was as simple as the attendance was great. Attendees included African American leaders from all parts of the continent, a host of whites, and multitudes of the simple, country folks Washington loved so much.

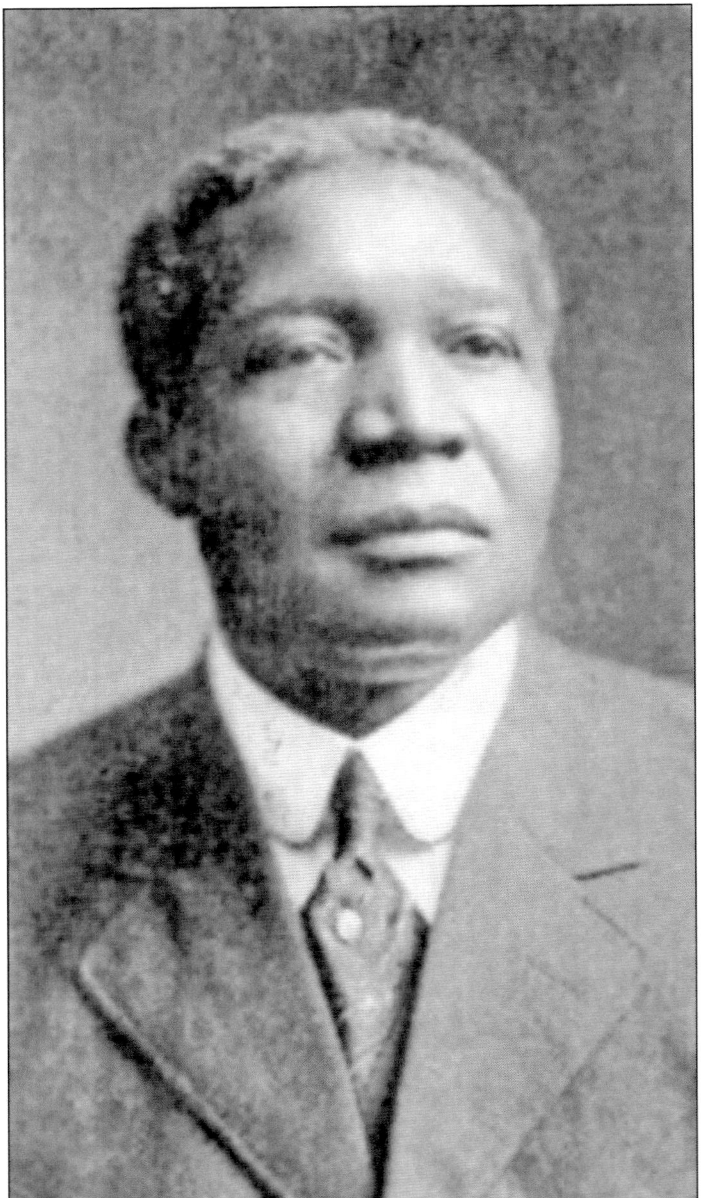

Maj. Robert Russa Moton (1867–1940) became the second principal of Tuskegee after Washington's death in 1915, continuing many of his predecessor's policies. Moton became chairman of the National League on Urban Conditions in 1919, was elected president of the National Negro Business League in 1921, maintained strong White House ties, and was a speaker at the Lincoln Memorial dedication in Washington, DC, in 1922. Academics expanded during his tenure, with liberal arts added to the curriculum and the school becoming a four-year, degree-granting institute in the fields of agriculture, home economics, mechanical industries, and education in 1925. Moton's title eventually changed to president, the school endowment more than tripled to $7.7 million, and, in 1923, Moton committed school land and secured the construction of the Veterans Administration hospital on campus, establishing the first and only such facility staffed exclusively by blacks.

William Levi Dawson graduated from Tuskegee Institute in 1921, as seen in this photograph by Cornelius M. Battey. He then trained at the American Conservatory of Music in Chicago and went on to play first trombone with the Chicago Civic Orchestra. Dawson returned to Tuskegee Institute to teach music in 1930, distinguishing himself as a composer and choral director. (Courtesy of the Manuscript, Archives, and Rare Book Library, Robert W. Woodruff Library, Emory University.)

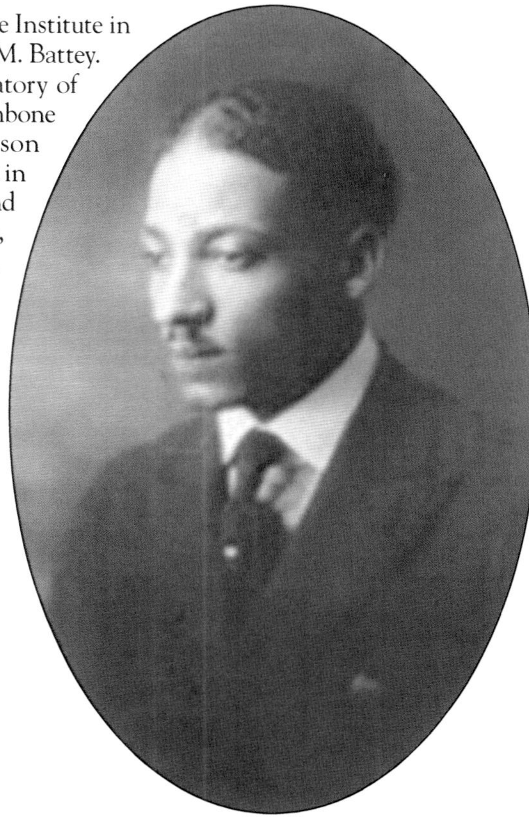

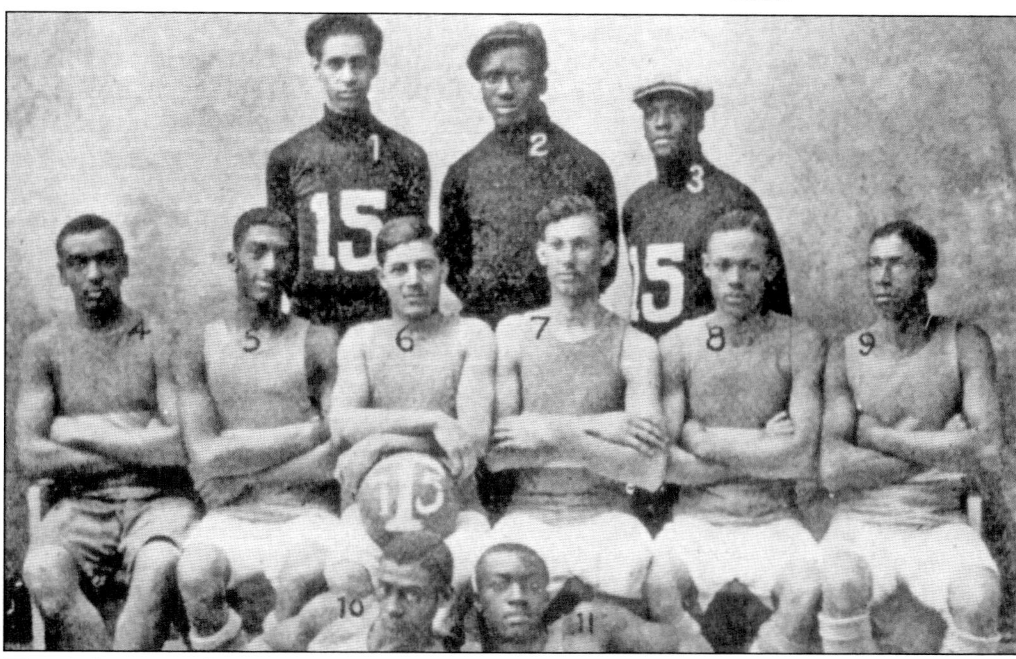

The 1915–1916 Tuskegee Institute varsity basketball team poses for a team photograph. While the emphasis was on football during the institute's early years, the Tigers gained national prominence in basketball in the 1920s.

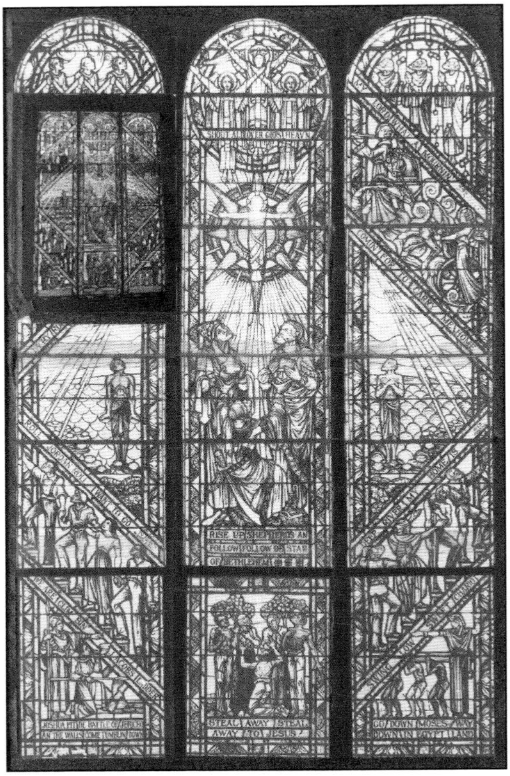

The stained-glass chapel windows, called "singing windows," were added to the chapel during President Moton's term. Other improvements during his tenure included a new wing to the John A. Andrew Hospital and the construction of Margaret Murray Washington Hall, Logan Hall, the Hollis Burke Frissell Library, and Samuel Chapman Armstrong Hall.

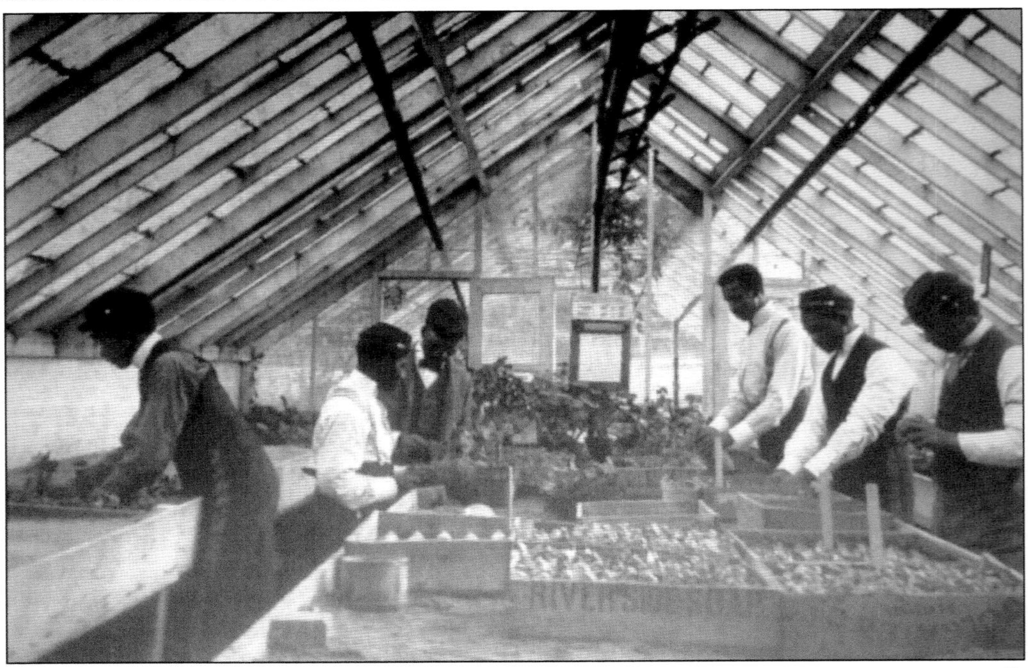

President Moton oversaw other structural additions and improvements on campus as well, including the new horse barn, the dairy, the Chambliss Children's House, the William G. Willcox Building, and the greenhouse shown here during a horticulture class around 1920. (Courtesy of the Library of Congress.)

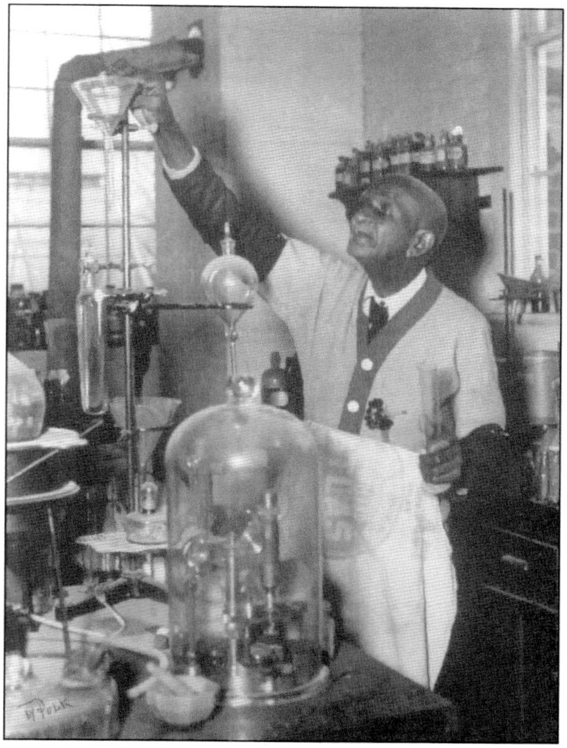

George Washington Carver is conducting research with test tubes in a laboratory in this 1929 P.H. Polk photograph. (Courtesy of the estate of P.H. Polk.)

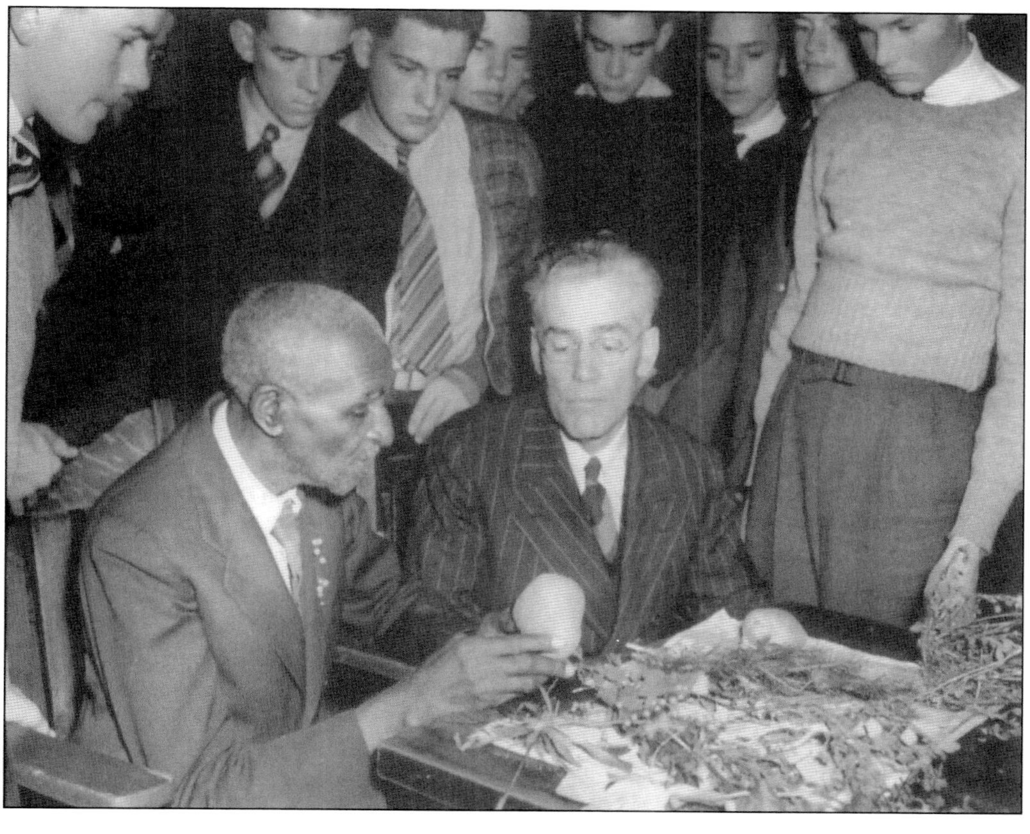

George Washington Carver is seen here giving a classroom demonstration at Tuskegee to a visiting class of white students in this P.H. Polk photograph from around 1930. The visitors are watching intently. (Courtesy of the estate of P.H. Polk.)

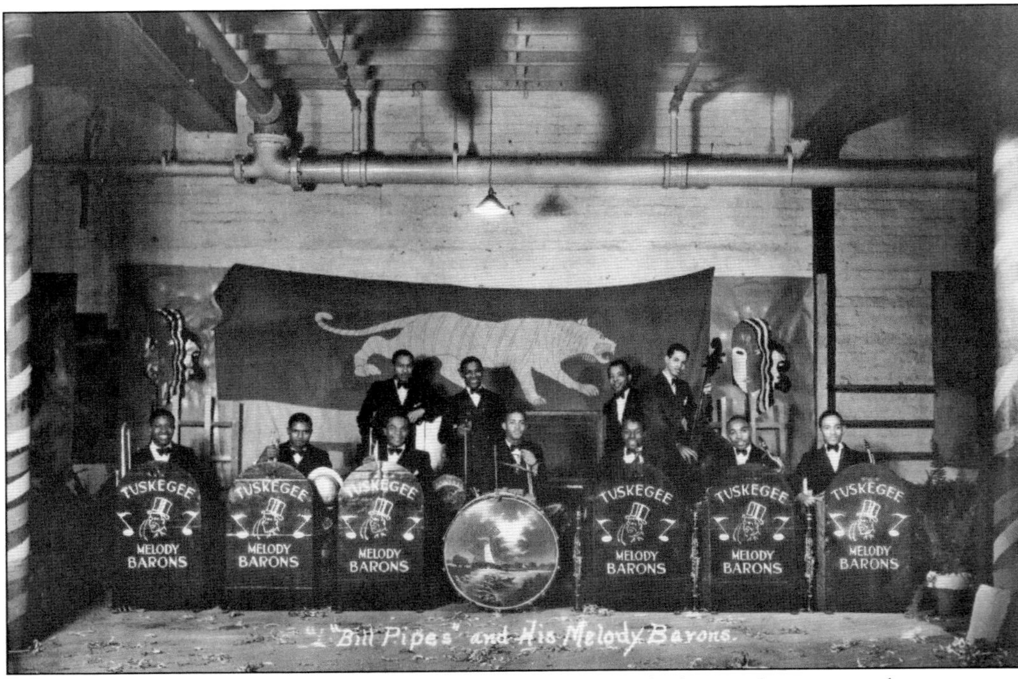

Bill Pipes and His Melody Barons pose for P.H. Polk's camera before performing at a homecoming event at Tuskegee in 1929. (Courtesy of the estate of P.H. Polk.)

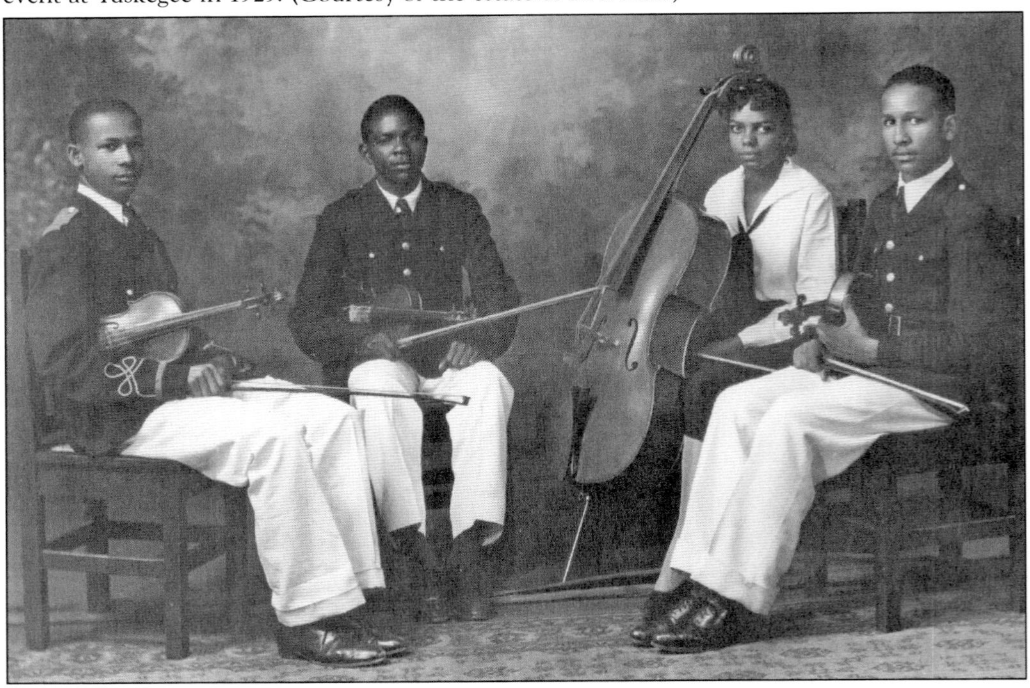

Unidentified students in the Tuskegee Institute string quartet pose for a formal portrait by P.H. Polk. Music became an important program at the institute due to the presence of William Levi Dawson, an alumnus who played first trombone for the Chicago Civic Orchestra before returning to head the music department. He had been back for two years when this photograph was taken in 1932. (Courtesy of the estate of P.H. Polk.)

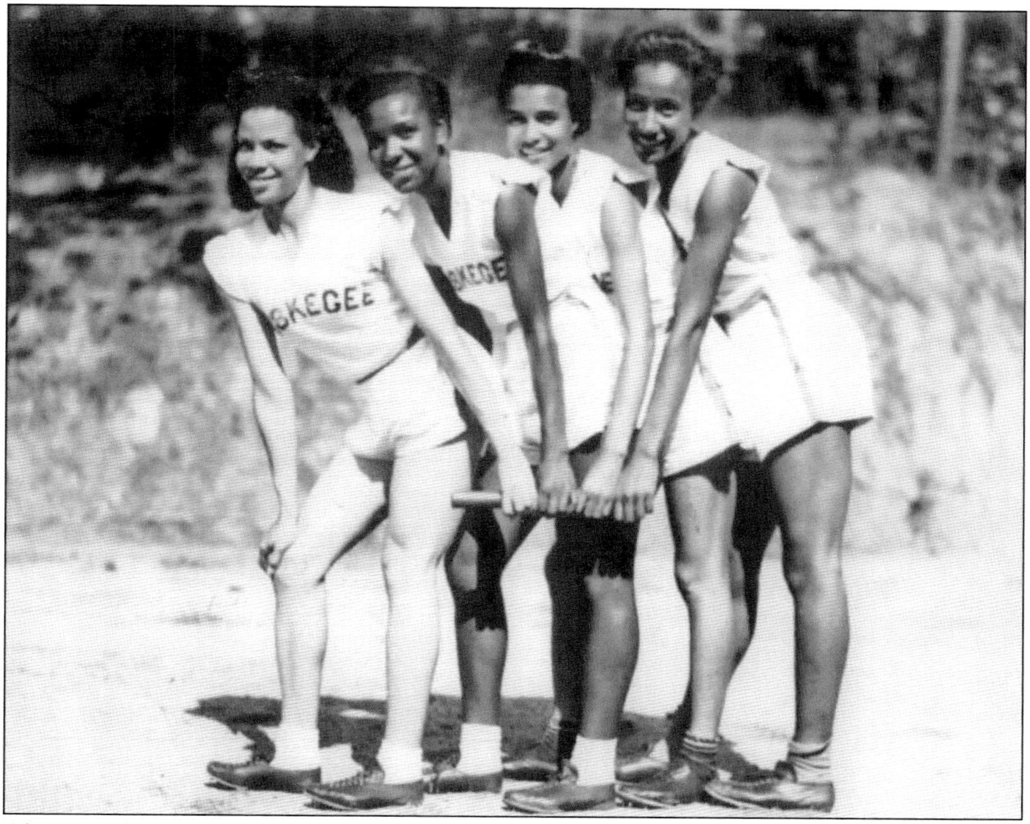

Alice Coachman, the Tuskegee Flash, anchored the female relay team at the institute. The 1942 Tuskegee Golden Tigerettes included, from left to right, Lucy Newall, Leila Perry, Rowena Harrison, and Coachman. In 1948, Coachman became the first African American woman to win an Olympic gold medal, winning in the high jump. (Courtesy of Tuskegee University Archives.)

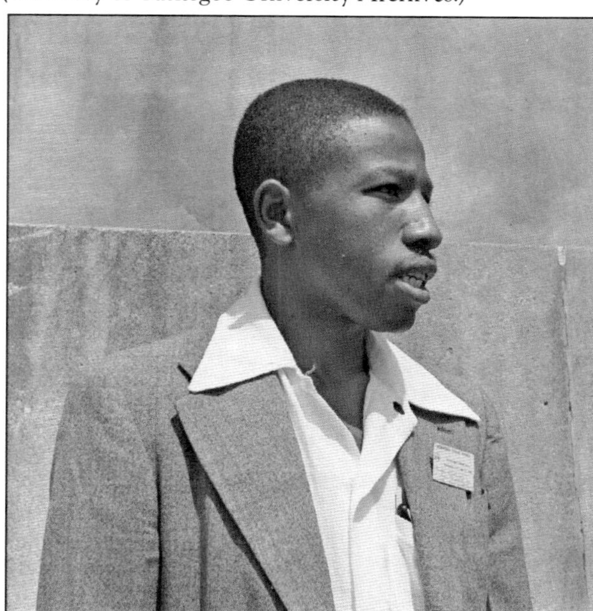

Theodore R. Johnson was the institute's delegate to the 1942 International Student Assembly in Washington, DC. Organized by the US Committee of International Student Service, 365 youths representing 56 nations gathered at George Washington University under the banner of the United Nations to discuss new ways to achieve a better global life. Pres. Franklin D. Roosevelt's keynote address was translated into 31 languages, and First Lady Eleanor Roosevelt facilitated the event.

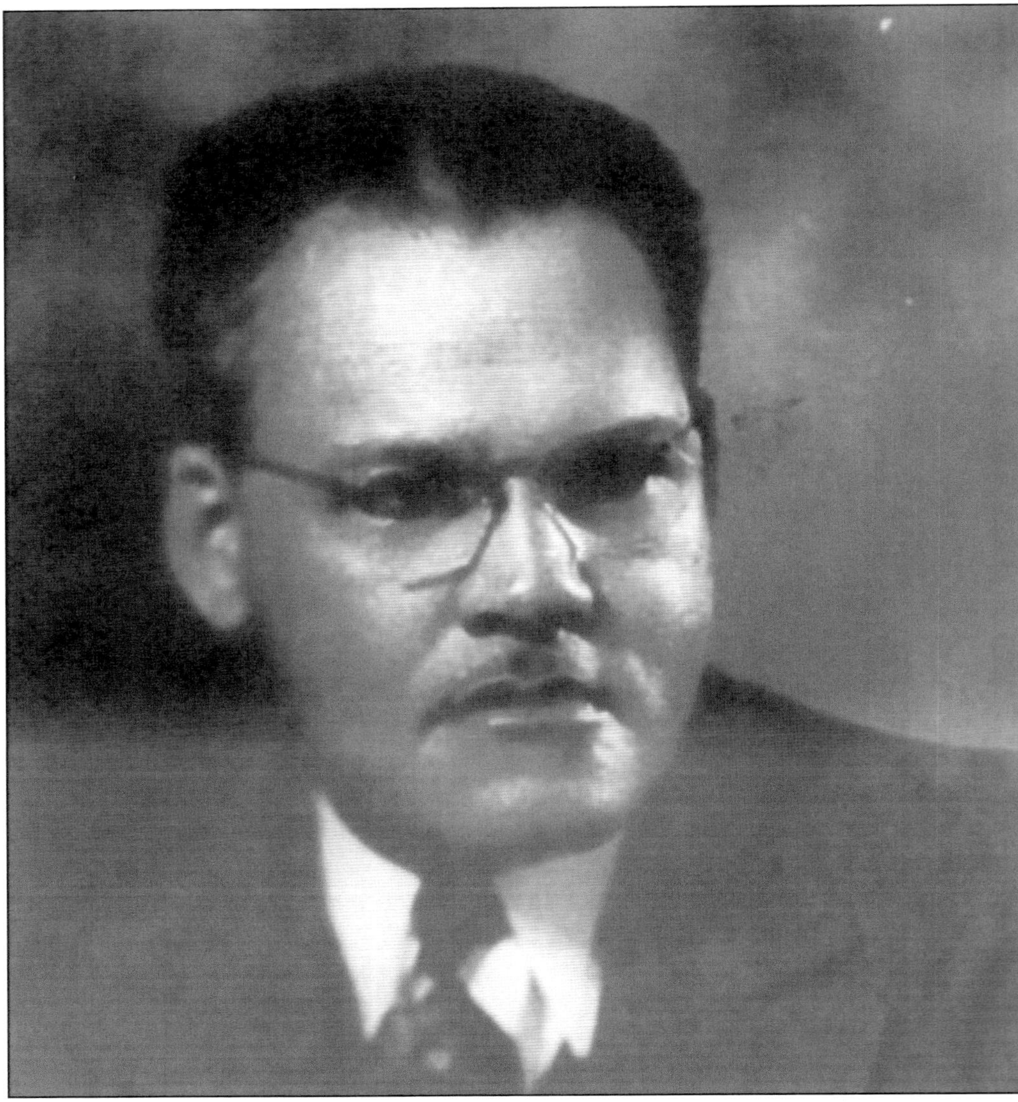

Frederick Douglass Patterson became the head of the veterinary division at Tuskegee Institute in 1928. Soon after, Patterson, who held a PhD in veterinary medicine from Iowa State and a PhD in bacteriology from Cornell University, became the director of the school of agriculture. In 1935, he succeeded Robert Moton, his father-in-law, to become the third president of the institute, a position he held until 1953. Tuskegee began offering graduate courses under his tenure. He also convinced the federal government to operate an air base on campus and persuaded the Alabama legislature to increase annual allocations to the institute from $2,500 to $110,000. Patterson also conceived the United Negro College Fund, which established a central organization to receive funds to support historically black colleges and universities, helping to relieve some of the burden of individual development, especially among small colleges with limited staff, and to minimize multiple institutions pursuing the same supporters.

Dr. Luther Hilton Foster Jr. was the fourth president of Tuskegee Institute, serving from 1953 to 1981. Dr. Foster led the institution through the era of the Civil Rights movement, including such events as the death of student Sammy Younge Jr., the first college student to die in the movement, and the important Gomillion v. Lightfoot Supreme Court decision.

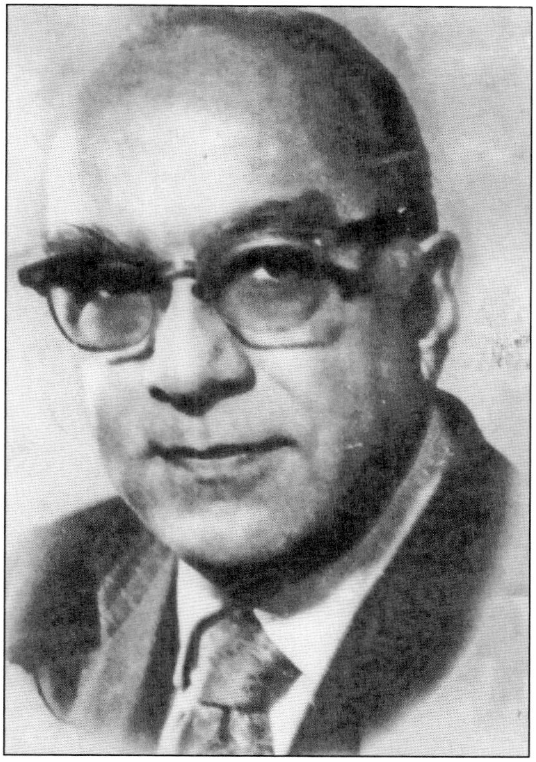

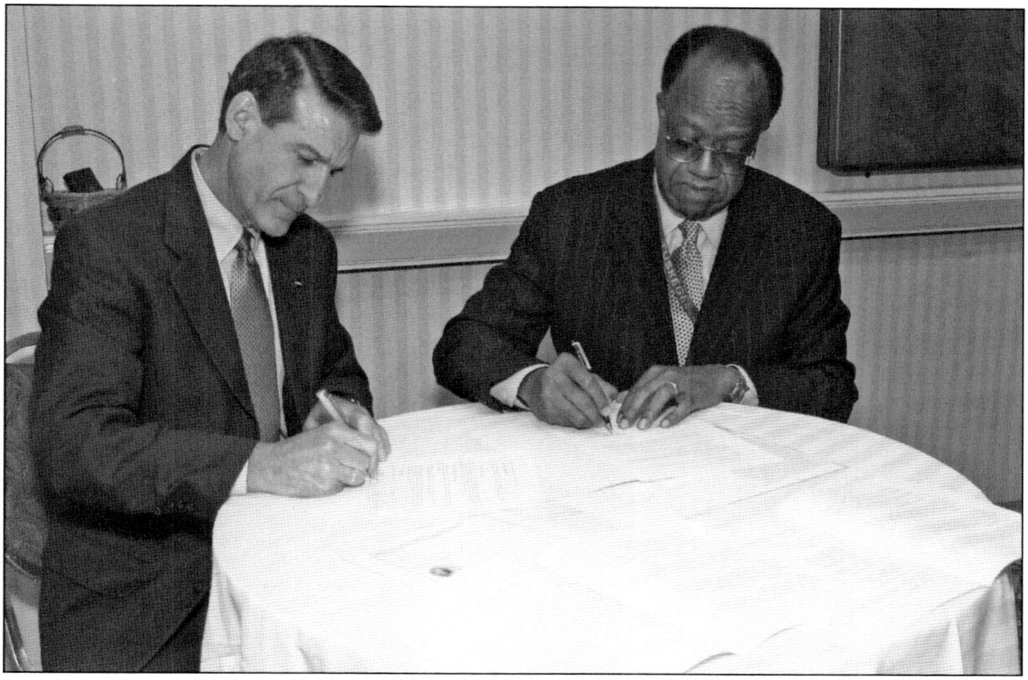

Art Stephenson (left) and Tuskegee president Benjamin F. Payton are seen here signing an agreement formalizing the addition of Tuskegee to the National Space Science and Technology Center in Huntsville. Dr. Payton was the fifth president of Tuskegee University, serving from 1981 to 2010.

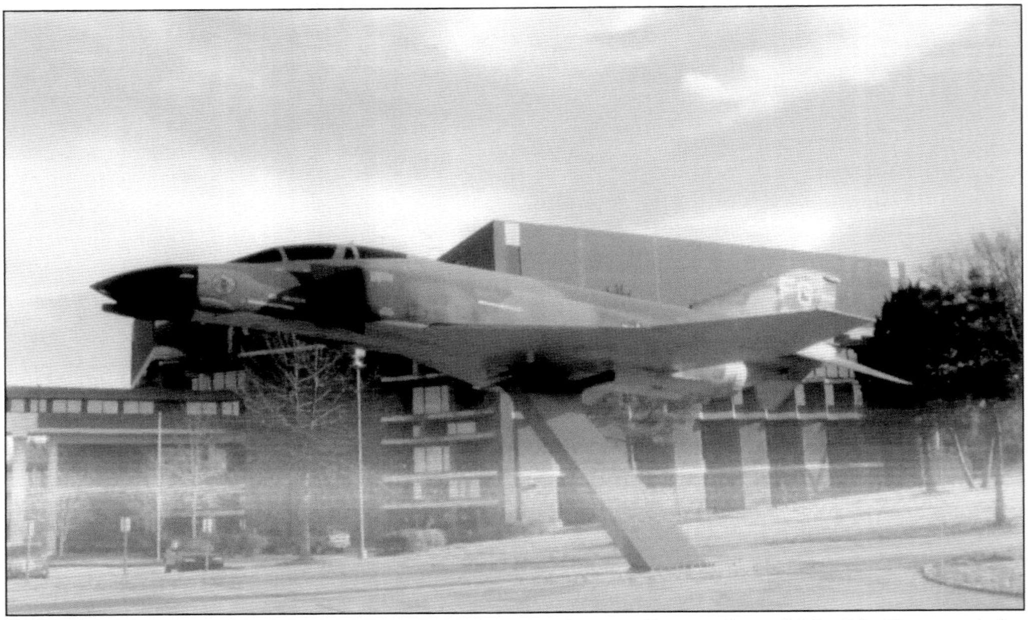

Dr. Payton developed the National Center for Bioethics in Research and Health Care and the Gen. Daniel "Chappie" James Center for Aerospace Science and Health Education, the largest athletic arena in the Southern Intercollegiate Athletic Conference (pictured). He also launched the first PhD programs at Tuskegee University. (Courtesy of Tuskegee University Archives.)

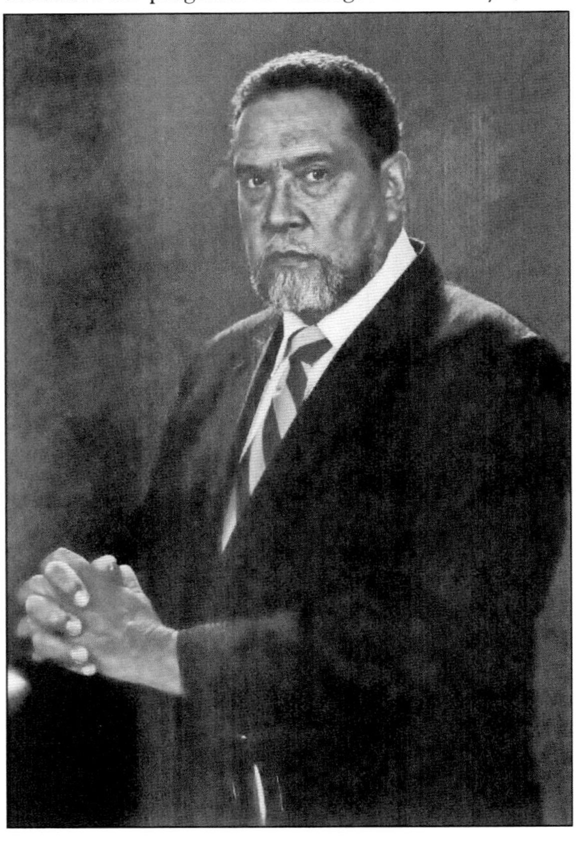

Dr. Gilbert Leonard Rochon became the sixth president of Tuskegee University in 2010. He has vowed "to bring the world to Tuskegee and Tuskegee to the world." Sharing a commitment with his alma mater, the Massachusetts Institute of Technology, to state-of-the-art excellence, Dr. Rochon has declared that Tuskegee is "not content with being a top baccalaureate college; we have our sights on becoming a top doctoral research institution." (Courtesy of Tuskegee University Archives.)

Four

"Mr. Polk, Take My Picture"

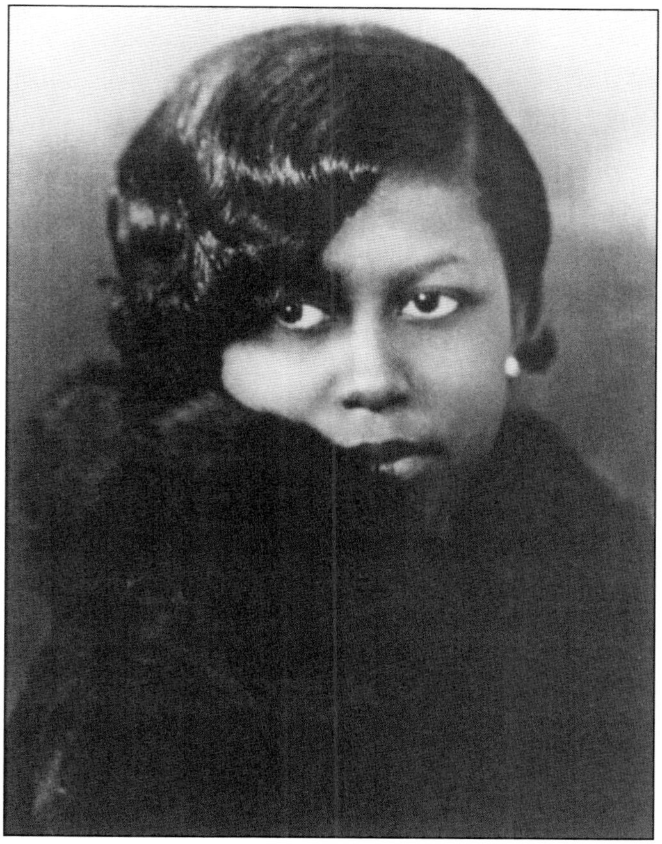

For most students, one advantage of attending Tuskegee Institute, aside from the educational opportunities it provided, was to have their portrait taken by "Mr. Polk." Though Polk's photographic work was essentially a Southern secret until the 1970s, he was considered a local treasure by many Macon County residents, particularly people affiliated with the school. Alberta Osborn posed for this photograph during her junior year in the winter of 1929. (Courtesy of the estate of P.H. Polk.)

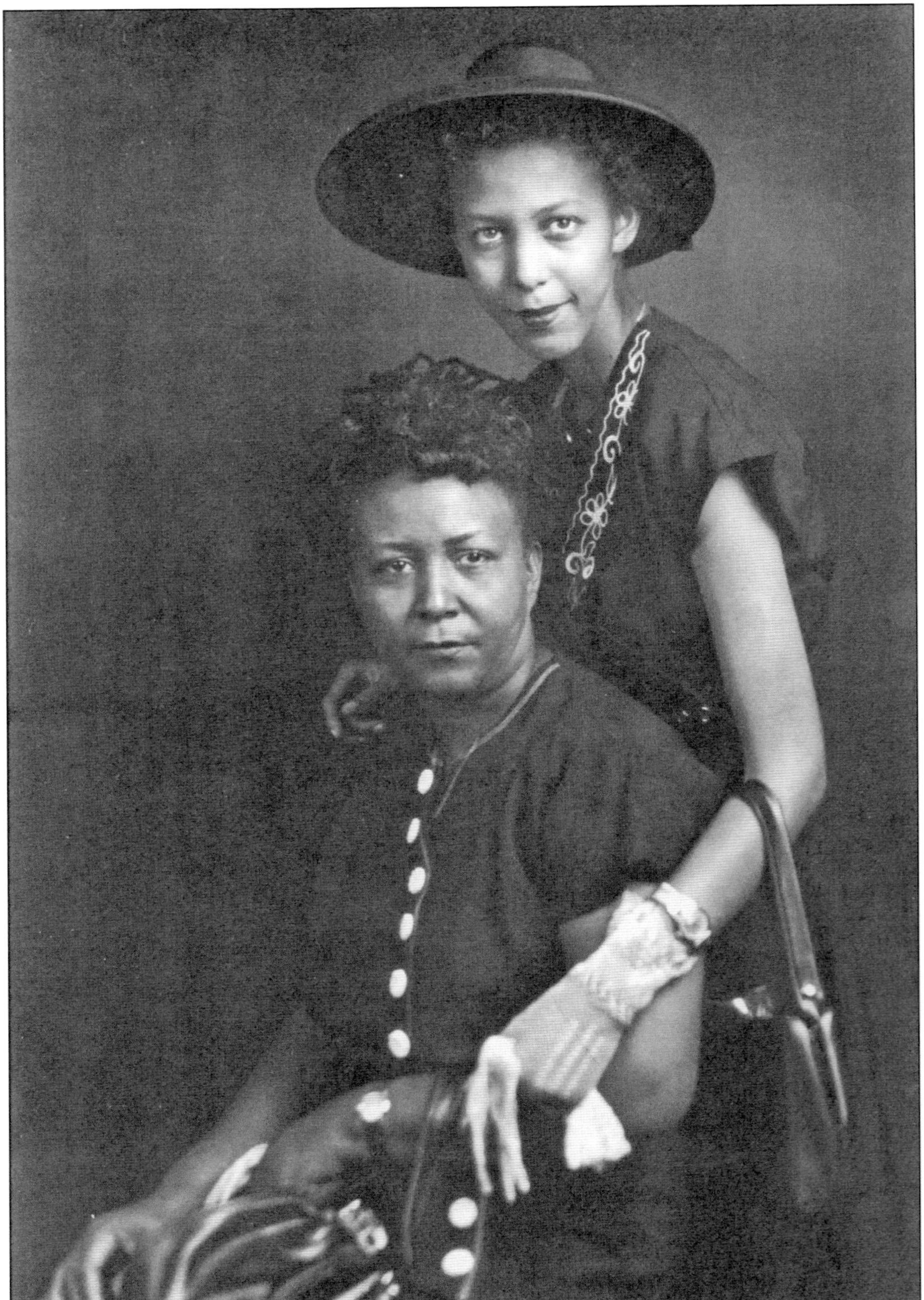

P.H. Polk's wife, Margaret Blanche Polk, and daughter Barbara Jean Polk pose in 1947 at the Polk Studio. The photograph reflects the closeness between mother and daughter and is an example of the body of portraits he created of family members. (Courtesy of the estate of P.H. Polk.)

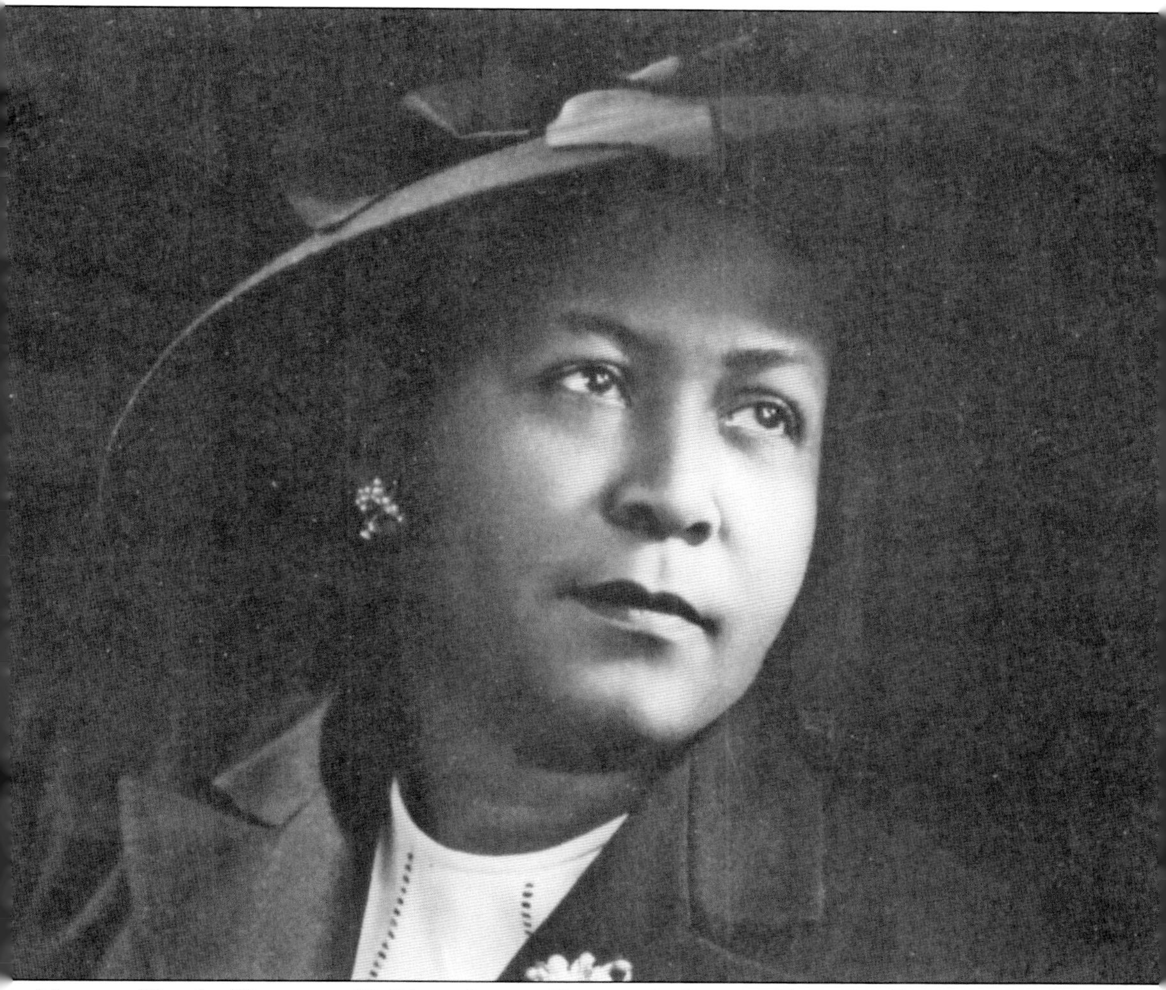

Margaret Blanche Thompson (Polk) was born in Brunswick, Georgia. She and Polk were married in Chicago in January 1926 and had nine children. They arrived in Tuskegee the following year with six-month-old Prentice Polk Jr., and their next eight children were born in Tuskegee. Margaret Polk focused initially on raising her family and then opened and operated a local restaurant in the 1940s called the Golden Tiger Café, named after the Tuskegee mascot. She also worked as a physical therapist, continuing the vocation for the remainder of her career. Family members were readily accessible as subjects for Polk's personal studio work. He took this photograph of his wife in 1946. It is considered one of the best examples of his preference for forming images around deeper tones, which he called working "from the dark side." (Courtesy of the estate of P.H. Polk.)

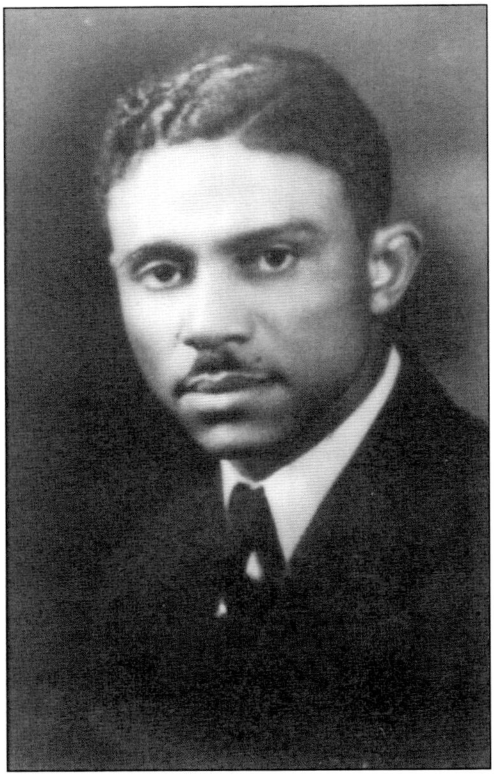

Prentice Herman Polk (1898–1984) was born Herman Polk but assumed his late father's first name in 1916. He attended Tuskegee Normal and Industrial Institute, first as a night student and then as the first day student to enroll in the school's new photography program. After three years of study under C.M. Battey, Polk graduated in 1920. He continued his training with a correspondence course and then worked as an apprentice in Chicago for photographer Fred A. Jensen. Polk worked odd jobs before returning to Tuskegee with his wife and young son in 1927. He began teaching at the institute and assisting Battey's successor, Leonard G. Hyman, in 1928. In 1933, Polk became the official photographer while also maintaining a successful private studio business. Except for 1938, when he attempted to set up a studio in Atlanta, Polk was professionally associated with Tuskegee for the rest of his life. (Courtesy of the estate of P.H. Polk.)

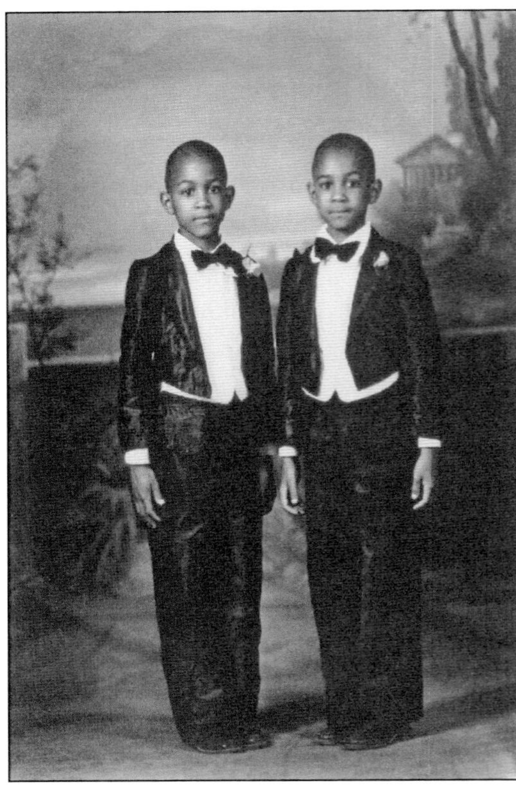

Theodore Clanville Polk (left) and Cornelius Wayman Polk were born in Tuskegee in 1929. In this 1936 photograph, Polk captured the twins dressed for a mock wedding. Polk later confessed that, looking back at the image, it was difficult even for him to tell which was which. (Courtesy of the estate of P.H. Polk.)

Twins Jacqueline and Jean Johnson posed for this birthday photograph in Polk's studio in 1932. Polk was known to tickle, make faces, play peek-a-boo with the black hood over his large-format camera, and use other lighthearted methods to get a desired response from his young subjects.

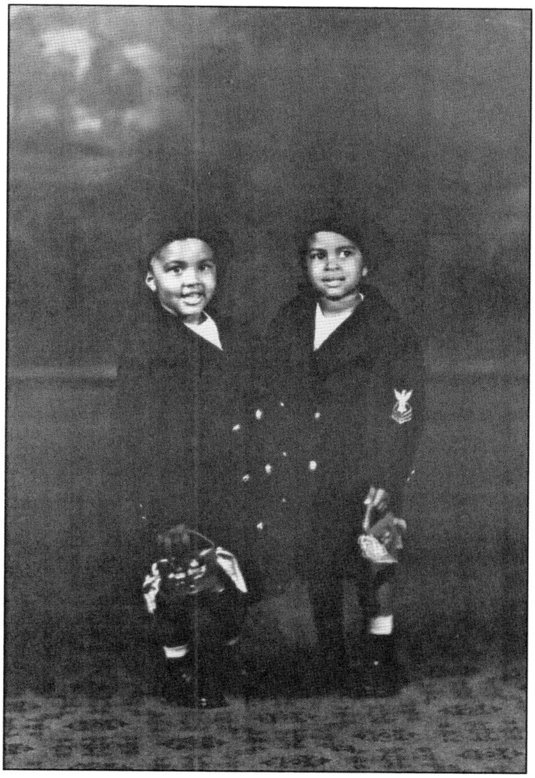

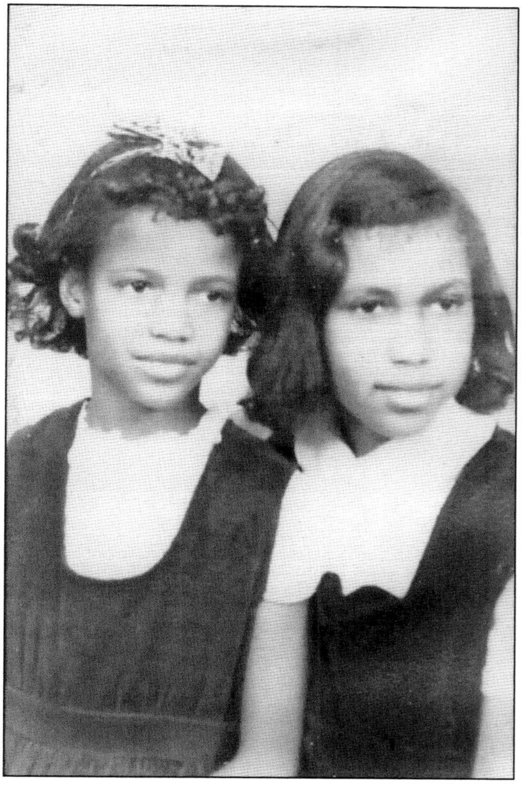

This photograph of two unidentified girls, most likely sisters, from around 1930, is typical of one type of formal portraiture produced by Polk in his private studio in Tuskegee.

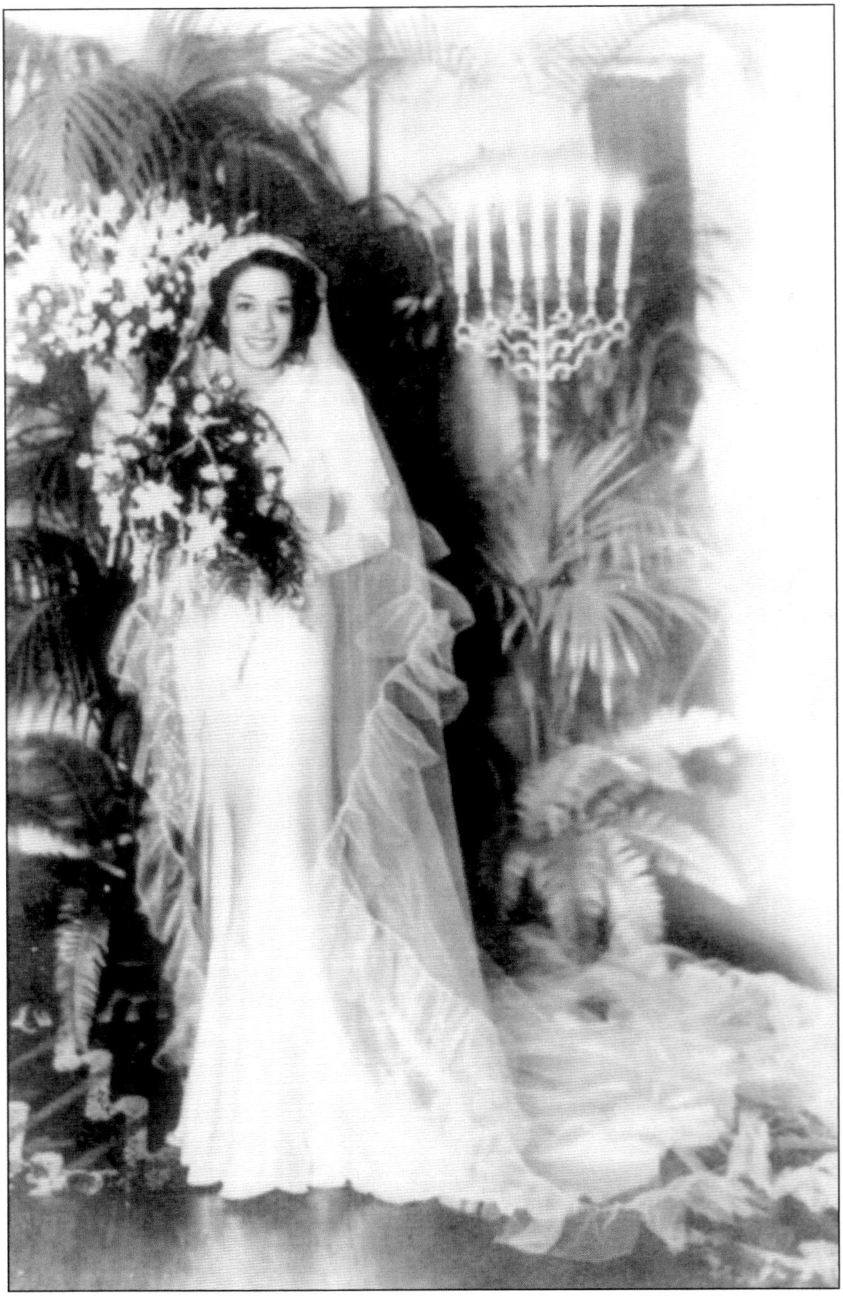

Choral director William Levi Dawson (1899–1990) met Cecile Demae Nicholson when he was the choir director at Ebenezer Church in Kansas City. She had earned a bachelor of arts degree from Howard University and a master of arts degree in home economics from Kansas State Teacher's College. The future Mrs. Dawson moved to Atlanta to chair the home economics department at Morris Brown College, and Dawson, a Tuskegee graduate, returned to the institute to teach in 1930. On September 21, 1935, the two were married at the Atlanta residence of artist Hale Aspacio Woodruff (1900–1980). The bride posed for this photograph before the ceremony. (Courtesy of the Manuscript, Archives, and Rare Book Library, Robert W. Woodruff Library, Emory University.)

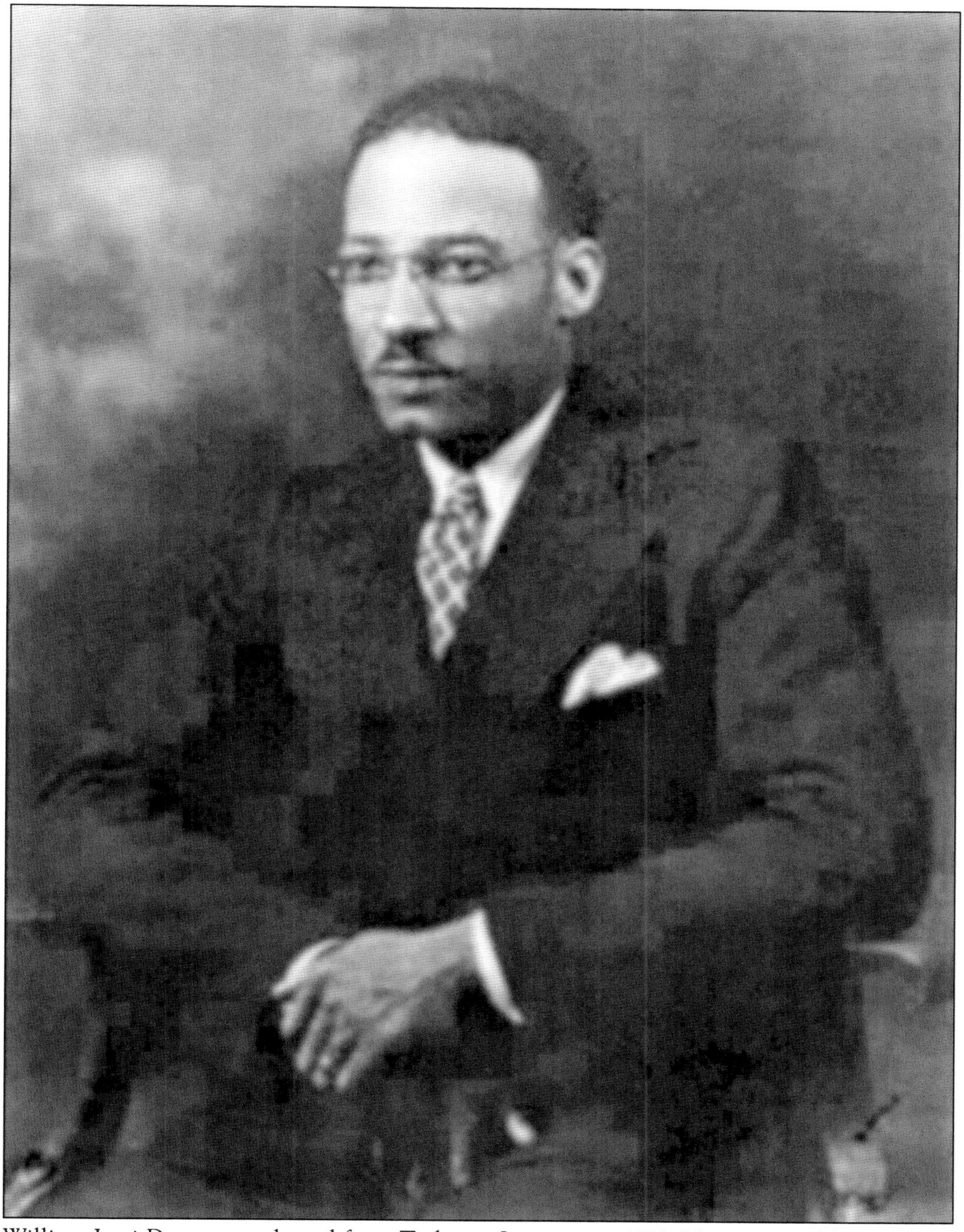

William Levi Dawson graduated from Tuskegee Institute in 1921. He continued his training at the American Conservatory of Music in Chicago and was playing first trombone with the Chicago Civic Orchestra about the time he sat for this Polk portrait in 1926. Dawson and Polk were acquainted from their time as students at the institute and renewed contact during their mutual time in Chicago. They were next reunited as teachers at Tuskegee, Polk in photography beginning in 1927 and Dawson in music starting in 1930. (Courtesy of the Manuscript, Archives, and Rare Book Library, Robert W. Woodruff Library, Emory University.)

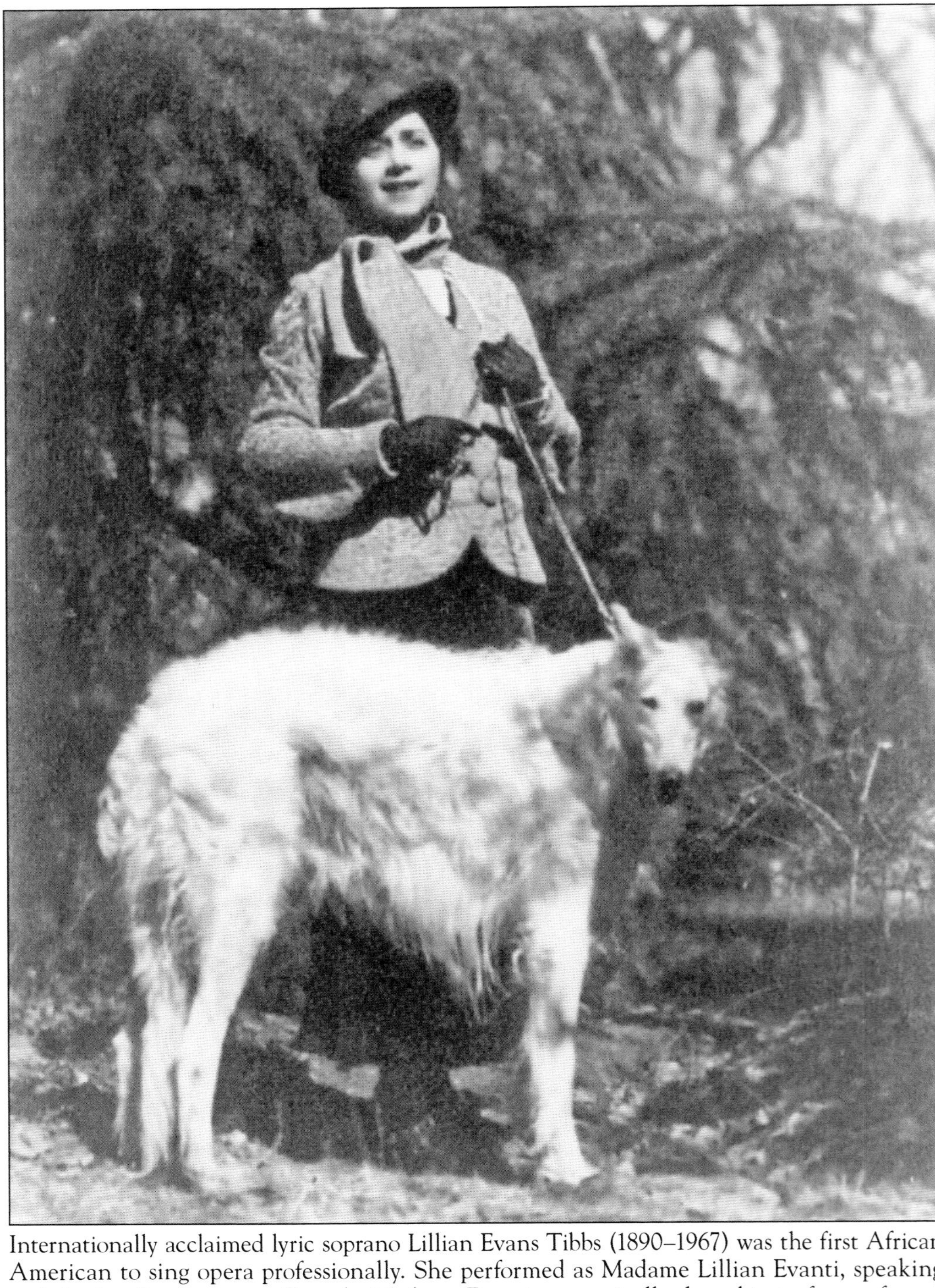

Internationally acclaimed lyric soprano Lillian Evans Tibbs (1890–1967) was the first African American to sing opera professionally. She performed as Madame Lillian Evanti, speaking and singing five languages fluently. Madame Evanti was typically the subject of more formal photographs. However, Polk chose to reveal something about her off-stage personality. While this 1937 photograph does capture her poise and grace, she is shown in a lighthearted, leisurely moment with her pet, minus the usual associations to her high-profile classical singing career. (Courtesy of the estate of P.H. Polk.)

This photograph of musician, playwright, lyricist, and singer Noble Sissle was commissioned in 1937, about the time he assumed leadership of the newly organized Negro Actors Guild of America. Sissle gained notoriety when he collaborated with songwriter Eubie Blake after World War I, performing in such Broadway shows as *Dixie Duo*. In 1921, they cowrote and coproduced *Shuffle Along*, the first Broadway musical written, produced, and performed by African Americans. (Courtesy of the estate of P.H. Polk.)

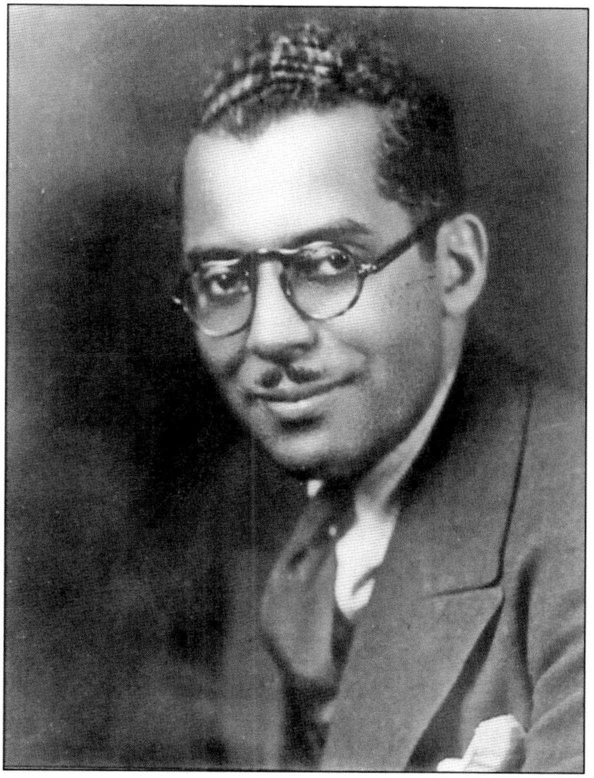

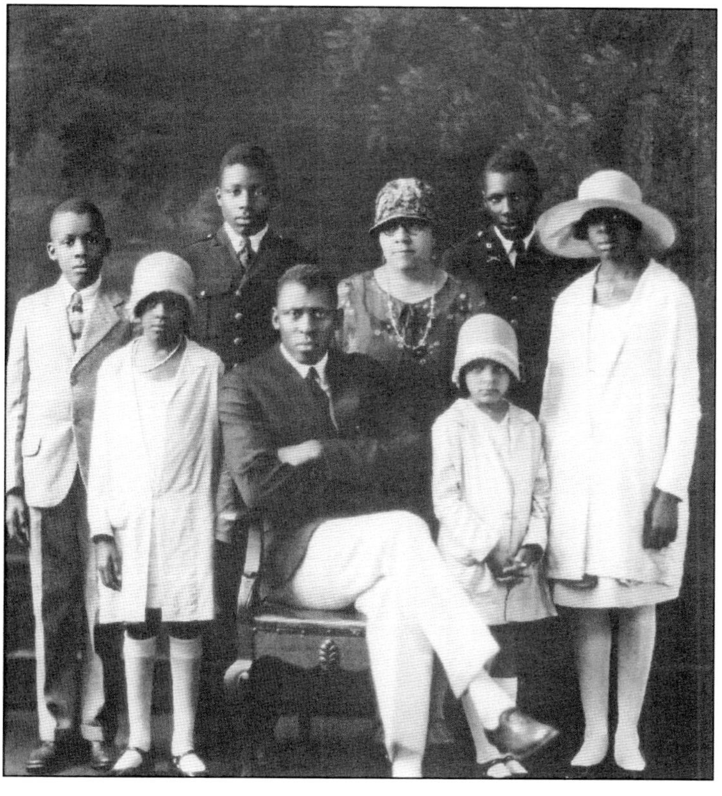

Tuskegee Institute instructor and agriculture agent T.M. Campbell (seated), his wife, Anna Ayers Campbell, and their six children are seen in this family portrait taken in Polk's studio after church on Easter Sunday 1932. Anna Campbell was a nurse trained at the institute, where the couple met. Their children also graduated from Tuskegee. (Courtesy of the estate of P.H. Polk.)

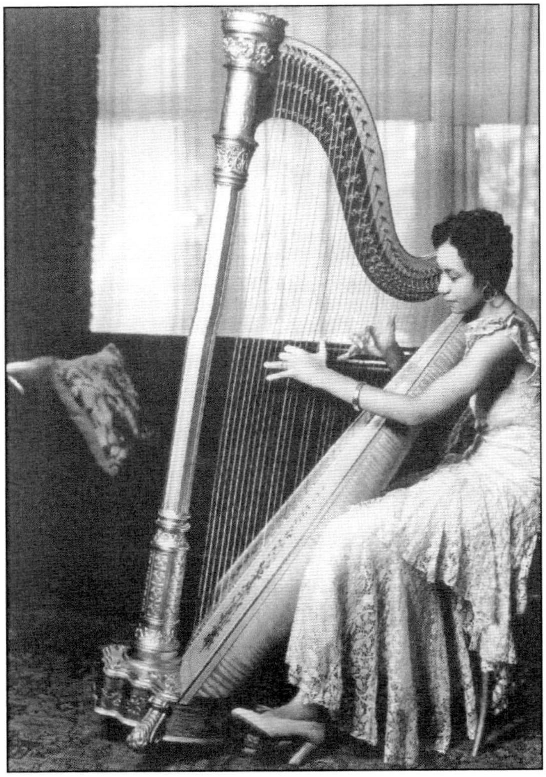

Catherine Moton Patterson, the daughter of Tuskegee president Robert Moton, continued to preside over the president's home as the wife of the next president, Frederick Douglass Patterson. She helped start the school of music and was highly regarded as a teacher and musician whose proficiency with the harp, violin, and piano was well known. As hostess to the almost continual stream of important visitors to Tuskegee's campus, she was also well known for her social skills and graces. She is seen here in 1936. (Courtesy of the estate of P.H. Polk.)

This photograph shows the Robinson-Ward wedding party in 1934. Mary Ward was the daughter of Zella and Col. Joseph Henry Ward, who was appointed chief medical officer of the Veterans Hospital at Tuskegee in 1922. He was the first African American to hold the position. (Courtesy of the estate of P.H. Polk.)

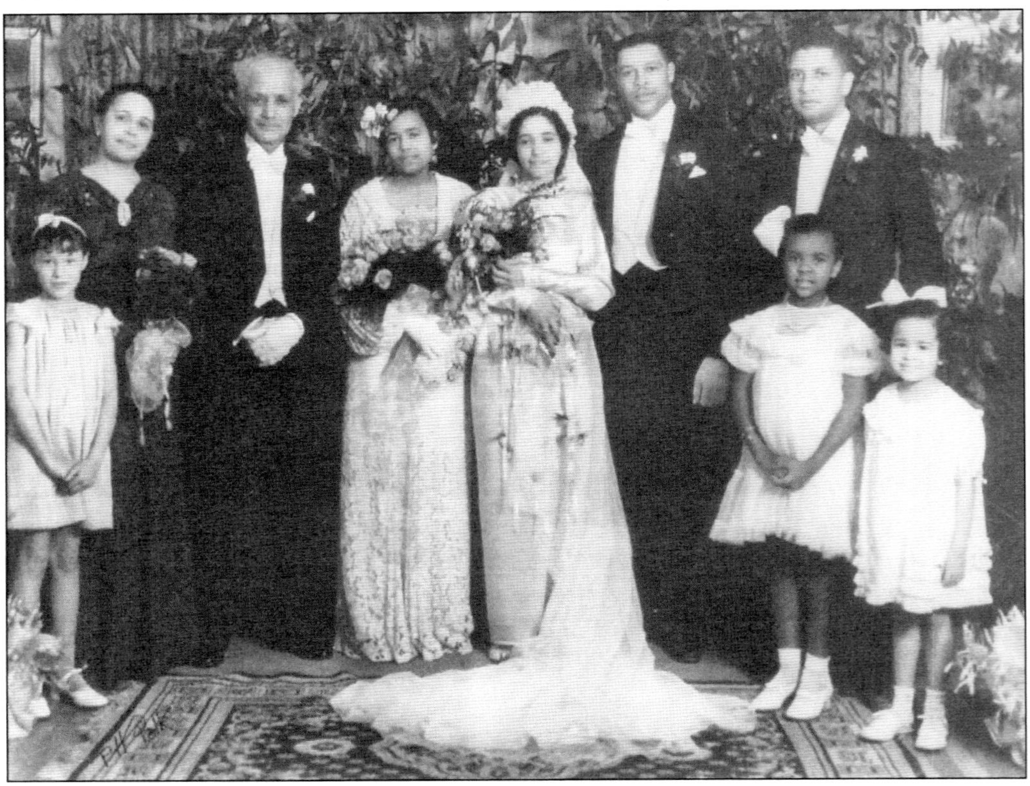

Nannie Helen Burroughs (1883–1861), an educator, activist, businesswoman, and orator, founded the National Training School for Women and Girls in 1901 in Washington, DC. She gained national attention for her speech "How the Sisters Are Hindered from Helping" at the 1900 National Baptist Convention, which made her in demand as a speaker. Burroughs was the first woman to deliver the commencement address at Tuskegee Institute, in 1934. This Polk photograph of her was taken in 1932. (Courtesy of the estate of P.H. Polk.)

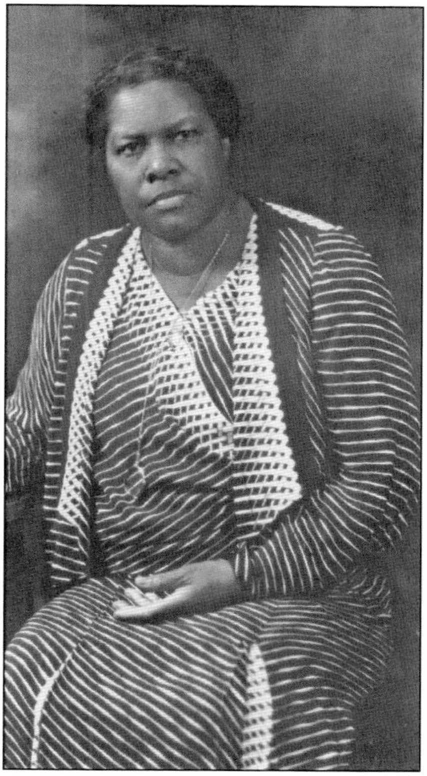

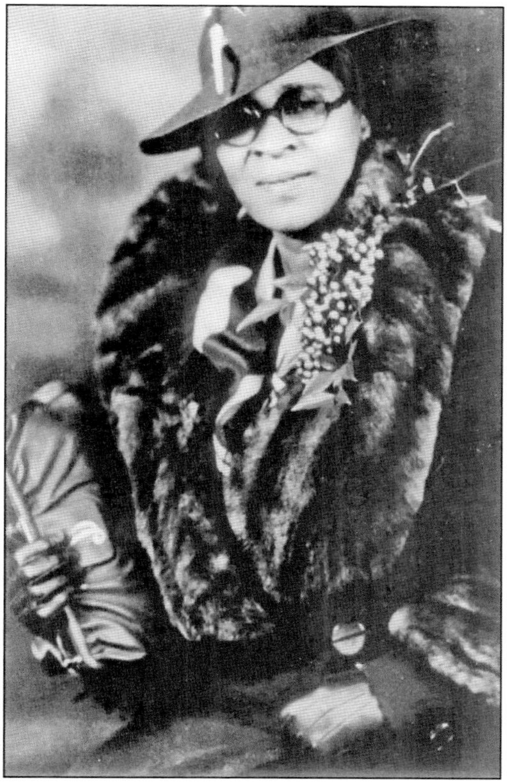

Dr. Charlotte Eugenia Hawkins Brown (1883–1961) founded the Alice Freeman Palmer Institute (later known as the Palmer Memorial Institute) in Sedalia, North Carolina, in 1905. Named after her friend and mentor Alice Palmer, who had become the first female president of Wellesley College in 1882, Brown shared Booker T. Washington's passion for educating people in the poorest and most rural communities. She initially followed the vocational curriculum at Tuskegee Normal, focusing on manual training and industrial education applied to rural living, earning praise and support from Washington for this mission. By 1933, when she sat for this portrait, Brown had shifted the curriculum towards liberal arts. Called the First Lady of Social Graces, Brown also incorporated basic social etiquette into her mission. (Courtesy of the estate of P.H. Polk.)

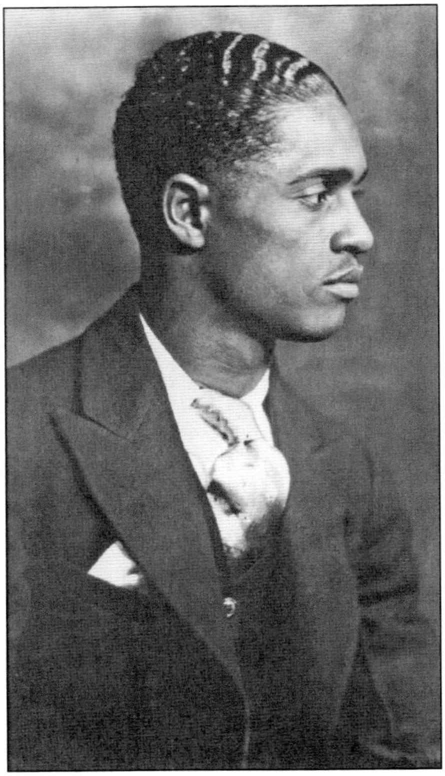

The unidentified young man in the 1935 portrait at left is believed to be a Tuskegee student. The photograph of J.L. Brown below, also dated 1935, is possibly John Louis Brown. The two images represent the small number of unknown or loosely identified portraits out of Polk's studio from the Depression era. Like other photographic commissions from his private patrons at the time, the two works present a more sophisticated image of African Americans in the South than were commonly seen in the New Deal era.

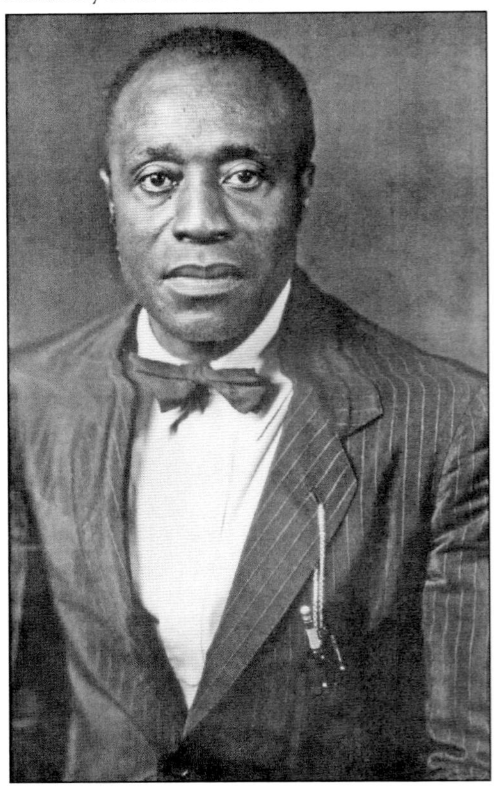

Emma Lee Randolph posed for this Polk portrait in 1933 when she was a student at the institute. As with the portraits on the opposite page, her refinement is in stark contrast to typical Depression-era images of African American women in the deep South. (Courtesy of the estate of P.H. Polk.)

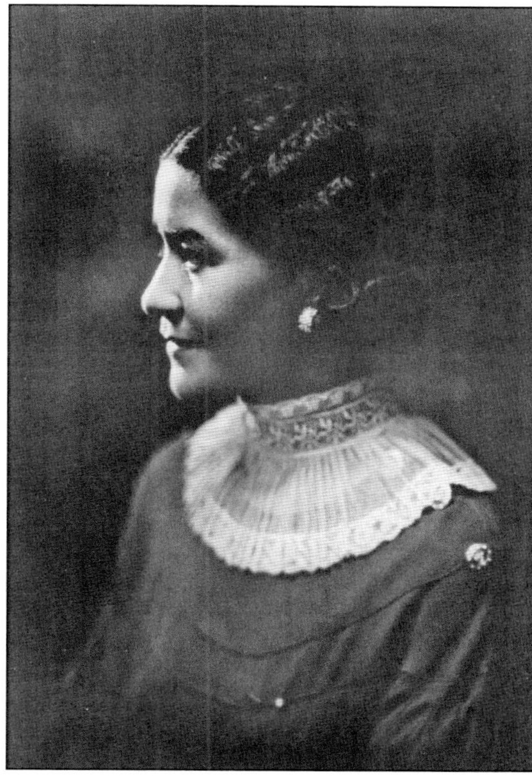

Mildred E. Hanson (Baker) wore the prom dress designed and made by her mother for this Polk portrait. She earned a business degree from Tuskegee Institute in 1938. A member of Tuskegee's first Civilian Pilot Training Program and among the first women with a private pilot's license, she was licensed by the Civil Aeronautics Authority as a parachute rigger, working with Alice Dungey Gray, who ran the parachute-rigging department at Moton Field. (Courtesy of the estate of P.H. Polk.)

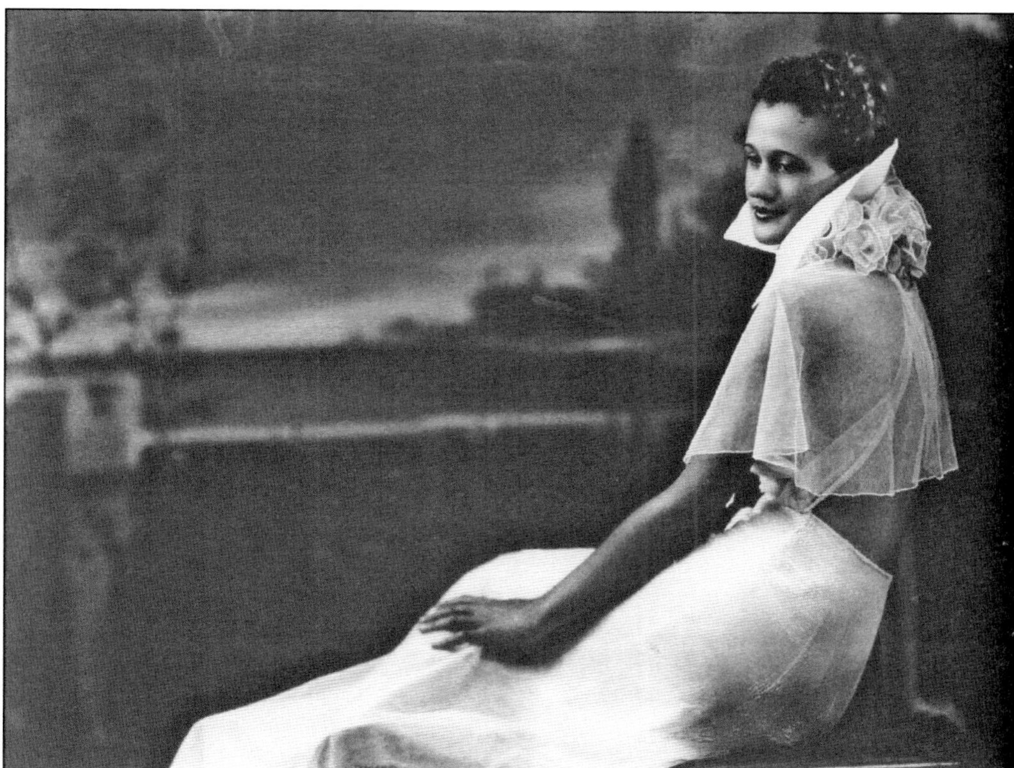

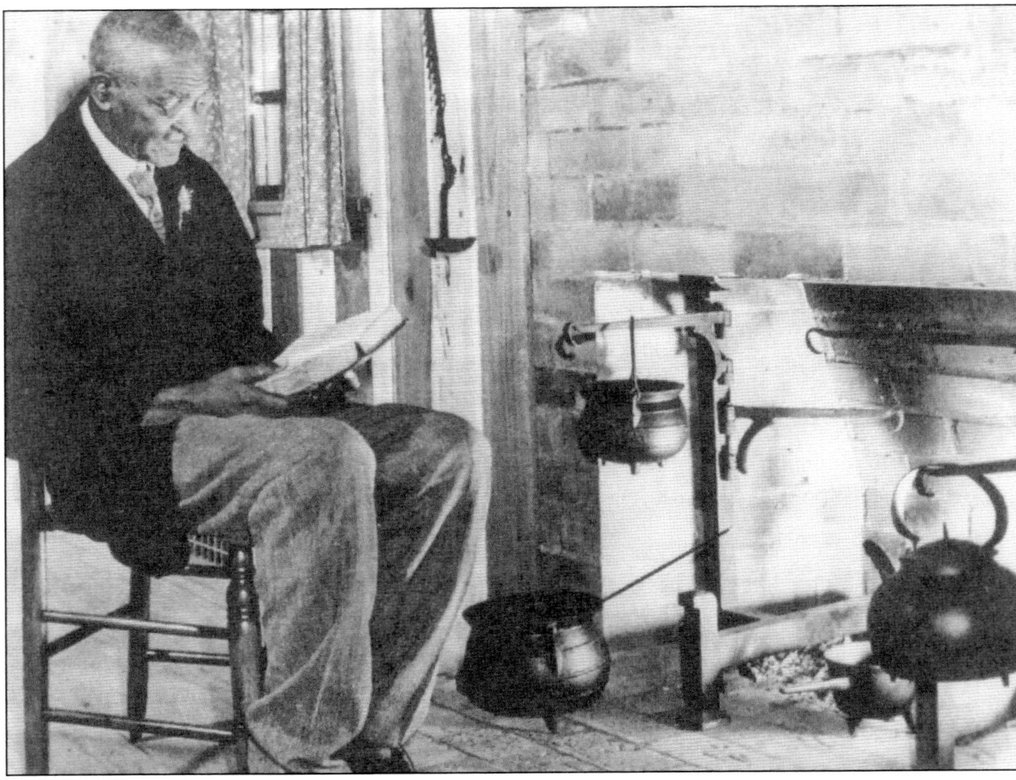

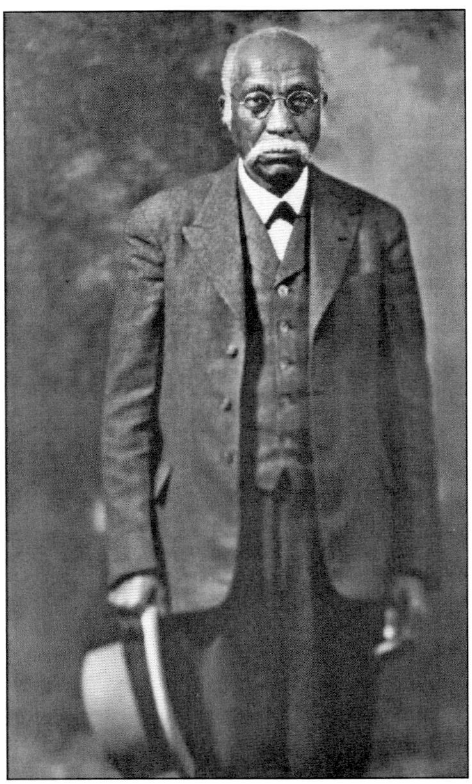

This photograph, titled *George Washington Carver: Reading At Fireside, 1942*, was a departure from Polk's usual photographs of the famous scientist in his role as official photographer. Carver is seen here in the modest quarters of a cabin just off the Village Green in Greenfield Village, which was built by Henry Ford to honor Carver and commemorate their friendship. Ford built it based on Carver's recollections of the Diamond, Missouri, cabin he was born in. The cabin was paneled with wood donated by governors of each of the then 48 states. Carver attended the dedication, living in the cabin for a few days, during which time Polk took this photograph. In a 1980 interview in his Tuskegee home, Polk clarified that "the photograph was really taken for Carver, not as official photographer for Tuskegee." (Courtesy of the estate of P.H. Polk.)

John H. Palmer (about 1863–1947) was the first registrar at Tuskegee Institute, a position he held for almost 40 years. He was also a member of the institute's executive council. Polk took this portrait in 1929.

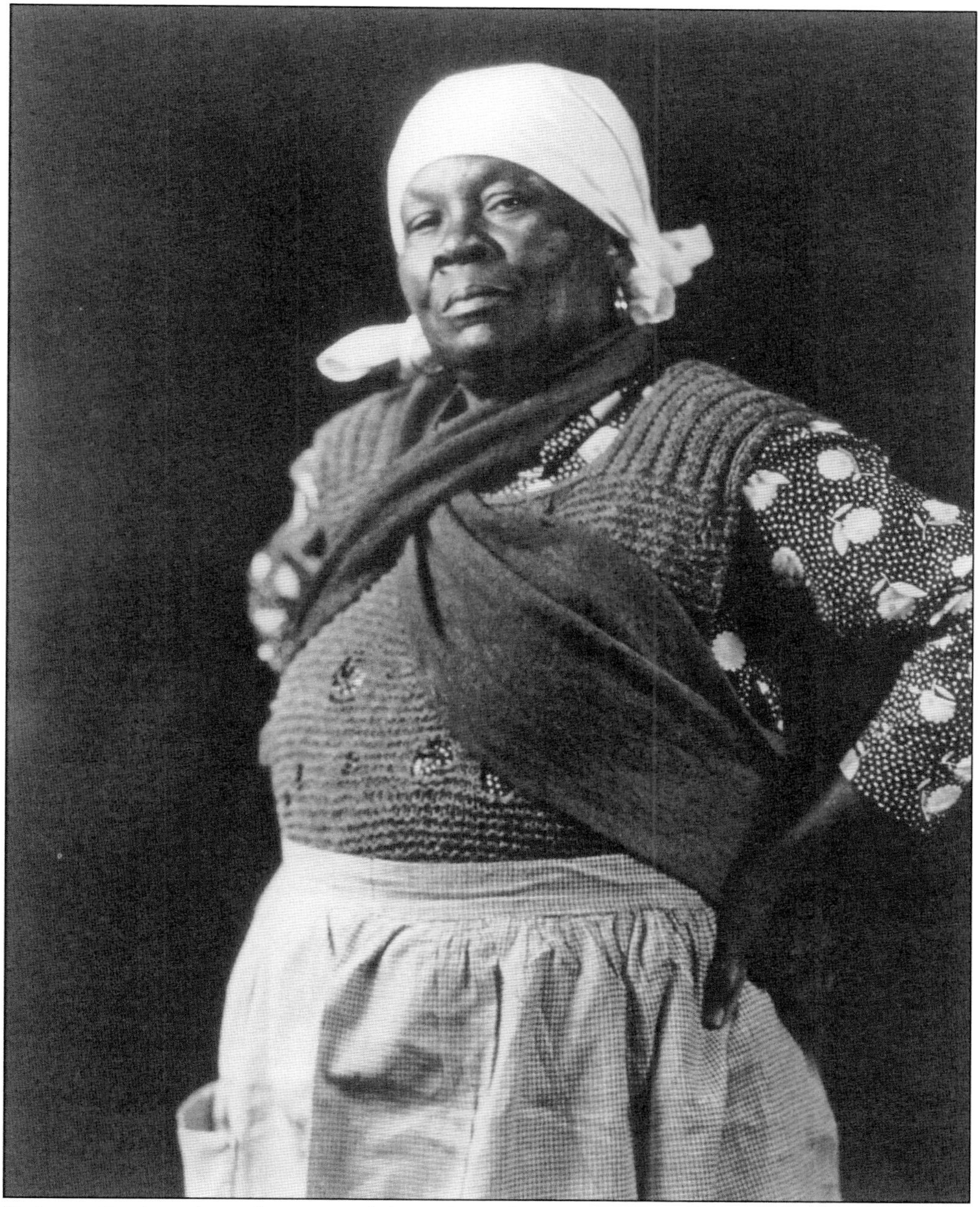

Tuskegee Institute hosted an annual farmer's conference for Macon County sharecroppers and small tenant farmers. In 1932, Polk spotted this unidentified woman, who was assisting with the open-air market, walking across campus from a second-story window. He rushed from the building, approached her, and, after a considerable amount of coaxing that included promising to pay her $1, convinced her to allow him to photograph her. He took his usual approach to getting his subject to assume a pose that was natural and characteristic of their personality. Not wanting to miss any of the conference, growing leery of Polk's antics, and ready to be paid, she struck this pose. Polk entitled the photograph *The Boss*. The image became the most popular in *Old Characters*, his series of rural subjects, and the best-known photograph of Polk's career. (Courtesy of the estate of P.H. Polk.)

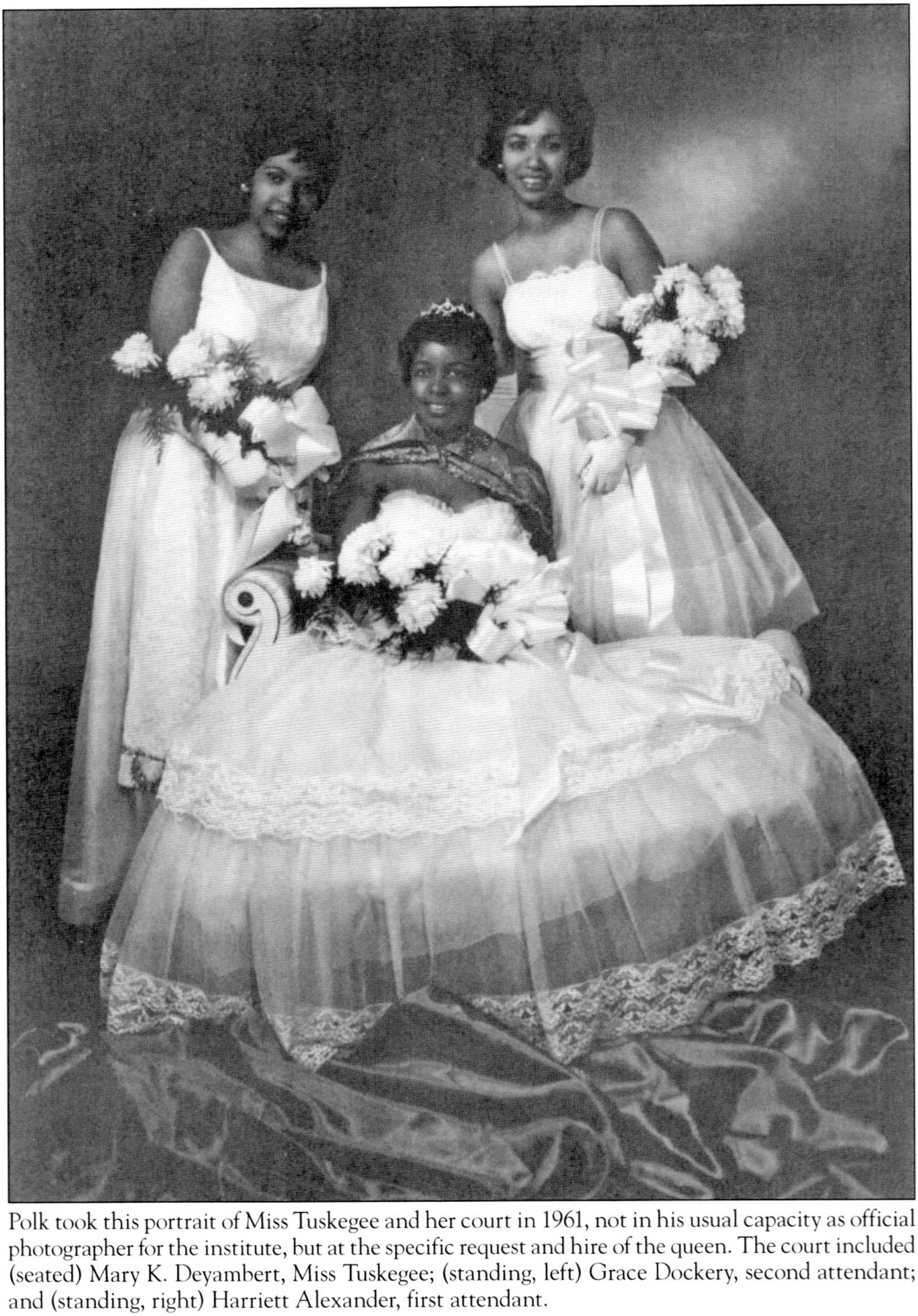

Polk took this portrait of Miss Tuskegee and her court in 1961, not in his usual capacity as official photographer for the institute, but at the specific request and hire of the queen. The court included (seated) Mary K. Deyambert, Miss Tuskegee; (standing, left) Grace Dockery, second attendant; and (standing, right) Harriett Alexander, first attendant.

Five

Tuskegee Airmen

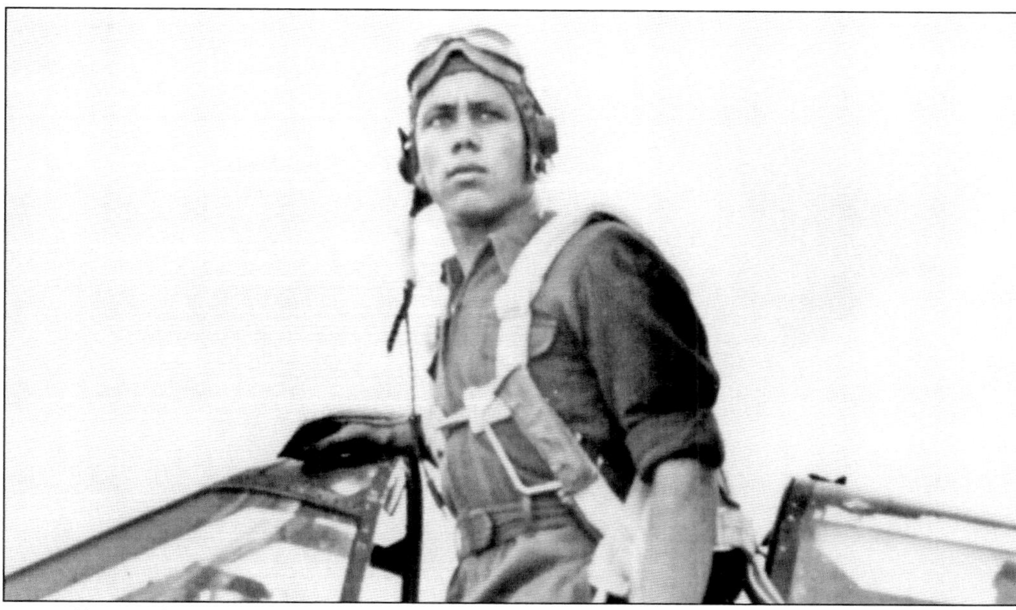

Lt. William Johnston was one of the "Western Pennsylvania Fly Boys" whose experiences in combat during World War II were the subject of a public television documentary on the unique journeys of the Tuskegee Airmen, beginning with their trek to the famous Alabama air field. Johnston was 17 years old when he persuaded his parents, after much deliberation, to allow him to enlist in the Army Air Corps in hopes of becoming a Tuskegee Airman. He was successful at both, and is seen here with his plane in 1944.

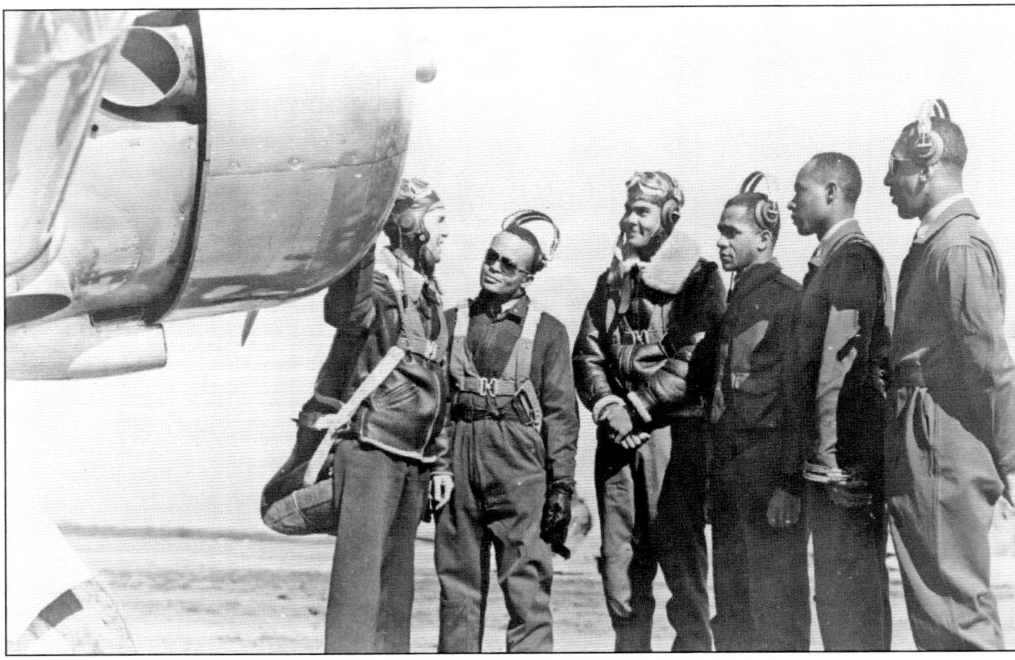

On March 7, 1942, five pilots became the first graduates of Tuskegee's flight training program and the first African American pilots in Army Air Corps history to complete advanced flying school as second lieutenants. Lt. Gen. George Edward Stratemayer (far left), the World War II chief of air staff, is seen here with the pilots (from left to right): George S. "Spanky" Roberts, Benjamin Oliver Davis Jr., Charles DeBow, Mac Ross, and Lemuel R. Curtis.

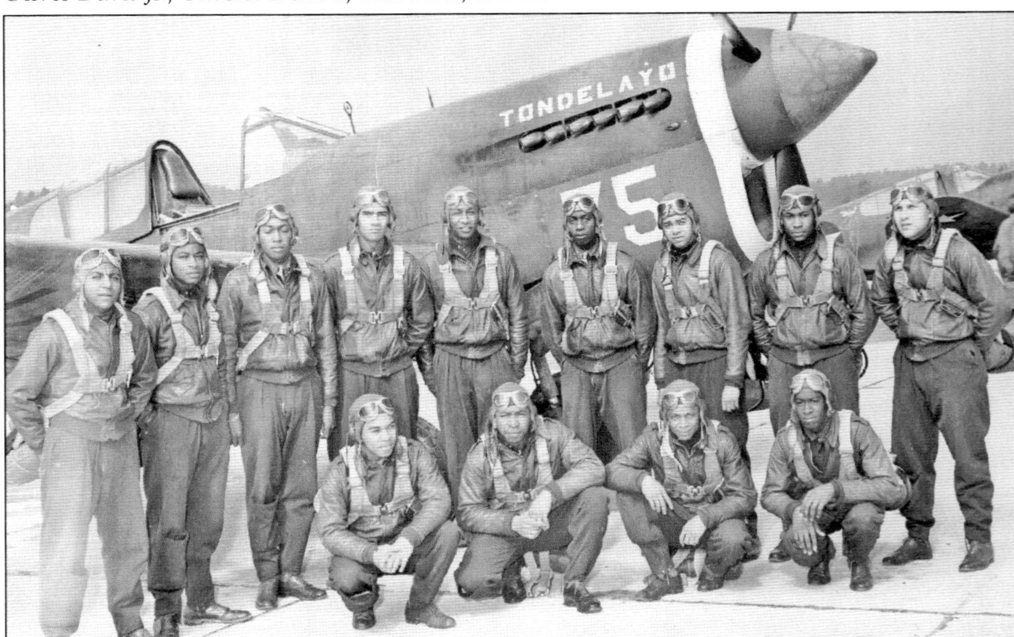

This photograph shows 13 unidentified members of Tuskegee Airmen Class 43C posed in front of the airplane *Tondelayo* at Moton Field in Tuskegee in 1943. (Courtesy of www.blackarchives.org.)

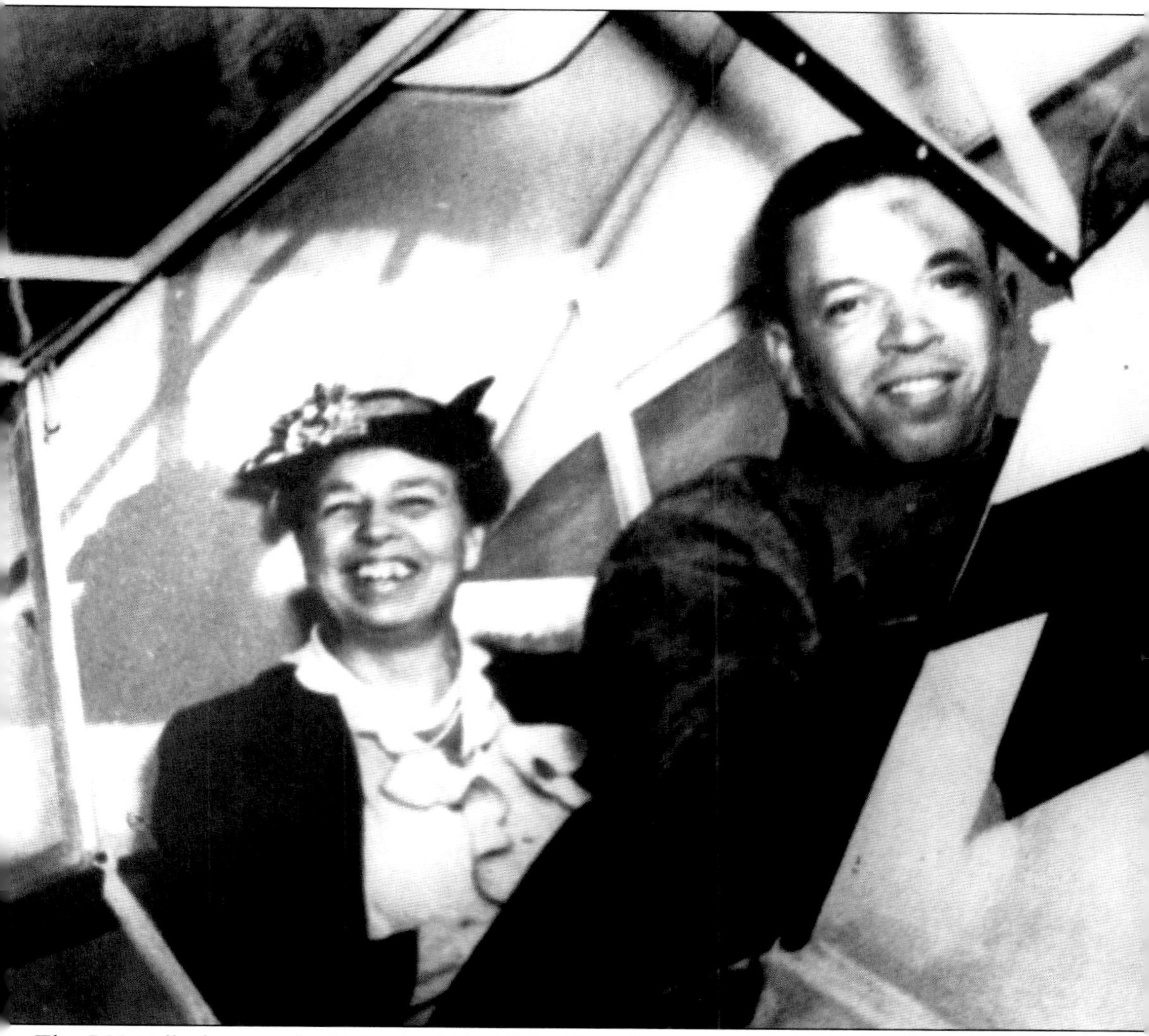

This P.H. Polk photograph of Charles Alfred "Chief" Anderson and First Lady Eleanor Roosevelt played a role in shifting opinions regarding African Americans as aviators. Taken in 1941 when Anderson gave Mrs. Roosevelt a plane ride during her Tuskegee visit, the photograph drew attention across the country. The First Lady was eager to discredit the idea that African Americans could not fly. The photograph served her wishes and gave validity to the training program. Anderson, a pioneer in African American aviation, became the head of Civilian Pilot Training at Tuskegee Institute in 1940. His successful program was a major factor in the Army Air Corps' decision to establish a primary training program at Tuskegee. As chief flight instructor at Moton Field, he oversaw the training of 1,000 African American pilots. (Courtesy of the estate of P.H. Polk.)

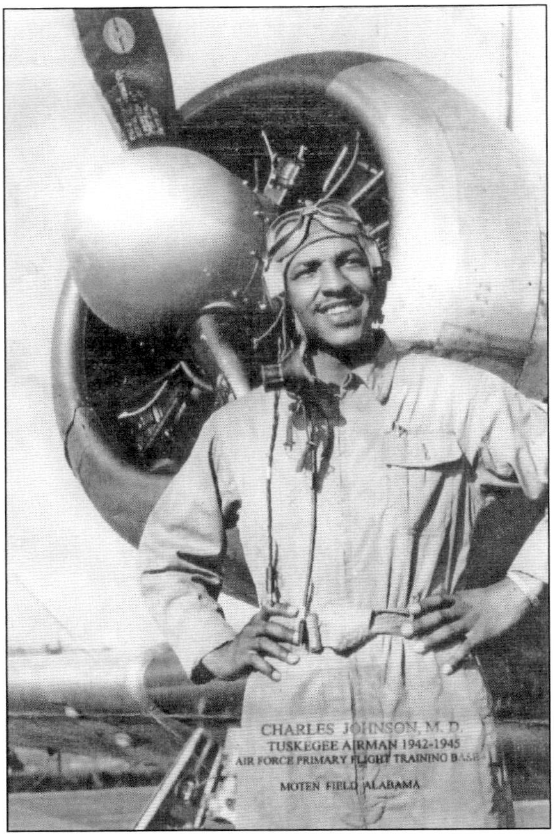

Charles Spurgeon Johnson Jr. (1921–2006) was a flight instructor at the Air Force Primary Flight Training Base at Moton Field from 1942 to 1945. In addition to overseeing cadets' routine flight times, trainers offered assistance in ground instruction, navigation training, aircraft maintenance, aerodynamics, cockpit training, emergency calls such as forced landing or mishap landings, and accident prevention. (Courtesy of Charles S. Johnson III.)

This group of African American women in the Army Air Corps poses in a casual formation during an assignment at the Tuskegee Army Air Field Hospital in 1943. They were at the base to assist pilots and cadets with physical and psychological problems. Part of their training included ground school instruction, though they flew no missions during World War II.

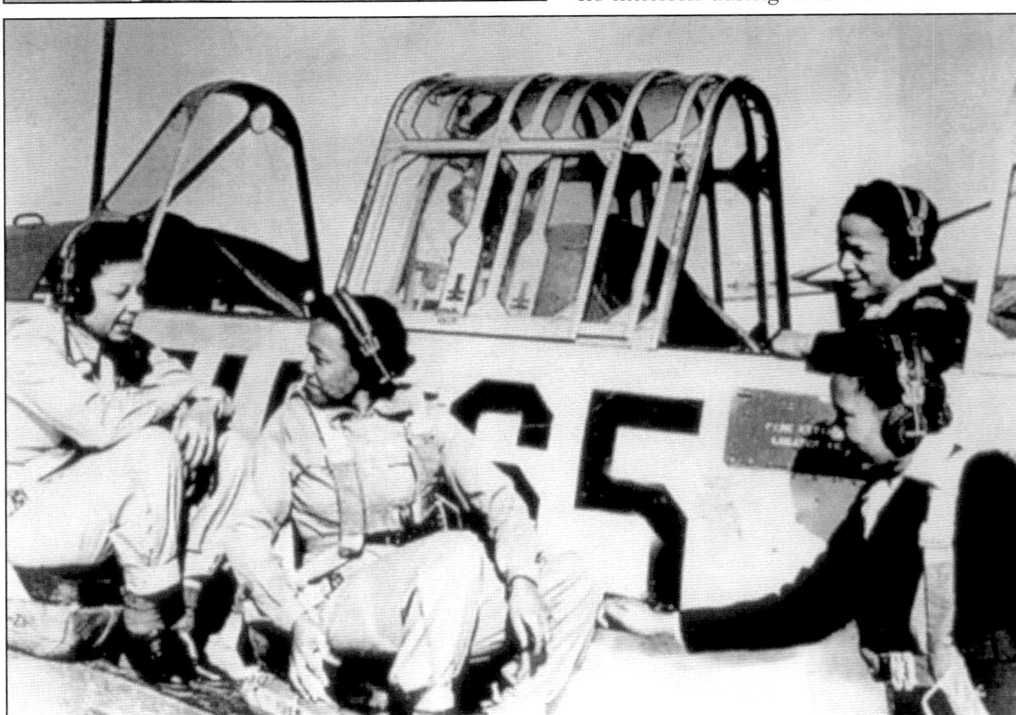

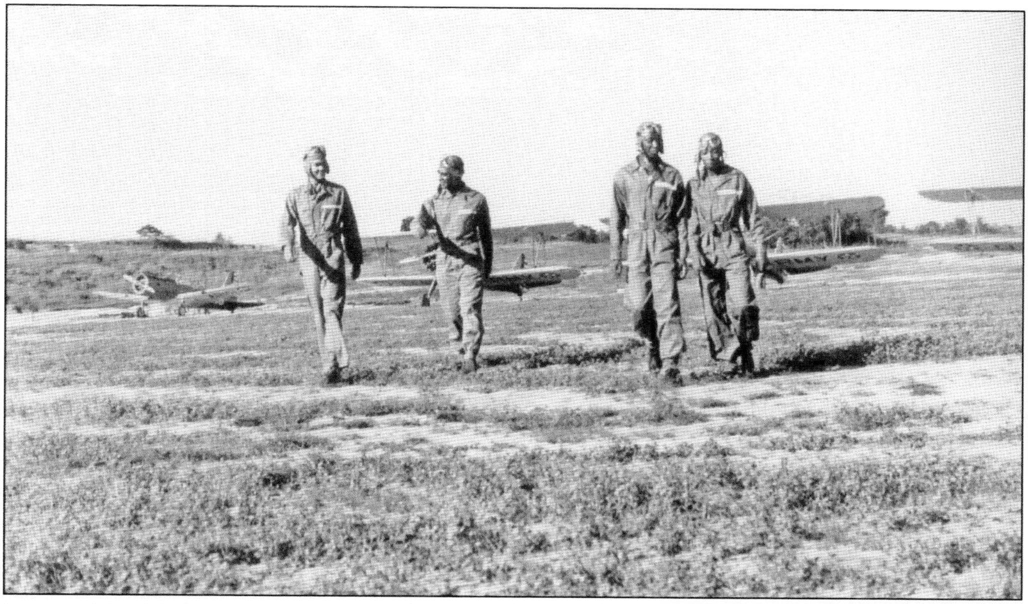

Four unidentified airmen walk leisurely across Moton Field in 1943, likely taking advantage of some down time from their training. As Tuskegee Institute official photographer, P.H. Polk took numerous photographs of pilots, cadets, and training staff in the 1940s. (Courtesy of the estate of P.H. Polk.)

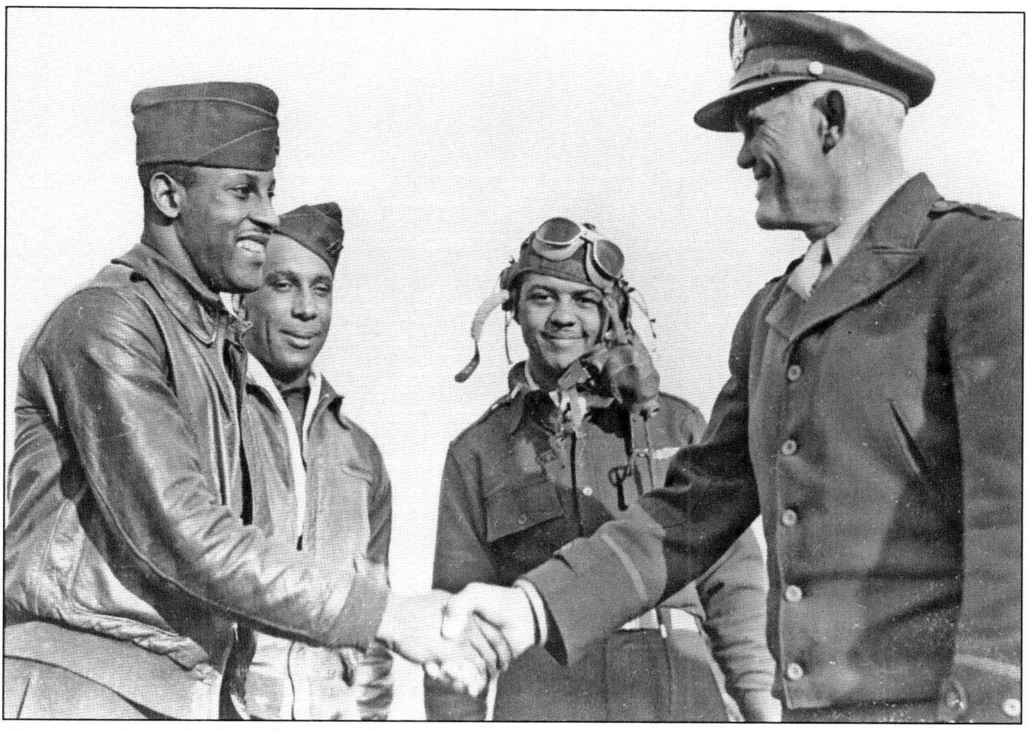

Capt. Charles B. Hall of Brazil, Indiana, was the first Tuskegee Airman to shoot down an enemy aircraft, and is seen here being congratulated by Maj. Gen. John Kenneth Cannon. Captain Hall's aerial victory against the Luftwaffe occurred on the morning of July 2, 1943. He was on his eighth mission.

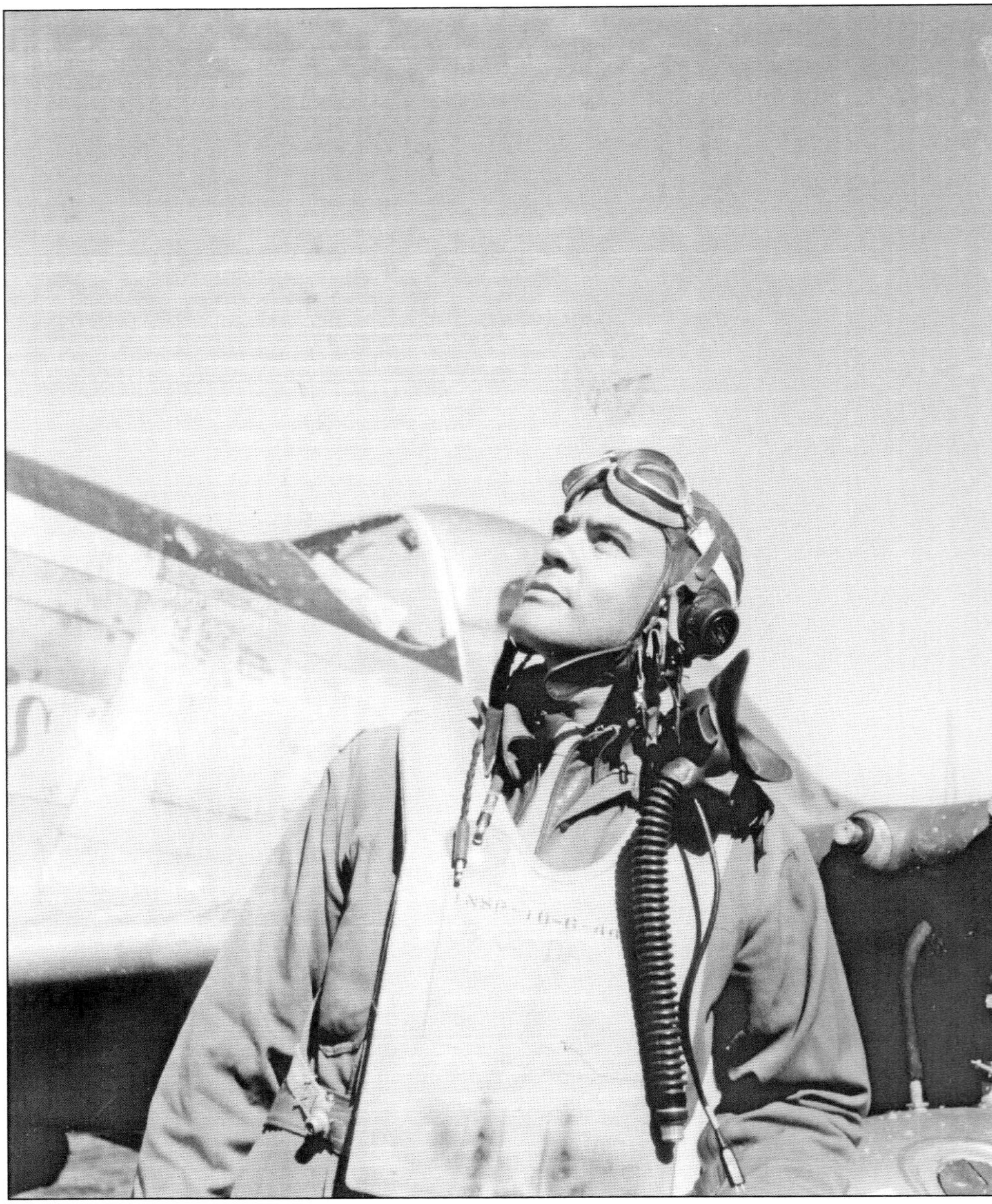

Capt. Benjamin Davis Jr. remembers: "On 2 July I led a 12-plane escort of 12 B-25s to Castelvetrano, southwest Sicily. I saw my first enemy aircraft, an element of two FW-190s and four Me-109s, far above my part of our formation, which was flying close escort to the B-25s. When the enemy planes dove on the bombers, our top cover turned into them and kept them out of range. During this mission we had our first pilot losses: Lts. Sherman White and James McCullin. We believed that both pilots had made forced landings along the Sicilian coast, but regrettably, it was not that way. The loss of fighter pilots was like a loss in the family. On each combat mission, members of the squadron watched the takeoff and were on hand in large numbers to count the planes as they returned and greet the pilots. On the brighter side of that mission, Lieutenant Hall shot down an FW-190, the first time a black pilot had downed an Axis plane, and damaged an Me-109. All other pilots returned to base."

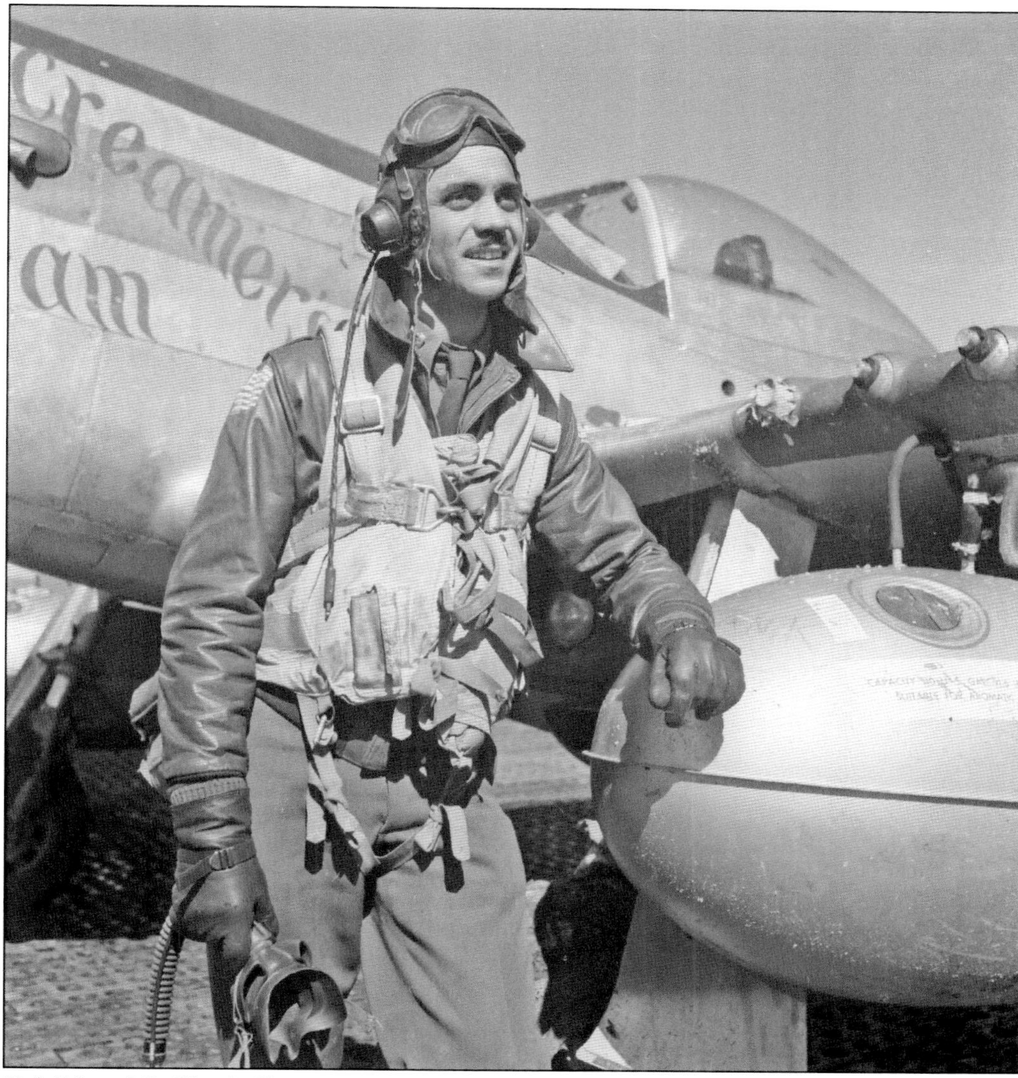

Col. Edward C. Gleed of Lawrence, Kansas, enlisted in the 9th Calvary in 1941 and was assigned to military intelligence. In 1942, he entered aviation cadet training at Tuskegee, graduating in December as a second lieutenant. During World War II, Gleed served in the European and Mediterranean theaters as a fighter pilot, as the squadron commander of the 301st Fighter Squadron, and as the operations officer of the 332nd Fighter Group. He is officially credited with two confirmed kills. He is seen here on December 31, 1944, in Ramitelli, Italy, with the aircraft *Creamer's Dream* in the background, a plane generally flown by Charles L. White of St. Louis.

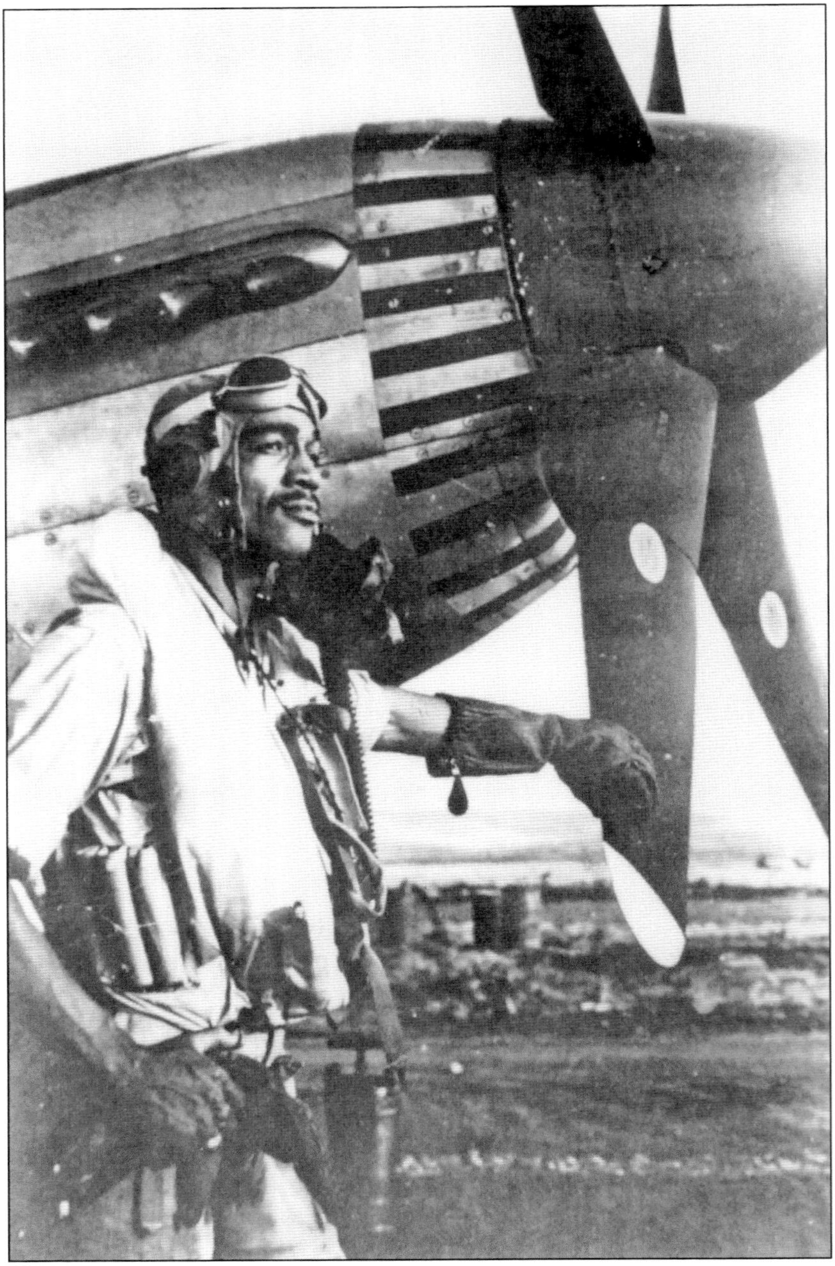

Lt. Col. Lee Archer (1919–2010) was a fighter pilot with the Tuskegee Airmen. He entered the Army in 1941, receiving training as a telegrapher and a field network-communications specialist. In 1942, he was accepted into aviation cadet training and reported to the Tuskegee Army Airfield. He graduated first in his class in 1943 and was commissioned a second lieutenant and assigned to the 302nd Fighter Squadron, under the 332nd Fighter Group, which was transferred to Italy during World War II. Lieutenant Colonel Archer flew 169 combat missions, flying cover and escorting long-range bombers over more than 11 countries, and strafing missions against enemy landing zones and troops on the ground. He earned the Distinguished Flying Cross and special citations from Presidents Eisenhower, Kennedy, and Johnson and the director of the CIA. His plane was named *Ina The Macon Belle* after his wife.

Dr. Leroy Bowman joined the Army Air Corps in 1941 and was eventually assigned to Tuskegee Army Air Field. He trained under Col. Benjamin O. Davis Jr. and fought extensively over Italy and Germany. Bowman flew 36 successful combat missions against the German Luftwaffe. He initially flew the P-40, P-47, and P-51, with dive-bombing as his main duty. Later, he escorted bombers to and from their targets. Bowman flew with the 301st Fighter Squadron.

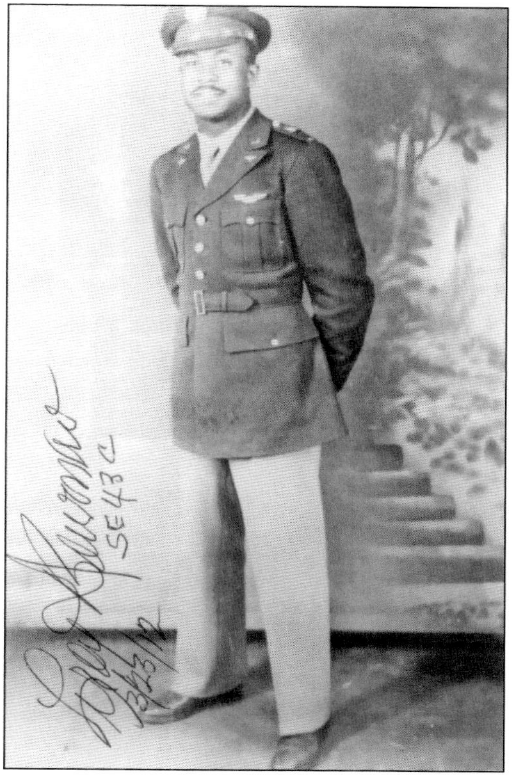

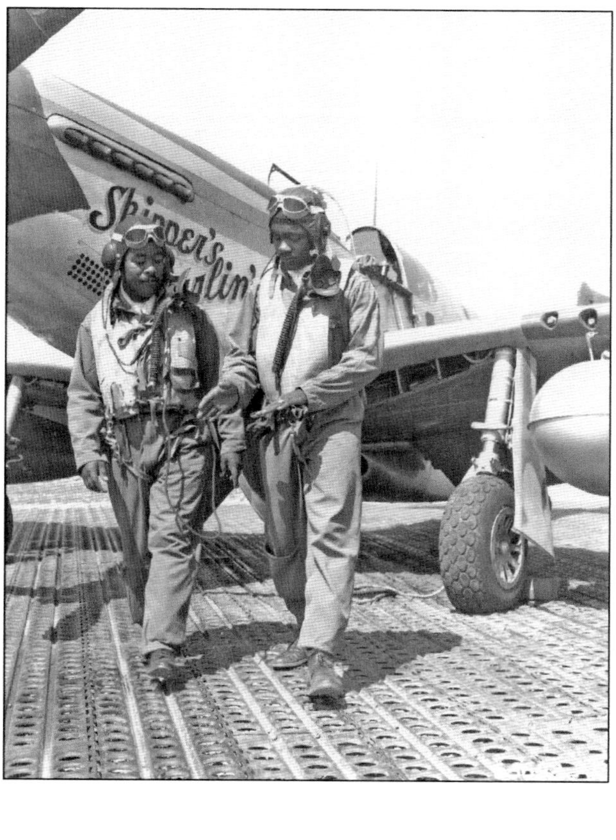

Red Tails commander Andrew D. Turner of the 15th Army Air Force 100th Fighter Squadron, 332nd Fighter Group (left) walks from his plane after being greeted by Lt. Clarence P. Lester. Turner had just landed the plane *Skipper's Darling III*, in Italy in September 1944.

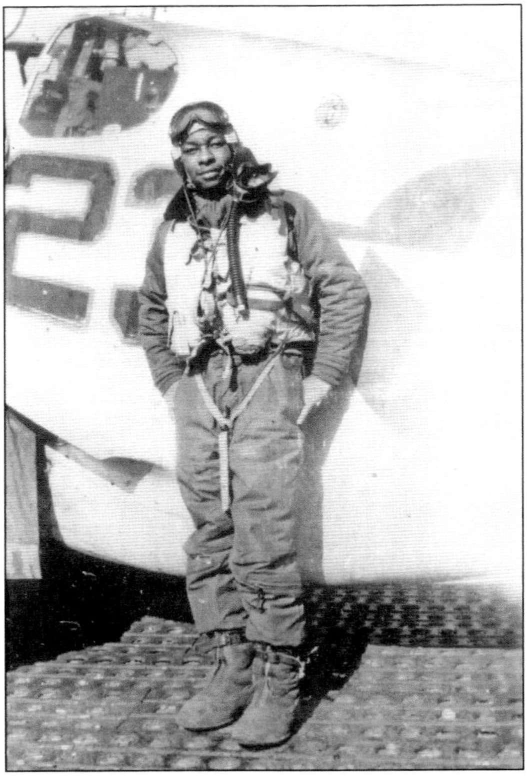

2nd Lt. Robert C. Robinson Jr. (1923–1945) stands beside his fighter plane, which he named *Tuxedo Junction*. From Asheville, North Carolina, 2nd Lt. Robinson made the ultimate sacrifice, being lost in action during a mission on March 25, 1945.

Pilots of the Tuskegee Airmen 332nd Fighter Group exit a parachute tent in Ramitelli, Italy, in March 1945. They are, from left to right, Richard S. "Rip" Harder, Brooklyn, class 44-B; an unidentified airman; Thurston L. Gaines Jr., Freeport, New York, class 44-G; Newman C. Golden, Cincinnati, class 44-G; and Wendell M. Lucas, Fairmont Heights, Maryland, class 44-E.

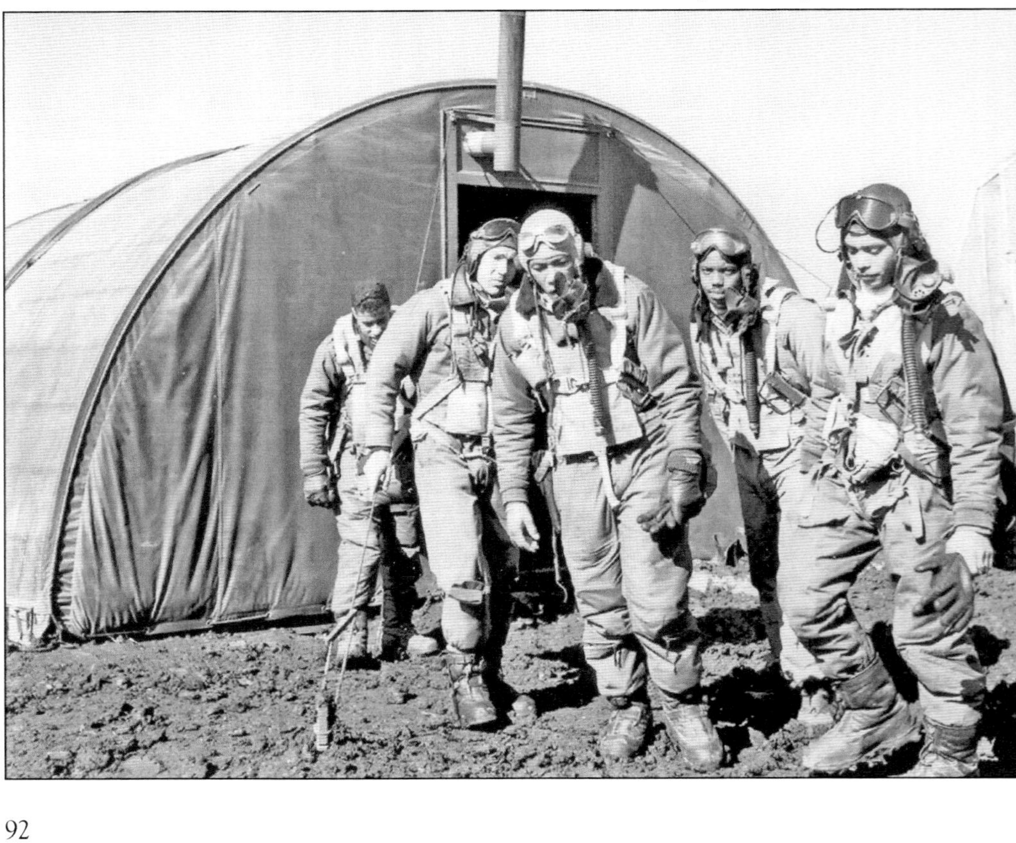

Sgt. William P. Bostic of the 301st Fighter Squadron is seen here in the control tower in Ramitelli, Italy, in March 1945. The control tower directed traffic with red, amber, and green lights and a flare gun to indicate special situations. (Courtesy of the Library of Congress Prints and Photographs Division.)

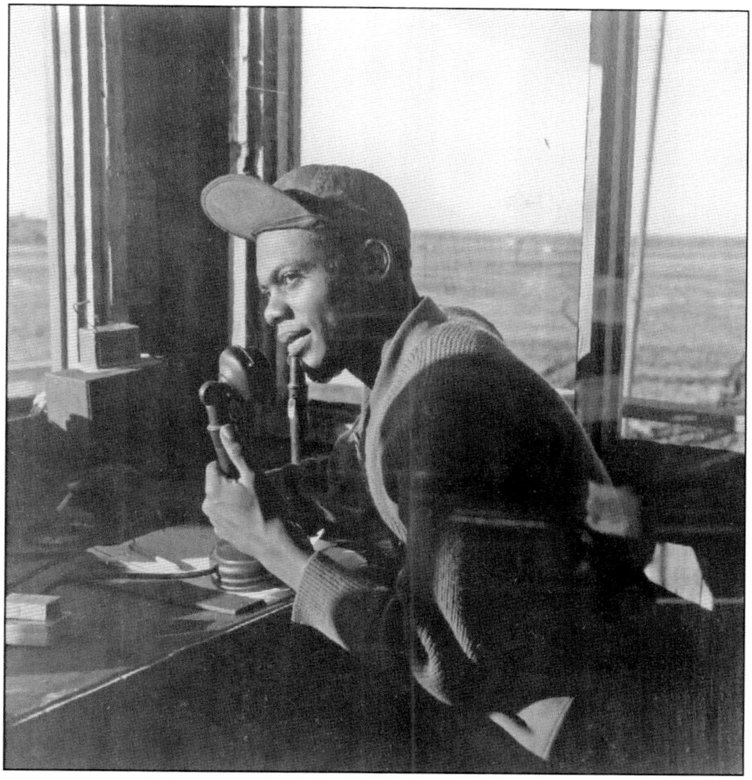

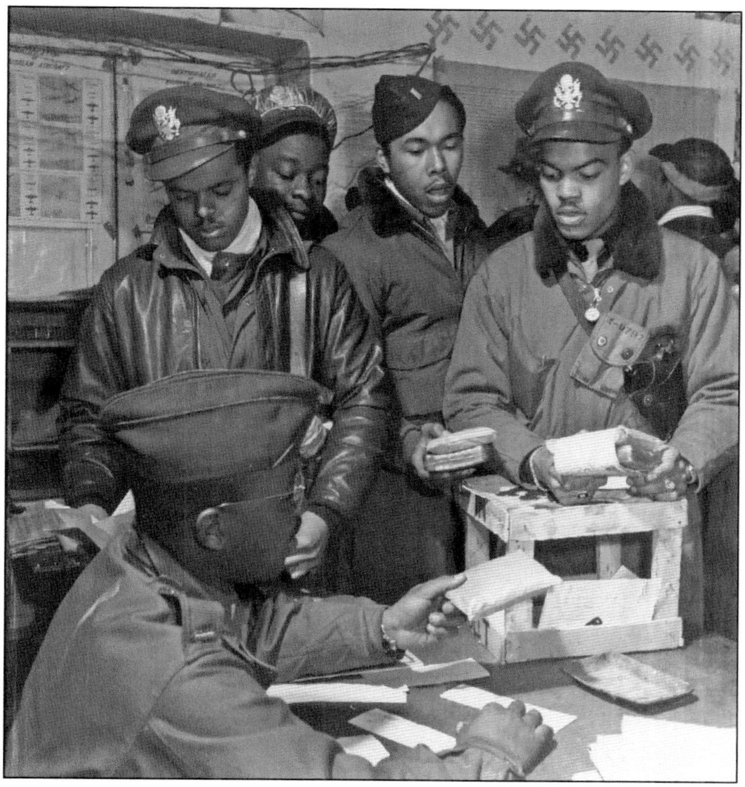

Fighter pilots are seen here receiving their "escape kits" (cyanide) at an air base in southern Italy in 1945. They are, from left to right, (seated) Theodore G. Lumpkin Jr.; (standing) Joseph L. "Joe" Chineworth, Memphis, class 44-E; Robert C. Robinson, Asheville, North Carolina, class 44-G; Driskell B. Ponder, Chicago, class 43-I; and Robert W. Williams, Ottumwa, Iowa, Class 44-E. (Courtesy of the Library of Congress Prints and Photographs Division.)

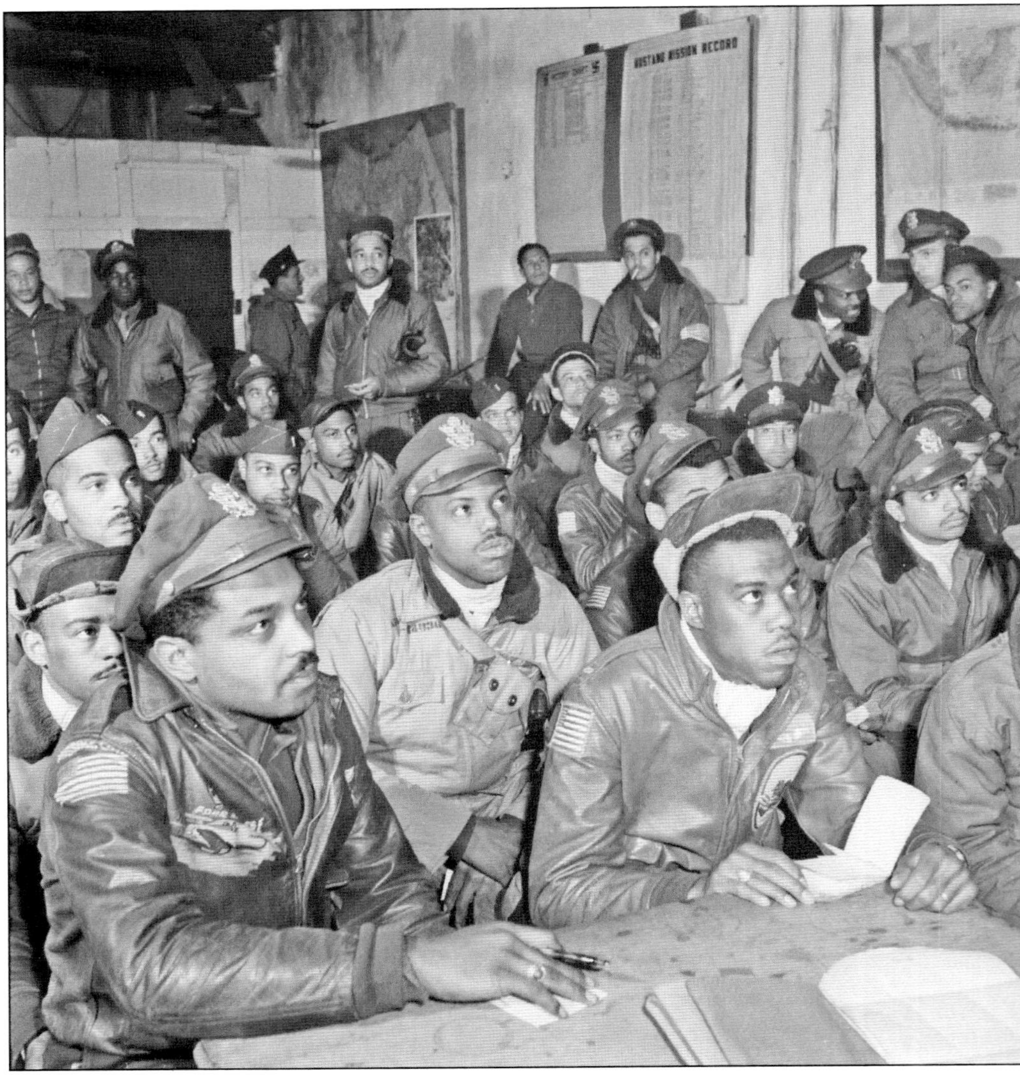

This photograph shows several Tuskegee Airmen attending a briefing in March 1945. They are, from left to right, (first row) Hiram E. Mann, Cleveland, class 44-F; an unidentified airman; Newman C. Golden, Cincinnati, 44-G; Bertram W. Wilson Jr., Brooklyn, 44-E; and Samuel W. Watts Jr., New York City, 44-E; (second row) Armour G. McDemoe, Martinsville, Virginia, 43-A; Howard C. Gamble, Charles Town, West Virginia, 43-K; Harry T. Steward Jr., Corona, New York, 44-F; Earle R. Lane, Wickliffe, Ohio, 44-D; Wyrain T. Shell, Brooklyn, 44-F; Harold M. Morris, Seattle, 44-D; John E. Edwards, Steubenville, Ohio, 44-C; John H. Porter, Cleveland, 44-C; James H. Fischer, Stoughton, Massachusetts, 44-G; and Wyrain T. Shell, Brooklyn, 44-F; (third row) William E. "Porky" Rice, Swarthmore, Pennsylvania, 44-G; Tony Weaver; Charles L. White, St. Louis, 44-C; George Arnold Lynch, Valley Stream, New York, 44-F; Samuel L. Washington, Cleveland, 44-F; Calvin J. Spann, Rutherford, New Jersey, 44-G; and Frank N. Wright, Elmsford, New York, 44-F. (Courtesy of the Library of Congress Prints and Photographs Division.)

Tuskegee Airmen spend an evening playing cards at the officer's club in Ramitelli, Italy, in March 1945. They are, from left to right, (seated) Robert "Bobby" Spurlock, Washington, DC; and Harold M. Morris, Seattle, class 44-D; (standing) Conrad A. Johnson, New York City, class 44-G; Ronald W. Reeves, Washington, DC, class 44-G; Leroy Roberts Jr., Toccoa, Georgia, class 44-E; and Calvin J. Spann, Rutherford, New Jersey, class 44-G. (Courtesy of the Library of Congress Prints and Photographs Division.)

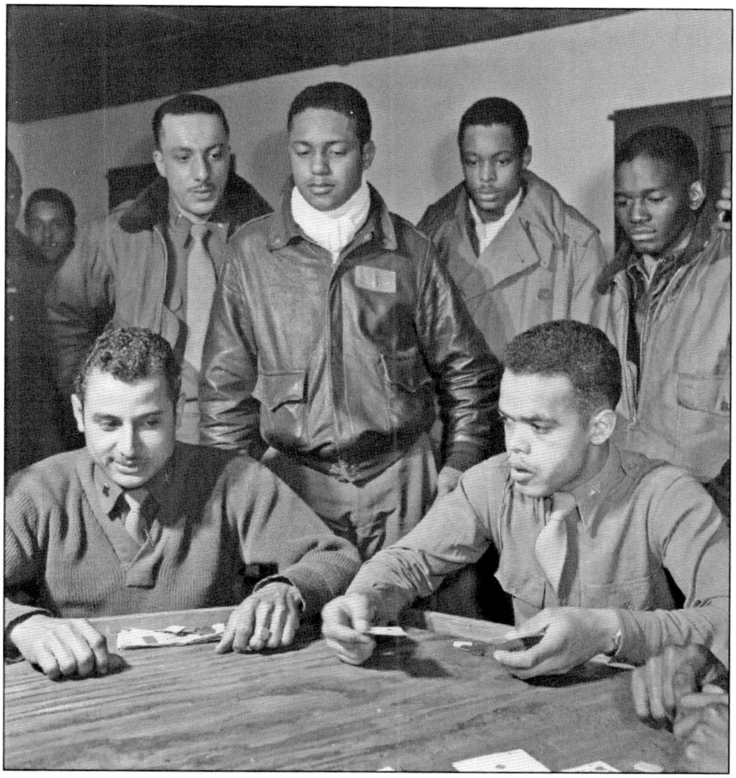

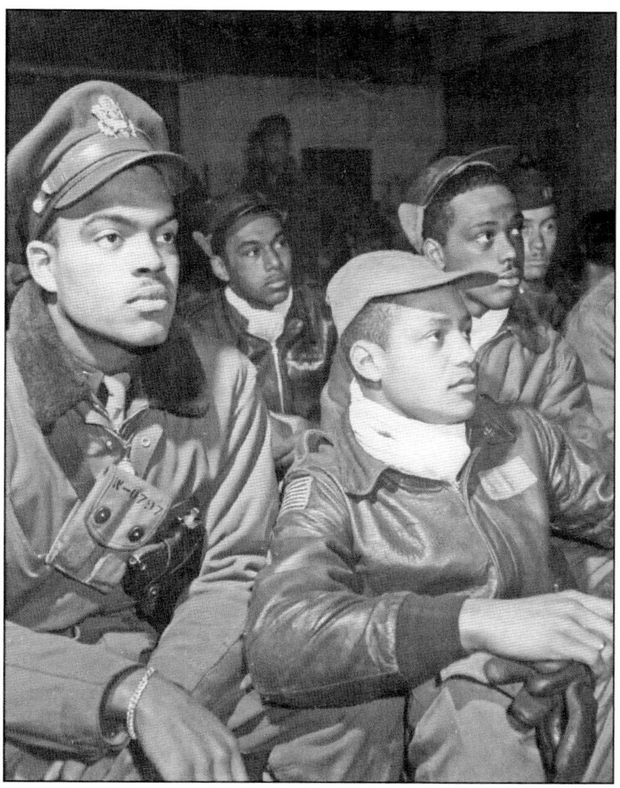

This close-up view shows members of the 332nd at a briefing. They are, from left to right, Robert W. Williams, Ottumwa, Iowa, class 44-E; William H. Holloman III, St. Louis; Ronald W. Reeves, Washington, DC, class 44-G; Christopher W. Newman, St. Louis, class 43-I; and Walter M. Downs, New Orleans, class 43-B.

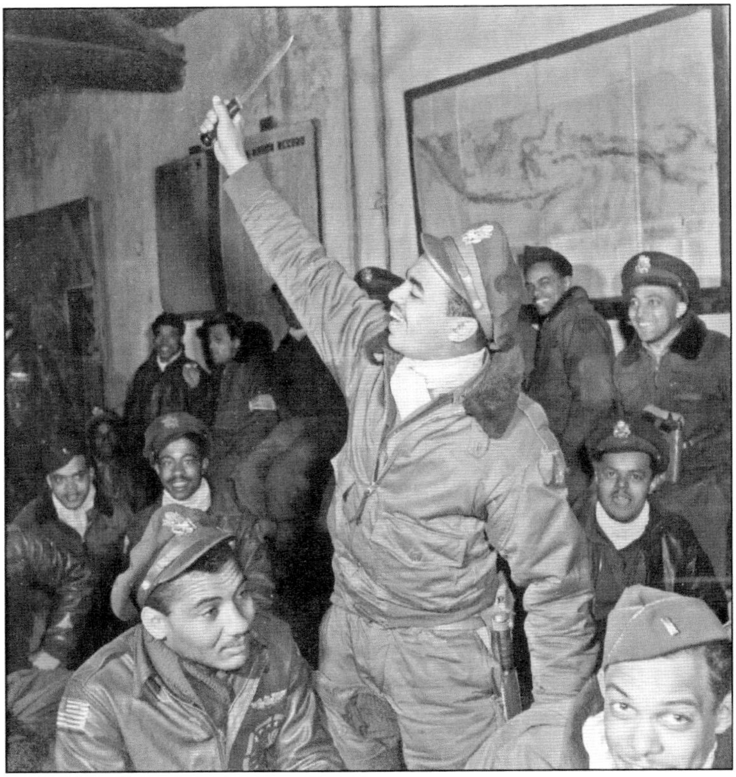

Members of the 332nd are seen here in a briefing room. They are, from left to right, (first row) Gentry E. Barnes, Lawrenceville, Illinois, class 44-D; Samuel W. Watts Jr., New York City, 44-E; and Wendell M. Lucas, Fairmont Heights, Maryland, 44-E; (second row) Harold M. Morris, Seattle, 44-D; John H. Porter, Cleveland, 44-C; and Joseph L. "Joe" Chineworth, Memphis, 44-E; (third row) three unidentified airmen and Wyrain T. Schell, Brooklyn, 44-F. (Courtesy of the Library of Congress Prints and Photographs Division.)

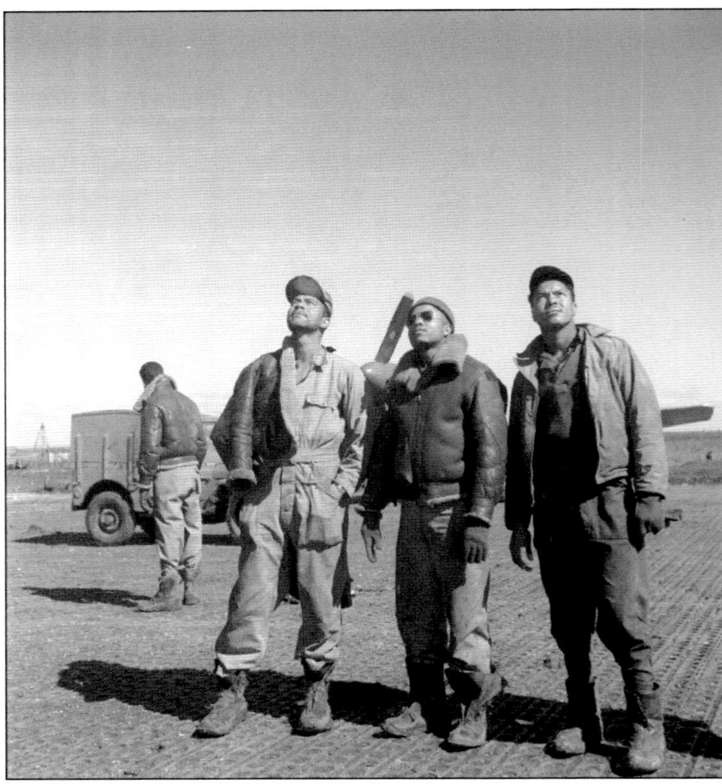

Three unidentified Tuskegee Airmen are seen here looking skyward moments after fellow pilots have taken flight in March 1945 in Ramitelli, Italy. A note on the back of the photograph reads, "These guys were stand-ins, but excellent 'mechanics,' as they were pilots."

Lena Horne visited servicemen during World War II, including the Tuskegee Airmen. After African American soldiers were barred from one of her concerts and forced to sit behind German prisoners at another, she quit the tours and performed for soldiers in the West and the South, paying multiple visits to the Tuskegee Airmen at their training base.

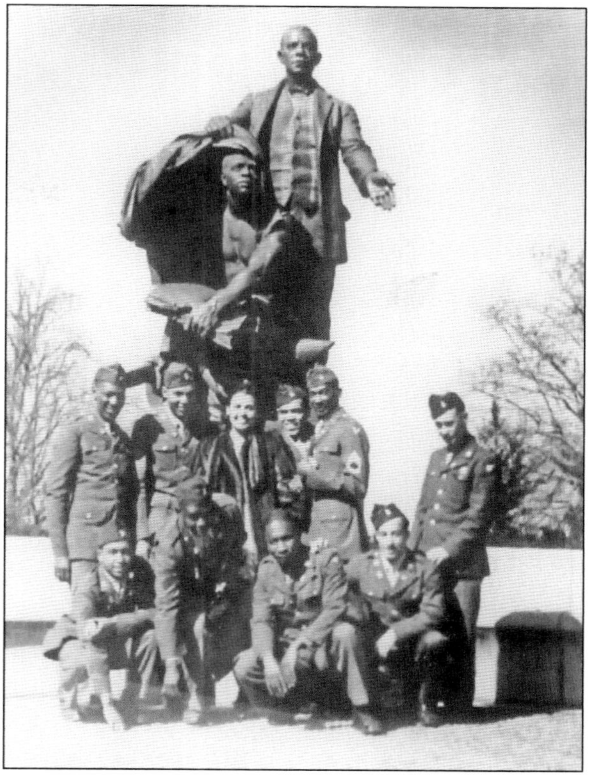

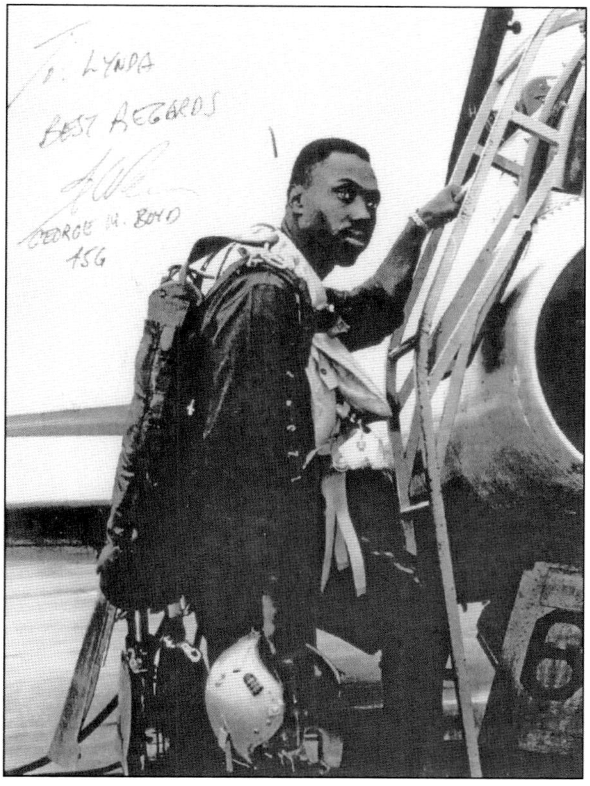

Col. George Mills Boyd is seen here in his flight gear about to board his plane in 1945. He was a skilled fighter pilot who trained in the Army Air Corps at Moton Field in Tuskegee. After completing training, Colonel Boyd was assigned to the 100th Fighter Squadron, under the 332nd Fighter Group, at Lockbourne Army Airfield in Ohio. He went on to be a 28-year veteran, serving in World War II, the Korean War, and Vietnam, and retired as a major. He then joined the Kansas Civil Air Patrol, where he earned the rank of colonel.

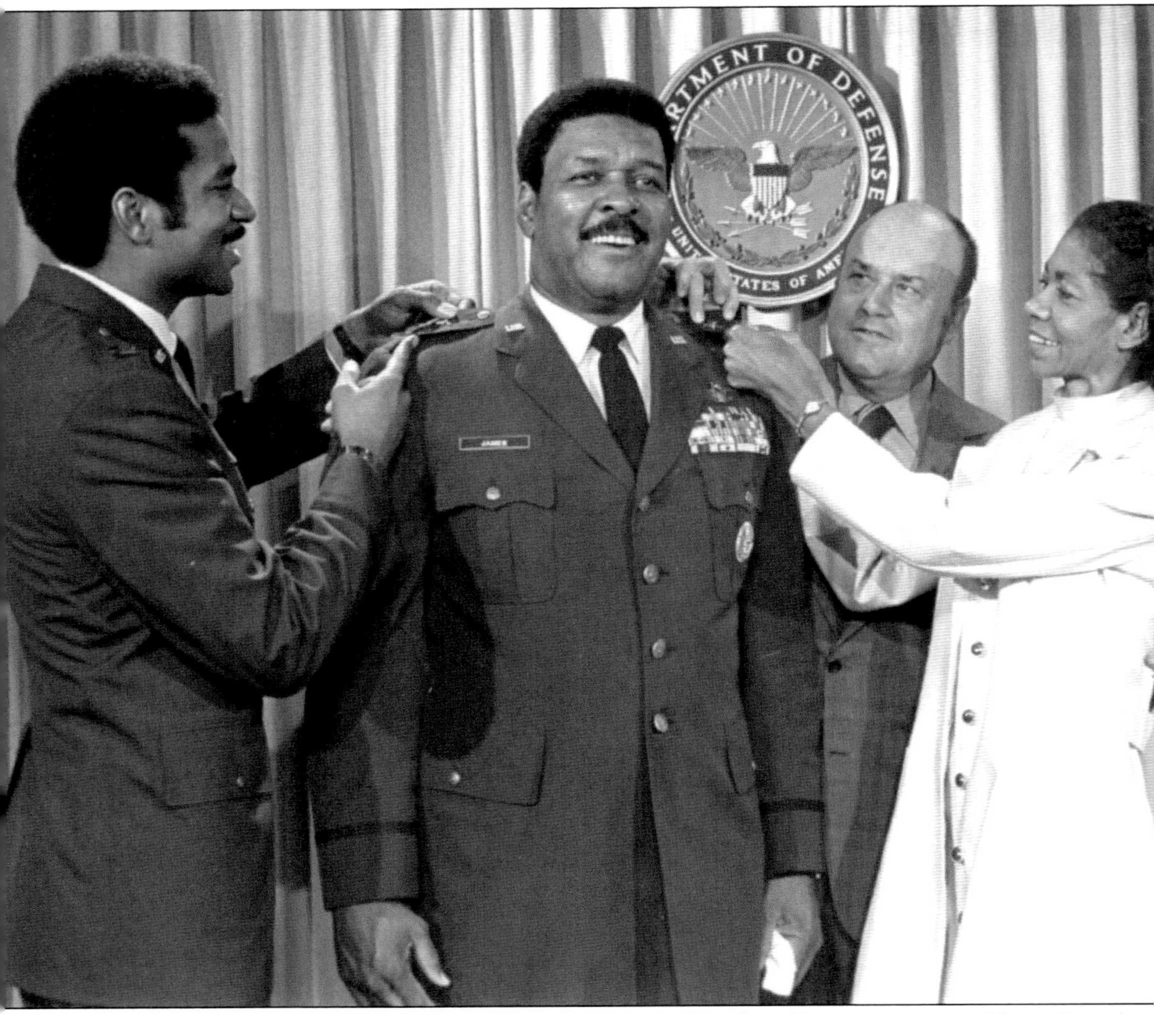

Maj. Gen. Daniel "Chappie" James Jr. (1920–1978) learned to fly at Tuskegee Institute. He graduated in 1942 and continued flight training, becoming a cadet in the Army Air Corps in January 1943. Commissioned in July, he trained pilots for the all-black 99th Pursuit Squadron and flew 101 fighter missions in the Korean War. Promoted to major while stationed at Otis Air Force Base, he graduated from the Air Command staff school in 1957 and was assigned in Washington, DC, England, and Arizona. Then a colonel, he flew 78 combat missions in Vietnam. James became vice commander of the 33rd Tactical Fighter Wing at Eglin Air Force Base in Florida, and then brigadier general. In 1970, he became the deputy assistant secretary of defense and reached the rank of major general. In 1975, James became the first African American four-star general in US military history.

Six

THEY CAME, THEY SAW

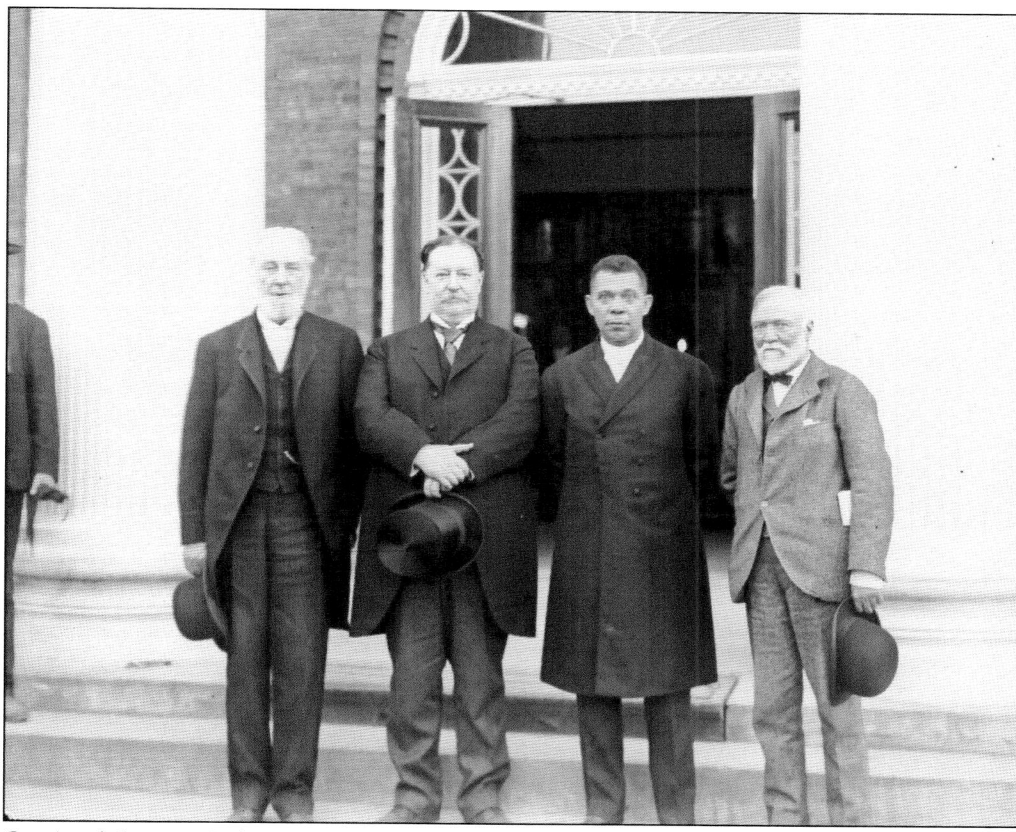

On April 5, 1906, Robert Curtis Ogden (1836–1913), Secretary of War William Howard Taft (1857–1930), Booker T. Washington, and Andrew Carnegie (1835–1919) pose for a photograph during the 25th anniversary festivities at Tuskegee Institute. Taft, who would later become the 27th president, delivered a major speech on the same day Frances Benjamin Johnston took this photograph. (Courtesy of Tuskegee University Archives.)

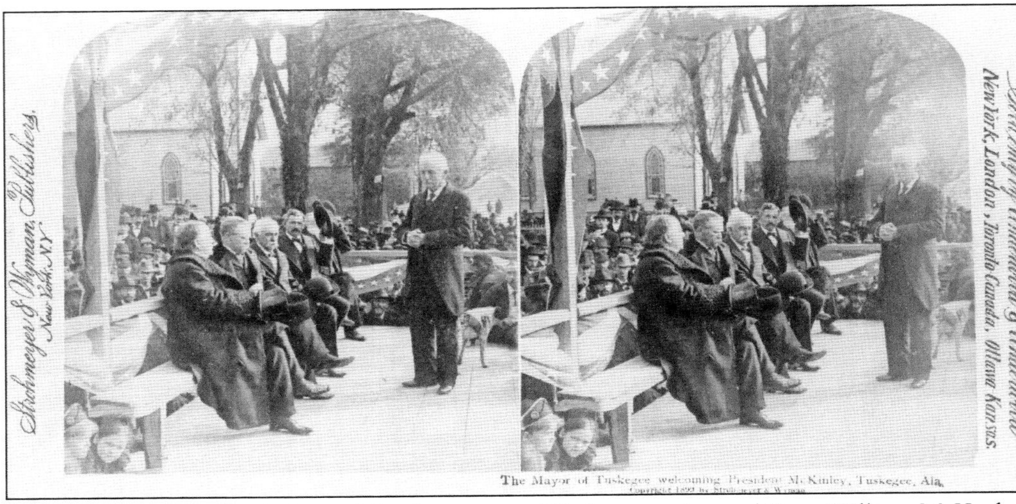

In this stereo photograph from 1899, the mayor of Tuskegee welcomed Pres. William McKinley to the city. Other platform guests included Gov. Joseph F. Johnston and leaders of the state legislature. Booker T. Washington, who invited the president to Tuskegee, joined the platform when the parade commenced.

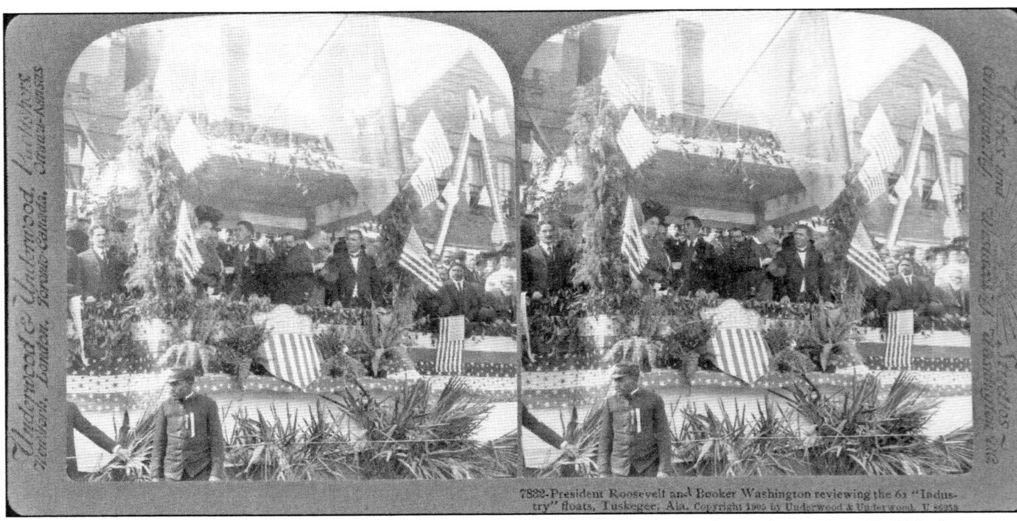

This stereograph, dated 1905, reads, "President Theodore Roosevelt and Booker T. Washington on the reviewing stand watching 61 'Industry Floats', Tuskegee, Ala." Washington invited the president to the city and held the parade in his honor. The 61 floats represented the areas of training and study offered at the institute.

George Washington Carver and Pres. Franklin D. Roosevelt are seen here in a friendly embrace during the president's visit to Tuskegee Institute on March 30, 1939. President Roosevelt, who had been invited 30 years prior by Booker T. Washington, jokingly stated in his speech that he finally made good on the invitation. The president made the stopover visit while en route to rest at Warm Springs, Georgia. P.H. Polk took the photograph. (Courtesy of the estate of P.H. Polk.)

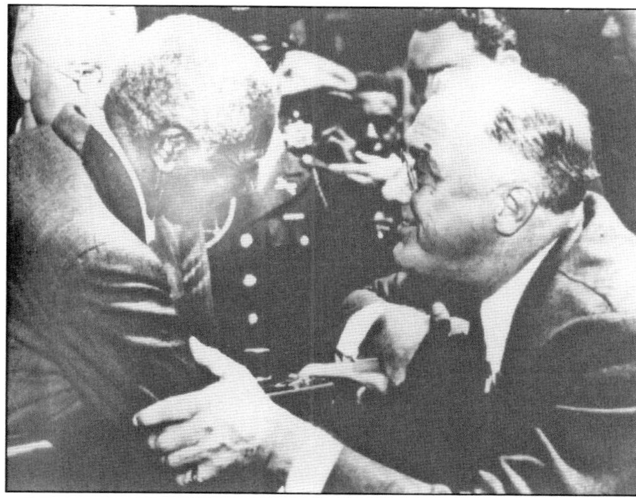

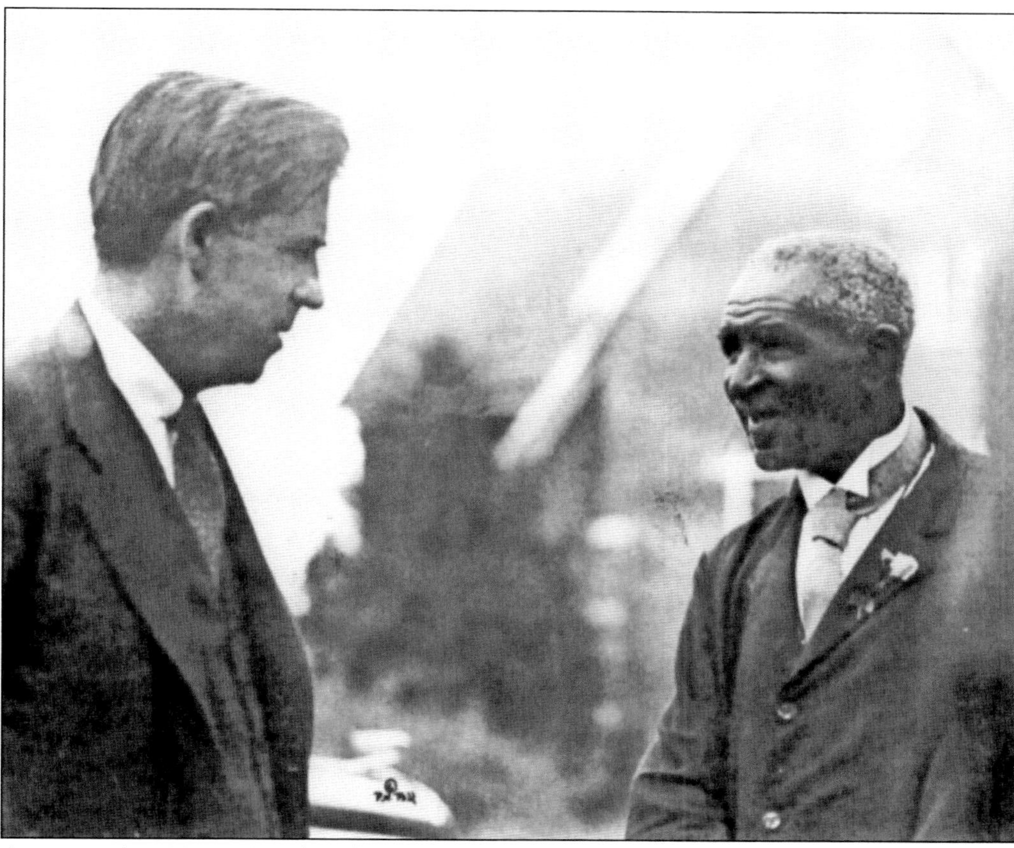

As a young boy, Henry Agard Wallace (1888–1965) tagged along with Iowa State graduate student George Washington Carver on nature walks. He attributed his interest in nature and agriculture to Carver, whom he called "the kindest, gentlest teacher I ever knew." Wallace went on to become the secretary of agriculture, the vice president, and the secretary of commerce. This P.H. Polk photograph shows him visiting Carver in 1940. (Courtesy of the estate of P.H. Polk.)

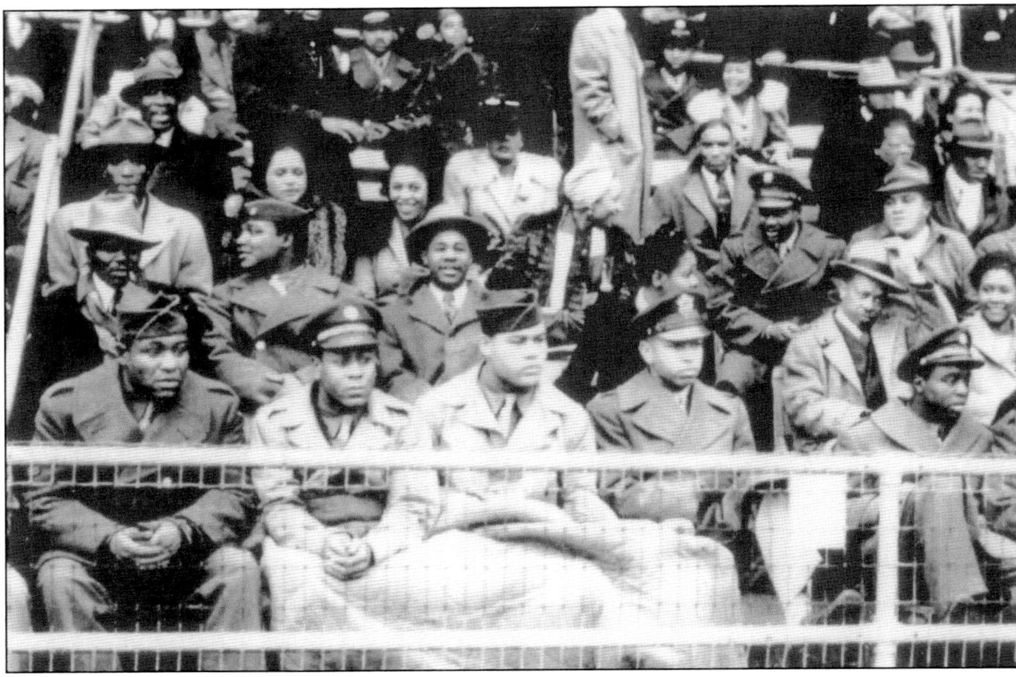

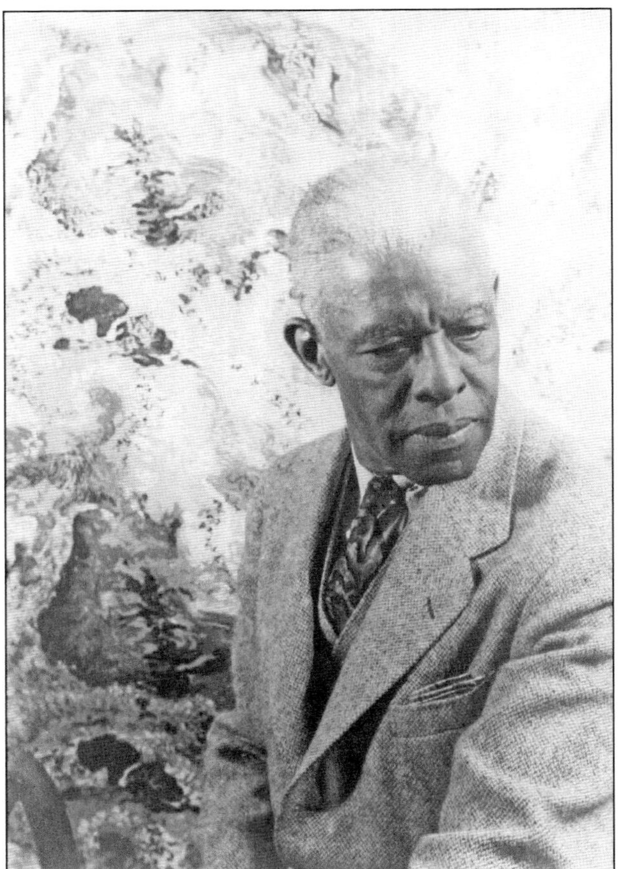

Boxer Joe Louis (1914–1981), known as the Brown Bomber, was the world heavyweight champion from June 22, 1937, to March 1, 1949. He visited the campus to enjoy a Tuskegee Golden Tigers football game in the early 1940s. He is seen here in the center of the stands at the stadium in a P.H. Polk photograph. (Courtesy of the estate of P.H. Polk.)

Lyric tenor Roland Hayes (1887–1977), noted for his masterful interpretation of classical songs and African American spirituals, performed sparingly between 1940 and 1973, giving special recitals at Carnegie Hall in New York and performing concerts at Fisk University and other colleges, including Tuskegee Institute. He performed at Tuskegee in 1948 on the invitation of Pres. Frederick Douglass Patterson. He is seen here in a 1954 Carl Van Vechten photograph. (Courtesy of the Library of Congress Prints and Photographs Division.)

Henry Ford made repeated trips to Tuskegee, beginning in 1932, in efforts to lure George Washington Carver to Dearborn, Michigan, to lead scientific explorations for alternative fuel sources with food crops. He offered to build Carver a home with a laboratory, an elevator, and a staff of his choosing. Carver maintained his commitment to Tuskegee. As of 1934, the two men communicated routinely via letters. By the time World War II began, the auto magnate sought Carver's help in developing a synthetic rubber to compensate for wartime rubber shortages. Carver arrived on July 19, 1942, and set up a laboratory in an old waterworks building in Dearborn. He and Ford experimented with different crops, including sweet potatoes and dandelions, eventually devising a way to make the rubber substitute from goldenrod, a weed plant. Ford is seen at right in a 1927 company stock photograph and below with Carver on July 22, 1942, in Dearborn at the opening of the food laboratory being donated to Carver. (Right, courtesy of the Library of Congress; below, courtesy of the National Archives and Records Administration.)

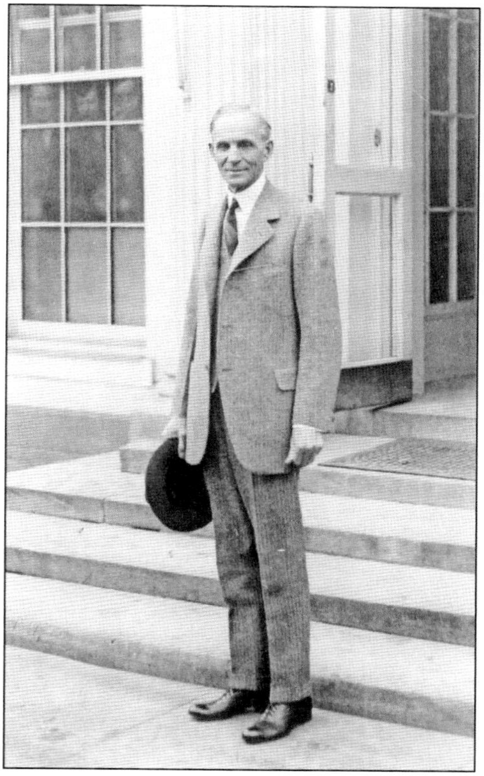

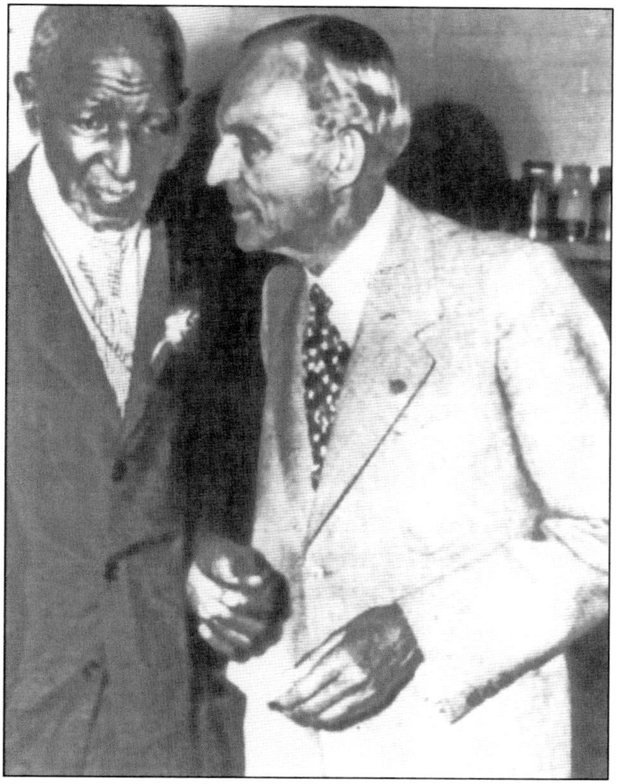

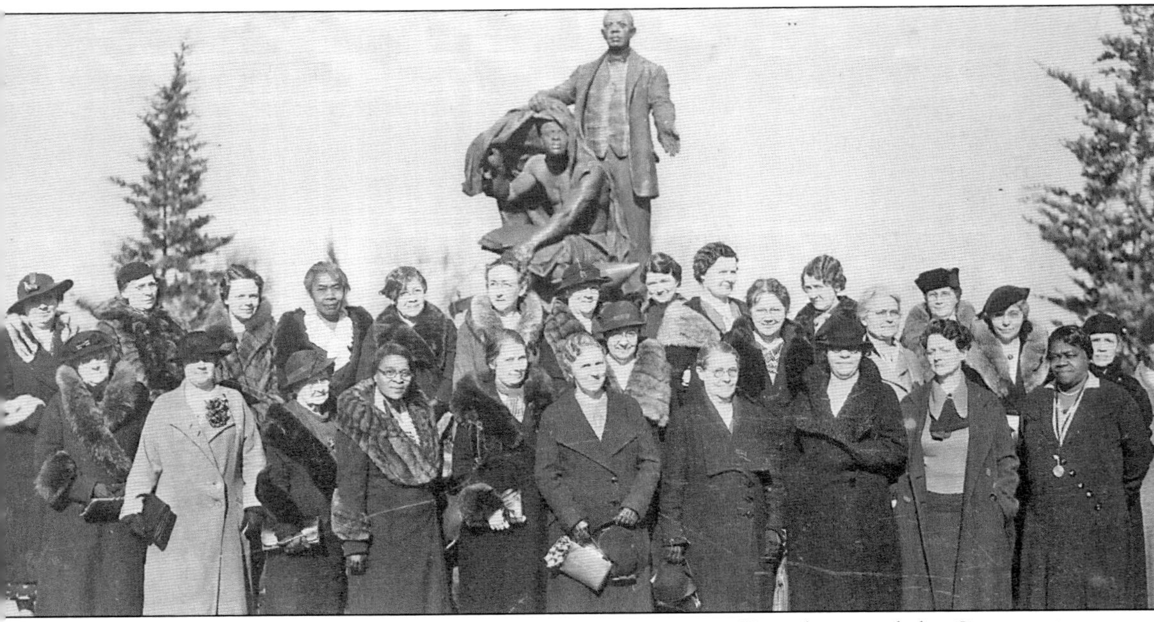

The Association of Southern Women for the Prevention of Lynching and the Commission on Interracial Cooperation met at Tuskegee in 1938. This photograph shows, from left to right, (first row) Sallie Little Hanna, Dallas; Mrs. C.H. Thorpe, Little Rock; Charlotte Hawkins Brown, Sedalia, North Carolina; Mrs. B.F. Zimmerman, Columbia, South Carolina; Mrs. C.L. Read, Zebulon, North Carolina; Mrs. W.A. Newell, Salisbury, North Carolina; Jennie Dee Booth Moton, Tuskegee Institute; Jessie Daniel Ames, Atlanta; and Mary McLeod Bethune, Daytona Beach, Florida; (second row) Mary Hedrick McCollum, Jacksonville, Florida; Mrs. Walter S. Jones, Jacksonville, Florida; Arlene Rogers Park, Lithonia, Georgia; Fannie C. Williams, New Orleans; Mrs. H.L. McCrory, Charlotte; Mrs. George E. Davis, Orangeburg, South Carolina; Mrs. J.W. Mills, Beaumont, Texas; Nannie Hite Winston, Louisville; Mrs. George Sexton, Shreveport, Louisiana; Mrs. J.D. Lawhon, Hugo, Oklahoma; Onilee Brown, Waxhaw, North Carolina; Mrs. C.M. Mullino, Montezuma, Georgia; Mrs. L.W. Alford, McComb, Mississippi; Mrs. J.A. Richardson, Richmond; Mrs. G.W. Hummel, Louisville; Florence Johnson Hunt, Fort Valley, Georgia; and Mrs. Robert O'Neal, Clarksville, Tennessee. (Courtesy of Triangle Research Libraries Network's Civilian Conservation Corps project, Jessie Daniel Ames papers.)

Seven

THE TUSKEGEE STUDY

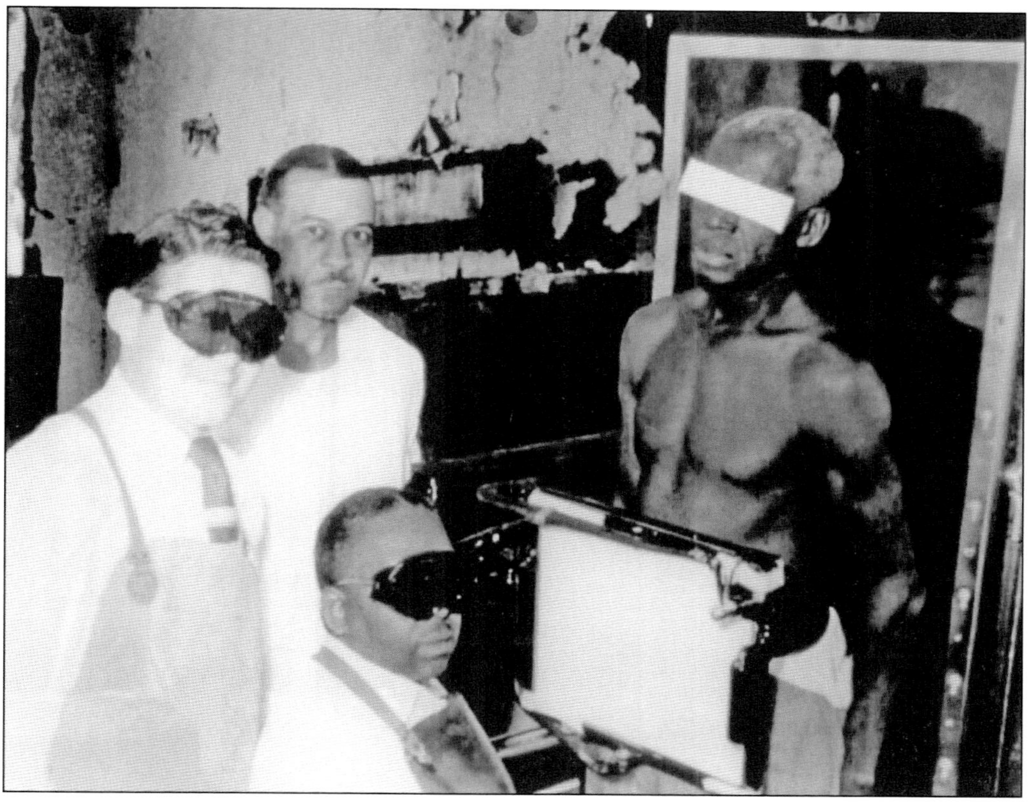

In 1932, US Public Health Service doctors contacted thousands of African American men in Macon County, offering free treatment for "bad blood," a generic term for several conditions, and most men were eager to receive free medical treatment. Of the 600 men chosen, 399 had syphilis and 201 were healthy. The latter group was then told they were sick, to serve as the control group, and the Tuskegee Study of Untreated Syphilis in the Negro Male was underway. (Courtesy of the National Archives and Records Administration.)

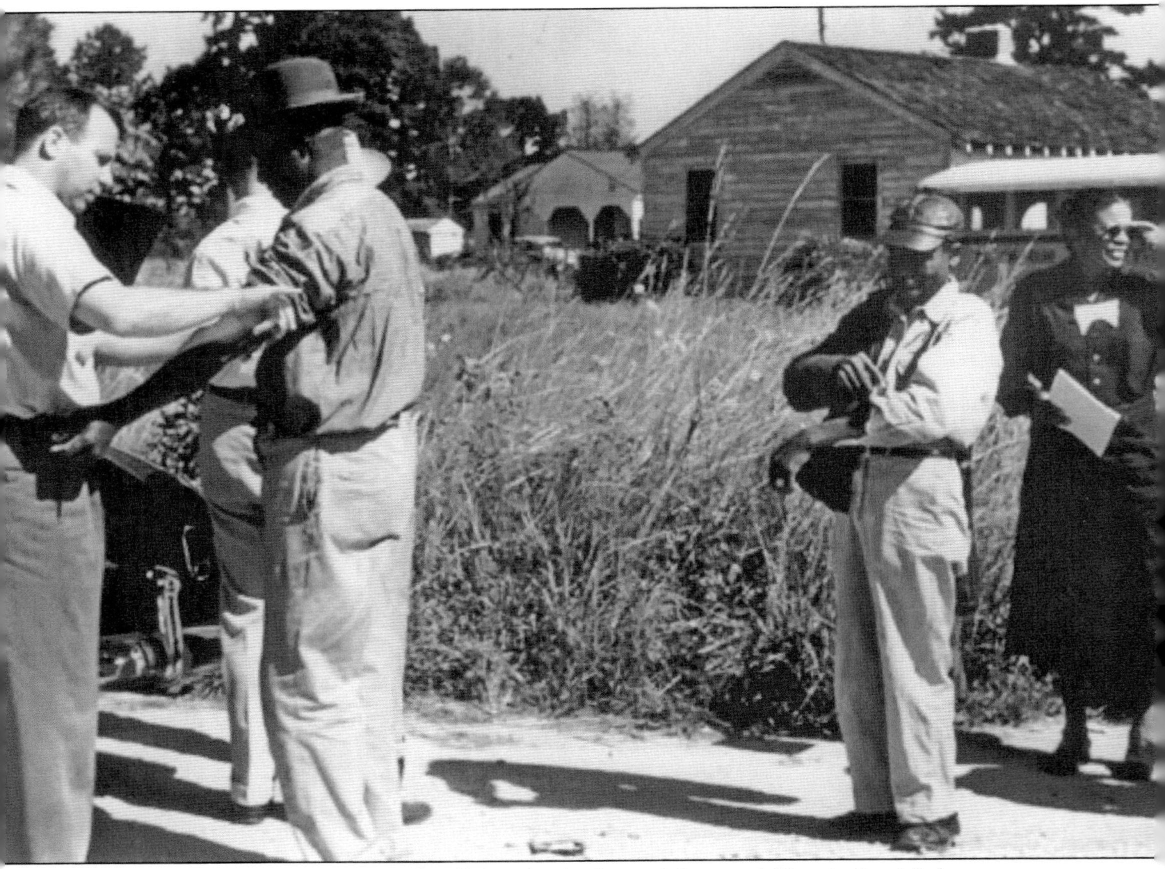

Some examinations occurred at John A. Andrews Memorial Hospital, with bogus treatments held at various other locations. Lasting 40 years, it was the longest non-therapeutic study of human disease in medical history and was intended to continue until all subjects had died. When news of the study broke in 1972, to the horror of many Americans and to the embarrassment of the government, the project abruptly ended. Two-thirds of the subjects had died of syphilis or syphilis-related conditions, 40 had infected their wives, and 19 children were born with congenital syphilis passed on by unsuspecting parents. (Courtesy of the National Archives and Records Administration.)

US Public Health Service (PHS) assistant surgeon general Dr. Taliaferro Clark devised the Tuskegee study to assess the long-term effects of syphilis and to determine if the disease affected blacks differently than whites. Macon County was targeted because 36 percent of its black male population had the disease, the highest rate of the six southern counties tested in 1930. (Courtesy of the National Archives and Records Administration.)

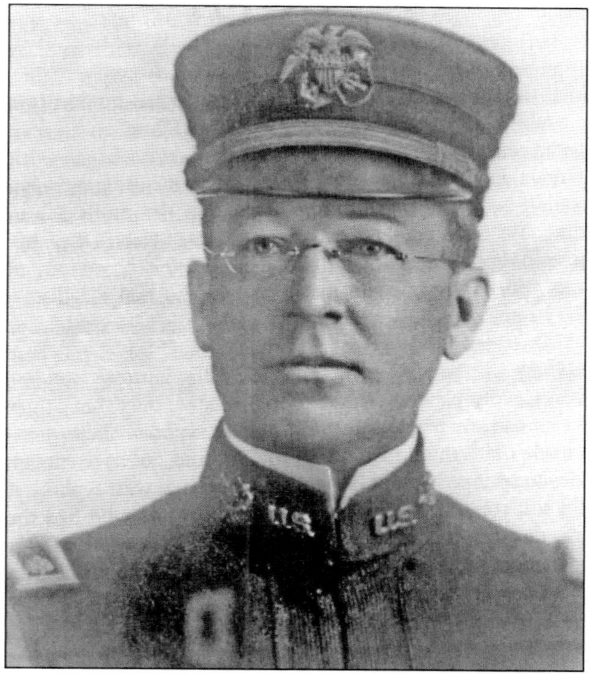

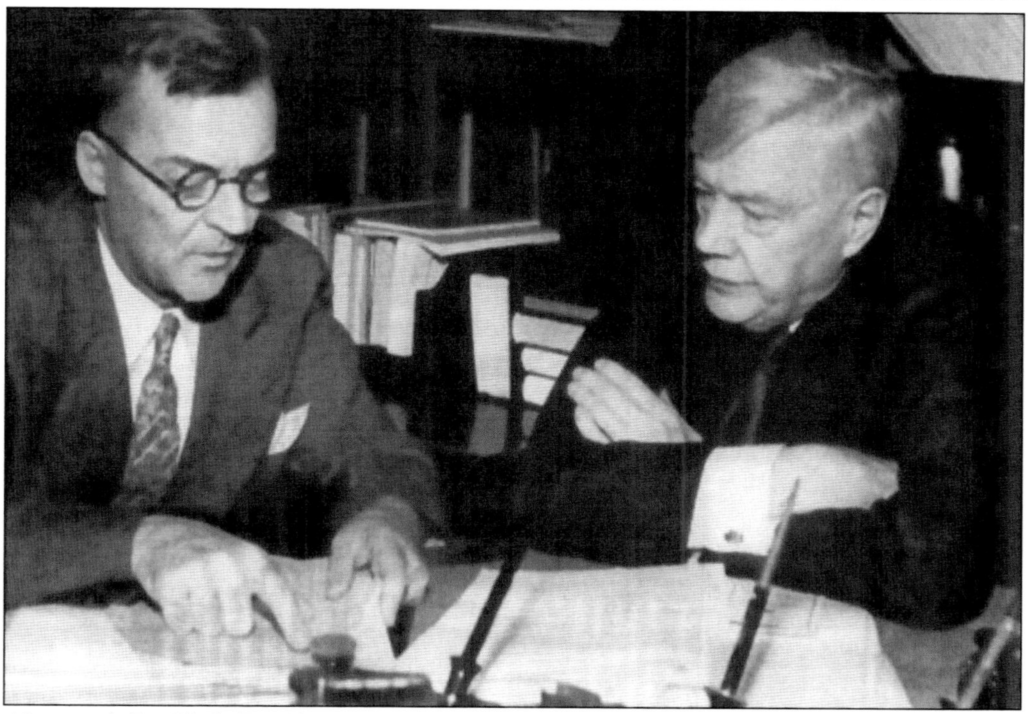

Along with Dr. Clark, Dr. Oliver C. Wenger (left), the PHS venereal disease clinic director in Hot Springs, Arkansas, lobbied state and county health agencies regarding the project. Dr. Wenger played a key role in establishing early study protocols. Though he historically favored mass screening and treatment programs for syphilis among African Americans, he advised, assisted, and supported the Tuskegee study, including the policy of concealing its objectives from subjects to secure their participation. (Courtesy of the National Archives and Records Administration.)

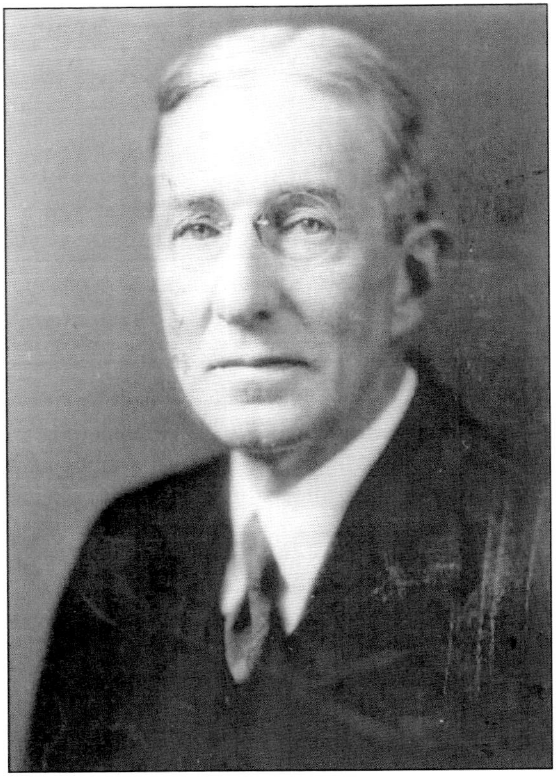

On September 30, 1932, PHS surgeon general Hugh S. Cumming solicited support from Tuskegee Institute president Robert Moton, stressing the need for a hospital to conduct examinations for unparalleled medical research that "could not be duplicated anywhere else in the world." Moton consented two days later, unaware that subjects would go untreated. With subsequent approval of the state and county boards of health, the Tuskegee study began. (Courtesy of the National Archives and Records Administration.)

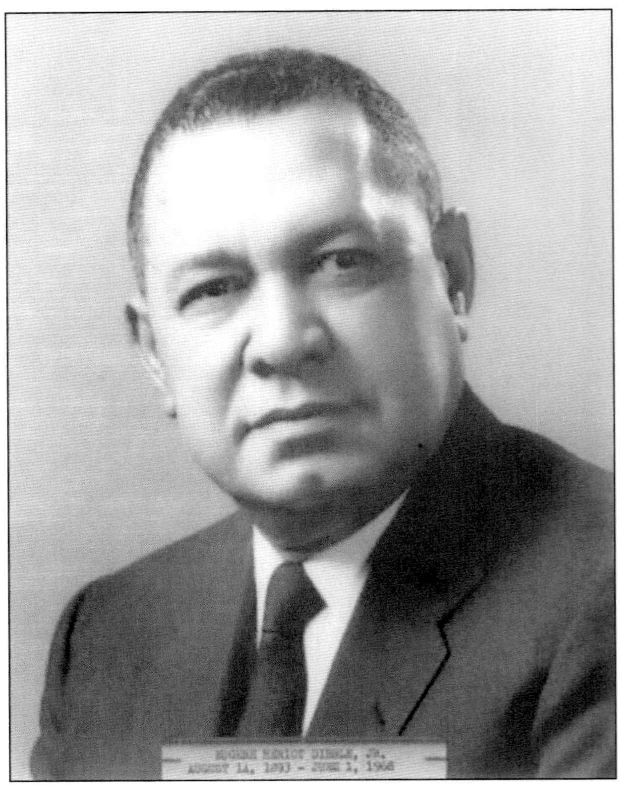

Dr. Eugene H. Dibble, the head of John A. Andrews Memorial Hospital, encouraged President Moton to cooperate with the study, believing it would offer valuable training for students and interns. Dr. Dibble recommended Eunice Rivers as the project's nurse. He and his staff assisted with some aspects of the study, including spinal taps. Dr. Dibble, like Moton, was told that the experiment would study the effects of syphilis on the "human economy." (Courtesy of Tuskegee University Archives.)

Dr. Taliaferro Clark named Dr. Raymond H. Vonderlehr the overall director of the study. Dr. Vonderlehr gained approval to extend the study beyond its initially authorized six-to-eight-month time frame. He also added autopsies to the study, considering the procedure necessary.

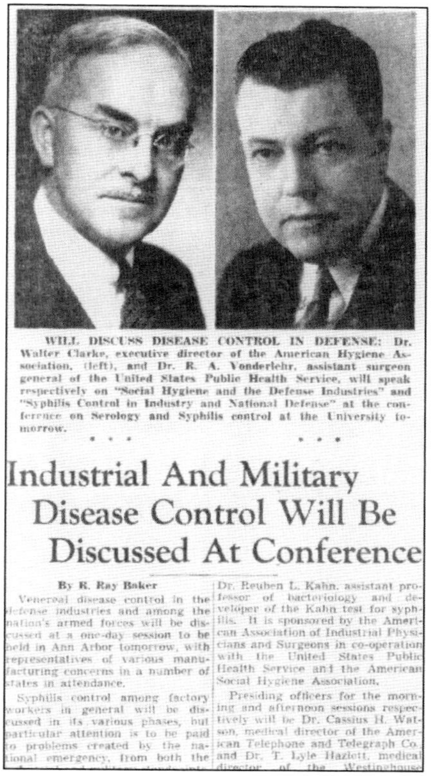

WILL DISCUSS DISEASE CONTROL IN DEFENSE: Dr. Walter Clarke, executive director of the American Hygiene Association, (left), and Dr. R. A. Vonderlehr, assistant surgeon general of the United States Public Health Service, will speak respectively on "Social Hygiene and the Defense Industries" and "Syphilis Control in Industry and National Defense" at the conference on Serology and Syphilis control at the University tomorrow.

* * * * * *

Industrial And Military Disease Control Will Be Discussed At Conference

By R. Ray Baker

Venereal disease control in the defense industries and among the nation's armed forces will be discussed at a one-day session to be held in Ann Arbor tomorrow, with representatives of various manufacturing concerns in a number of states in attendance.

Syphilis control among factory workers in general will be discussed in its various phases, but particular attention is to be paid to problems created by the national emergency, from both the

Dr. Reuben L. Kahn, assistant professor of bacteriology and developer of the Kahn test for syphilis. It is sponsored by the American Association of Industrial Physicians and Surgeons in co-operation with the United States Public Health Service and the American Social Hygiene Association.

Presiding officers for the morning and afternoon sessions respectively will be Dr. Cassius H. Watson, medical director of the American Telephone and Telegraph Co. and Dr. T. Lyle Hazlett, medical director of the Westinghouse

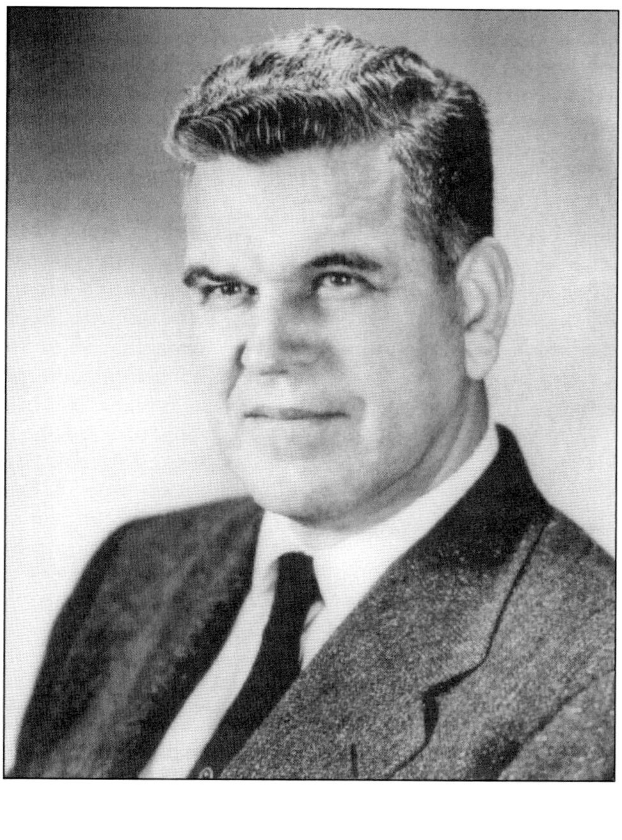

Dr. Vonderlehr appointed Dr. John Roderick Heller to handle on-site medical operations. Even though penicillin was routinely used to treat syphilis in PHS clinics across the country, and the Nuremberg Code, protecting the rights of research subjects, was established and in effect, Dr. Heller distributed colored aspirin, iron tonic, and vitamins to subjects, creating the false impression that their "bad blood" was being treated. He also deliberately focused on older men and advanced stages of the disease, deceptively examining healthy men of similar age for comparisons. (Courtesy of the National Archives and Records Administration.)

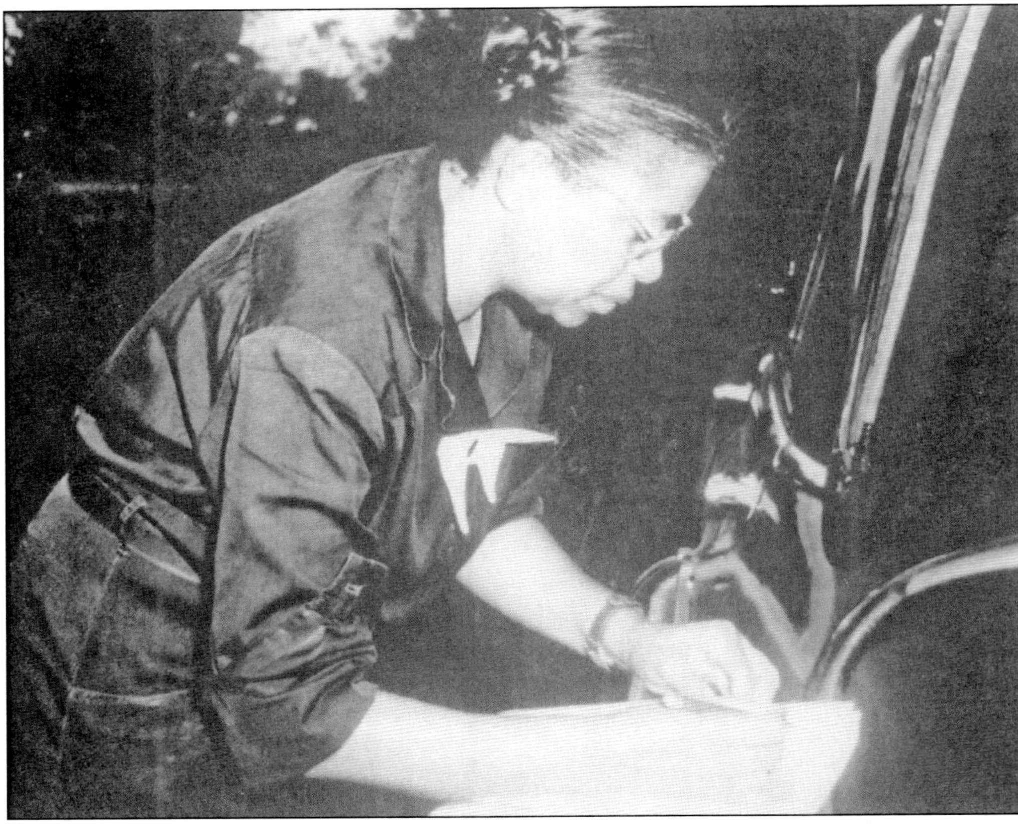

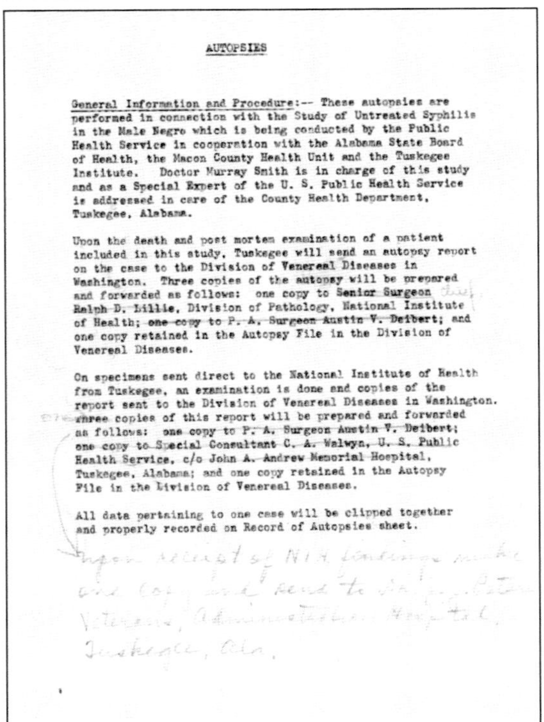

AUTOPSIES

General Information and Procedure:-- These autopsies are performed in connection with the Study of Untreated Syphilis in the Male Negro which is being conducted by the Public Health Service in cooperation with the Alabama State Board of Health, the Macon County Health Unit and the Tuskegee Institute. Doctor Murray Smith is in charge of this study and as a Special Expert of the U. S. Public Health Service is addressed in care of the County Health Department, Tuskegee, Alabama.

Upon the death and post mortem examination of a patient included in this study, Tuskegee will send an autopsy report on the case to the Division of Venereal Diseases in Washington. Three copies of the autopsy will be prepared and forwarded as follows: one copy to Senior Surgeon Ralph D. Lillie, Division of Pathology, National Institute of Health; one copy to P. A. Surgeon Austin V. Deibert; and one copy retained in the Autopsy File in the Division of Venereal Diseases.

On specimens sent direct to the National Institute of Health from Tuskegee, an examination is done and copies of the report sent to the Division of Venereal Diseases in Washington. Three copies of this report will be prepared and forwarded as follows: one copy to P. A. Surgeon Austin V. Deibert; one copy to Special Consultant C. A. Walwyn, U. S. Public Health Service, c/o John A. Andrew Memorial Hospital, Tuskegee, Alabama; and one copy retained in the Autopsy File in the Division of Venereal Diseases.

All data pertaining to one case will be clipped together and properly recorded on Record of Autopsies sheet.

Eunice Verdell Rivers was the supervisor of night nurses at Andrews Hospital when she was hired by Dr. Clark. She was the principal liaison between test subjects and the agency, and gained their trust. Leadership changed over the years, but Rivers remained a fixture, always diligently ensuring that subjects were not accidentally treated via other avenues. (Courtesy of the National Archives and Records Administration.)

Autopsies became key to the experiment under Dr. Vonderhelr in 1933, making nurse Rivers's role more vital. Her ability to calm the fears of skeptical families regarding autopsies led the men in the study to jokingly refer to themselves as members of "Miss Rivers' Lodge." Consenting families received $50 for funeral expenses. By 1953, only one family of the 146 men who died refused to permit an autopsy. (Courtesy of the National Archives and Records Administration.)

Participants received a certificate from the Public Health Service after being in the study for 25 years. When a subject died, the family received $50 for their burial, usually on the condition that survivor(s) consented to an autopsy being performed on the deceased person's remains.

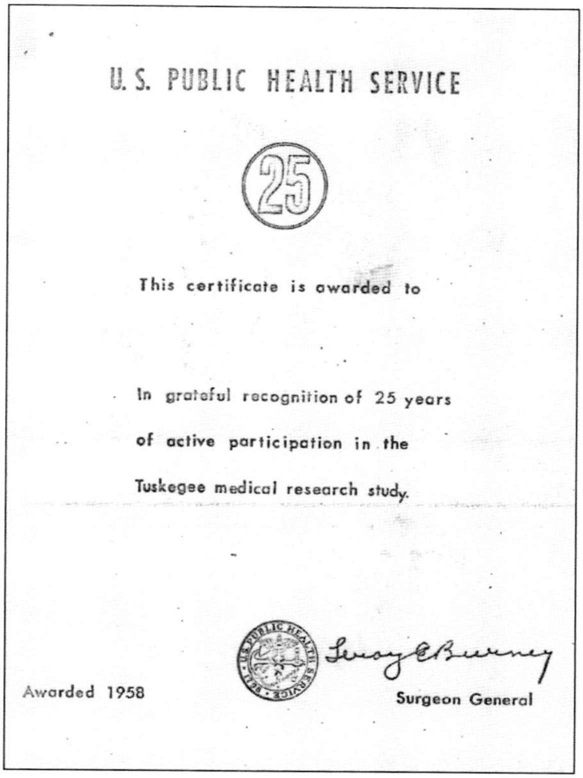

U. S. PUBLIC HEALTH SERVICE

25

This certificate is awarded to

In grateful recognition of 25 years of active participation in the Tuskegee medical research study.

Awarded 1958

Surgeon General

British medical research scientist Alexander Fleming discovered the bacteria-killing drug penicillin in 1928. It was accessible to the general public by the late 1940s and was being used to effectively treat many diseases, including syphilis, by 1950. Since the Tuskegee study was intended to study long-term effects of syphilis in black men without treatment, penicillin was not administered to them.

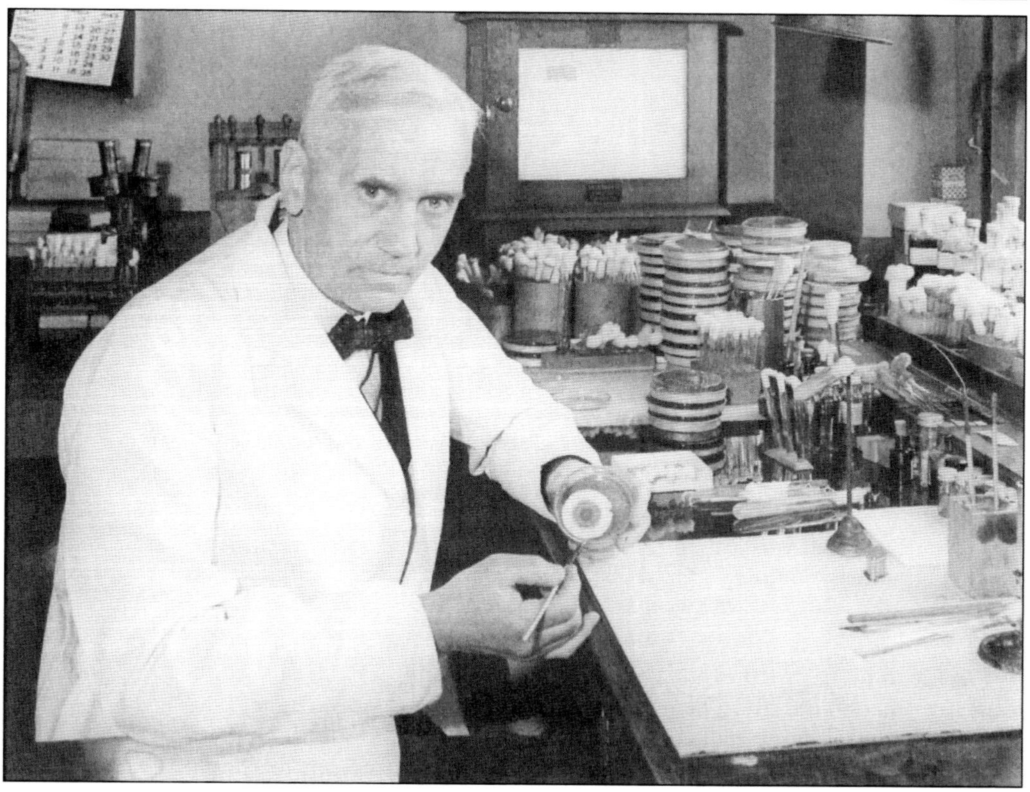

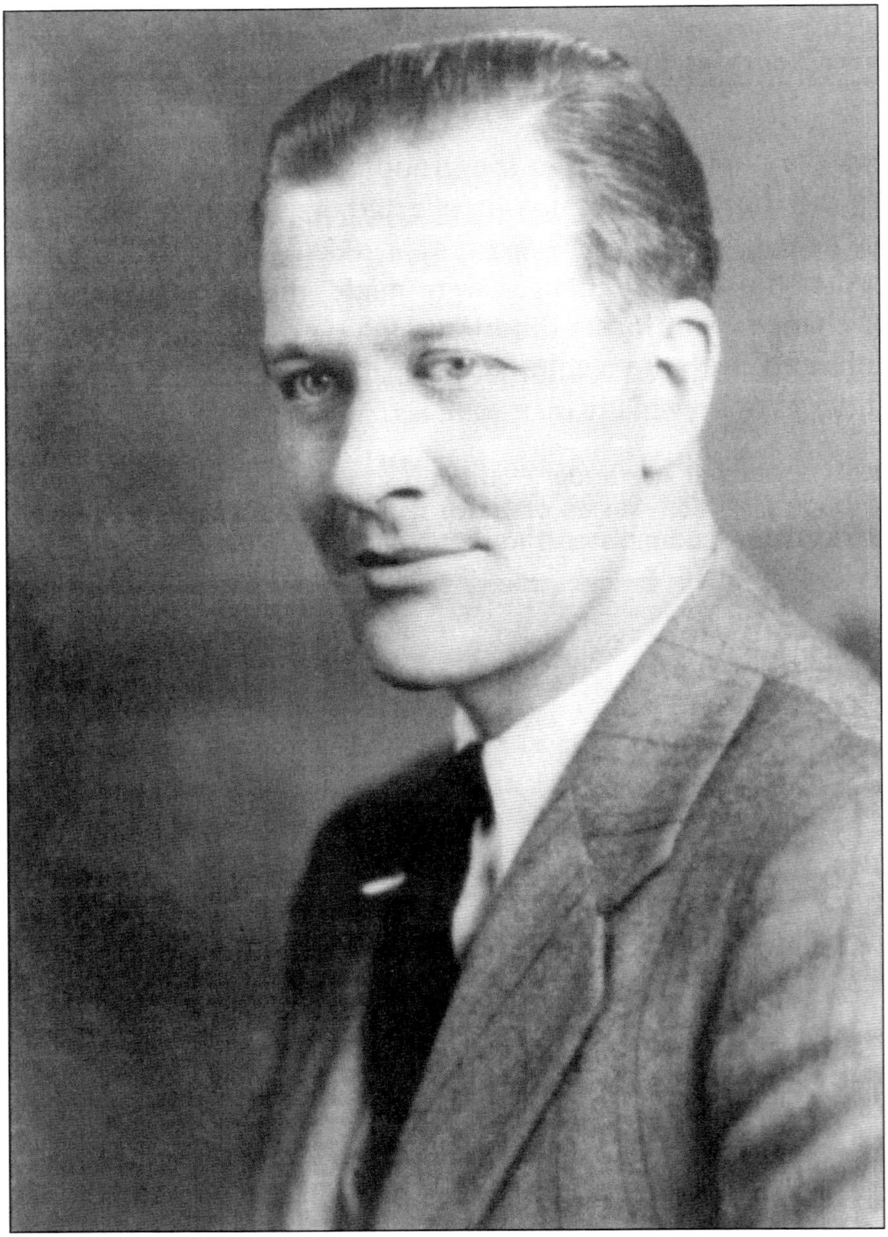

In 1938, Dr. Vonderhelr sent PHS official Dr. Austin V. Deibert to Tuskegee to administer the first complete physical examinations of the test subjects. Checking their medical histories, he discovered that many had received some medical care—doses of neoarsphenamine and applications of mercury ointment—during a 1930 Rosenwald Fund syphilis control project. He concluded that this technically classified the respective subjects as undertreated rather than untreated. In an effort to correct this flaw and validate the research, Dr. Deibert chose to replace the more than 100 people who had undergone some treatment with others diagnosed with the disease who likely had not. Limited funds allowed for the exchange of only 14. During further examinations, Dr. Deibert learned that 12 men in the control group had contracted syphilis. He and Dr. Vonderhelr decided to move the infected men to the syphilis roster, even though this would impact long-term statistical results. (Courtesy of the National Archives and Records Administration.)

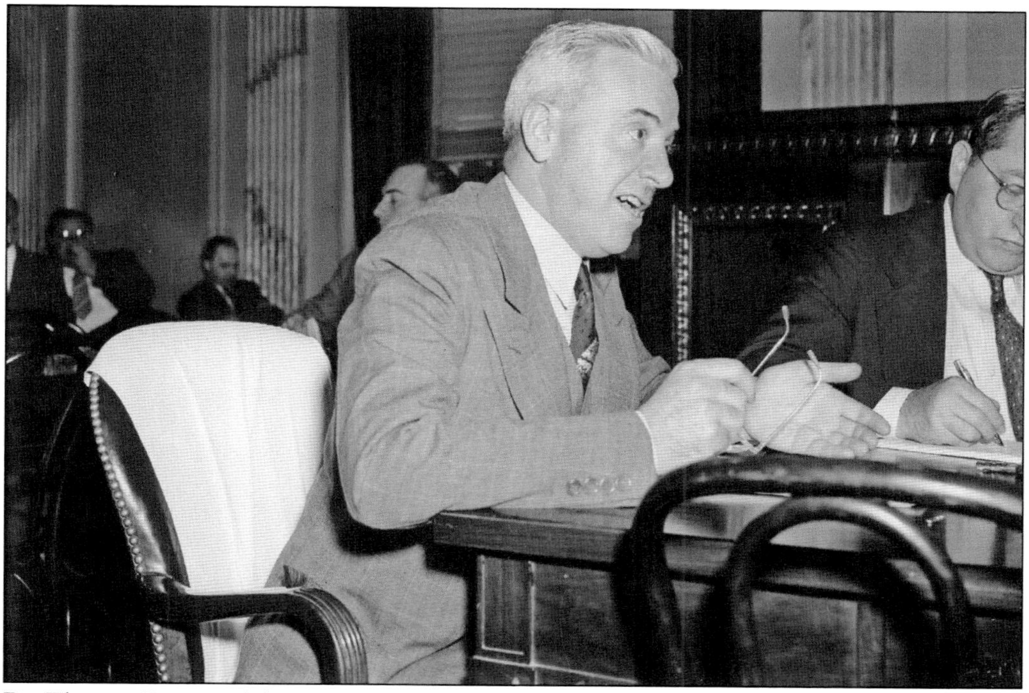

Dr. Thomas Parran of the PHS pointed out in 1937's *Shadow on the Land: Syphilis, the White Man's Burden* that whites introduced syphilis to blacks, and that the relative high rate of syphilis among African Americans was directly related to social and economic factors. He concluded: "Wherever education and living conditions among the Negro race approximates that of the white race, the syphilis rate approximates that of the white." (Courtesy of the National Archives and Records Administration.)

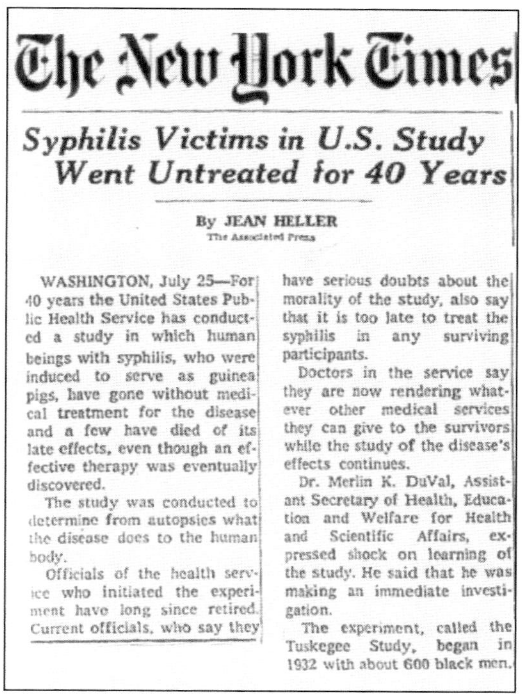

The New York Times

Syphilis Victims in U.S. Study Went Untreated for 40 Years

By JEAN HELLER
The Associated Press

WASHINGTON, July 25—For 40 years the United States Public Health Service has conducted a study in which human beings with syphilis, who were induced to serve as guinea pigs, have gone without medical treatment for the disease and a few have died of its late effects, even though an effective therapy was eventually discovered.

The study was conducted to determine from autopsies what the disease does to the human body.

Officials of the health service who initiated the experiment have long since retired. Current officials, who say they have serious doubts about the morality of the study, also say that it is too late to treat the syphilis in any surviving participants.

Doctors in the service say they are now rendering whatever other medical services they can give to the survivors while the study of the disease's effects continues.

Dr. Merlin K. DuVal, Assistant Secretary of Health, Education and Welfare for Health and Scientific Affairs, expressed shock on learning of the study. He said that he was making an immediate investigation.

The experiment, called the Tuskegee Study, began in 1932 with about 600 black men.

Associated Press investigative reporter Jean Heller broke the story of the Tuskegee study in the *New York Times* on July 25, 1972. The article exposed the government's sanction of the experiment, the deception of subjects, the lack of treatment, and how officials who initiated the study had long since retired while the project continued. Heller's story sparked public expressions of shock throughout medical research and health communities, including with Dr. Merlin Du Val, the assistant secretary of health, education, and welfare for the Department of Health and Scientific Affairs.

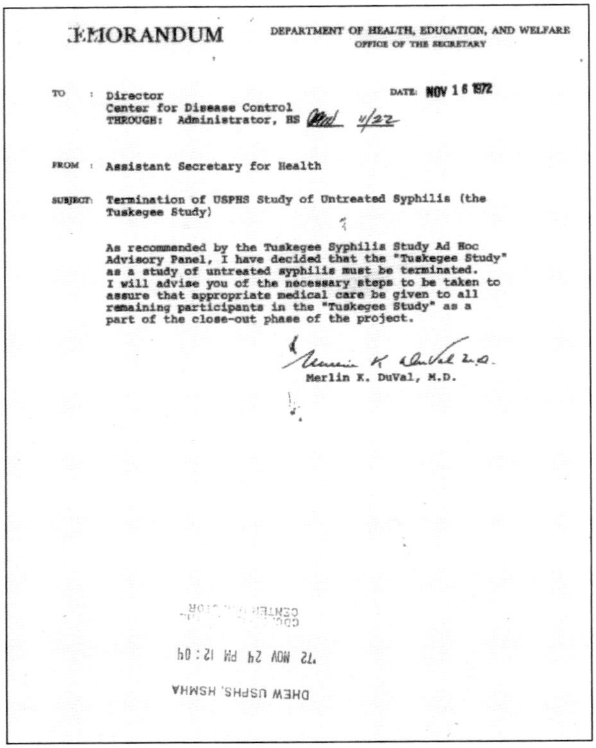

MEMORANDUM

DEPARTMENT OF HEALTH, EDUCATION, AND WELFARE
OFFICE OF THE SECRETARY

TO : Director
Center for Disease Control
THROUGH: Administrator, HS

DATE: NOV 16 1972

FROM : Assistant Secretary for Health

SUBJECT: Termination of USPHS Study of Untreated Syphilis (the Tuskegee Study)

As recommended by the Tuskegee Syphilis Study Ad Hoc Advisory Panel, I have decided that the "Tuskegee Study" as a study of untreated syphilis must be terminated. I will advise you of the necessary steps to be taken to assure that appropriate medical care be given to all remaining participants in the "Tuskegee Study" as a part of the close-out phase of the project.

Merlin K. DuVal, M.D.

The Tuskegee Syphilis Ad Hoc Advisory Panel was formed and, in October 1972, recommended the termination of the study. The federal government complied in November. The panel's final report, on April 28, 1973, condemned the study, indicating that the men with syphilis should have received penicillin when it became available, and that participants should have been informed about the nature of the study and the risks. (Courtesy of the National Archives and Records Administration.)

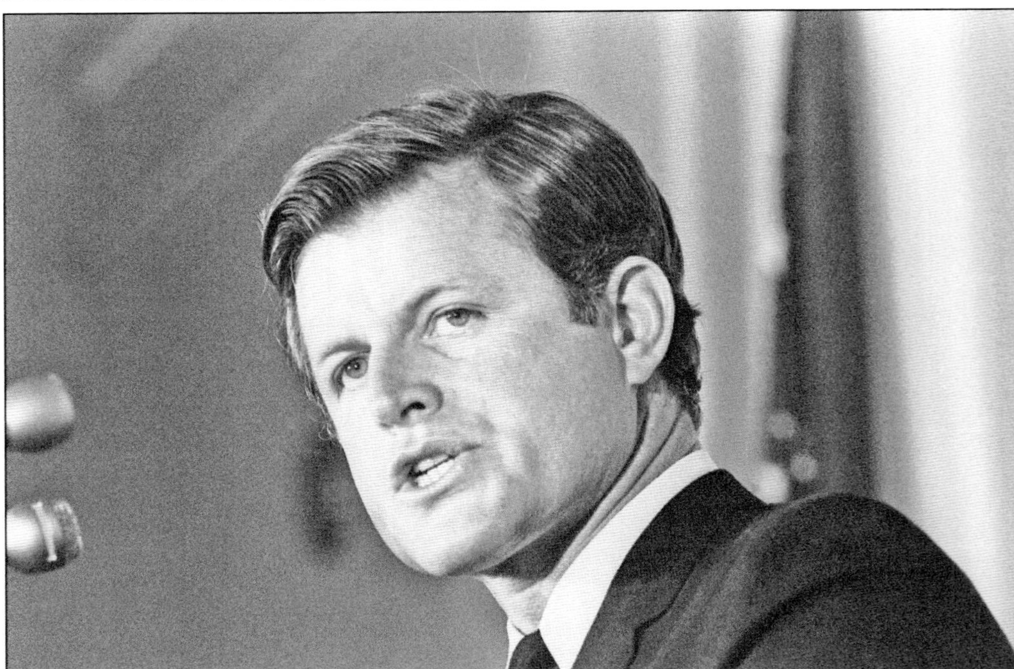

In February and March 1973, the Congressional Subcommittee on Health, chaired by Massachusetts senator Edward Kennedy, held hearings on the Tuskegee experiment to investigate possible civil rights and medical ethics abuses of the study. The hearings brought national attention to the need for federal regulations to protect participants in human medical studies.

Attorney Fred D. Gray was most appalled that the study was sanctioned by the federal government. On July 24, 1973, he filed a $1.8 billion lawsuit against the federal government on behalf of all the men in the study for damages to them and their families. The case was settled out of court in December 1974 for $10 million, which was dispersed to 6,000 people. Syphilis survivors received $37,500, control group survivors received $16,000, and descendants of deceased participants received smaller amounts.

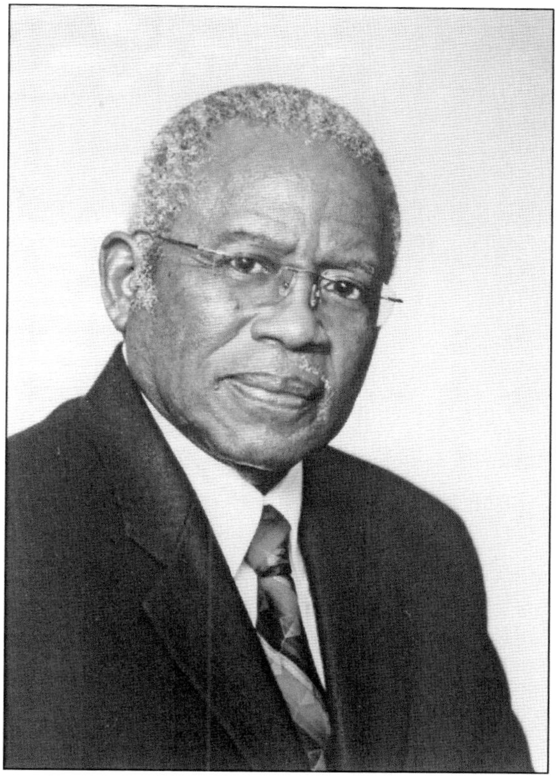

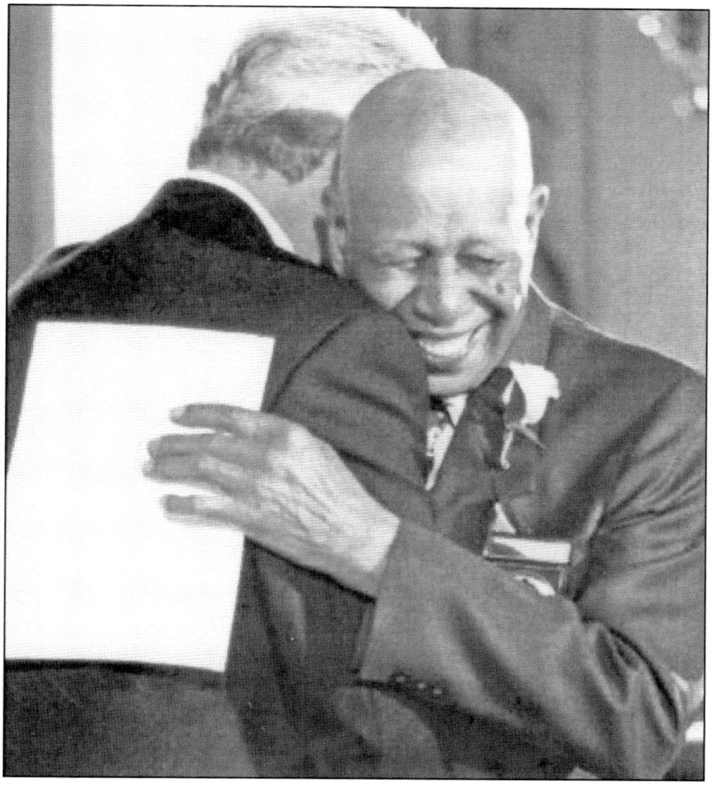

Herman Shaw, seen here, a subject in the study for its entire 40 years, condemned it as racist and as inflicting deep psychological wounds that eroded the faith and trust subjects and their families had in the government, in addition to the physical damage done. When the government's apology came, Shaw, Charles Pollard, Carter Howard, Fred Simmons, and Frederick Moss were five of the eight survivors present. (Courtesy of the National Archives and Records Administration.)

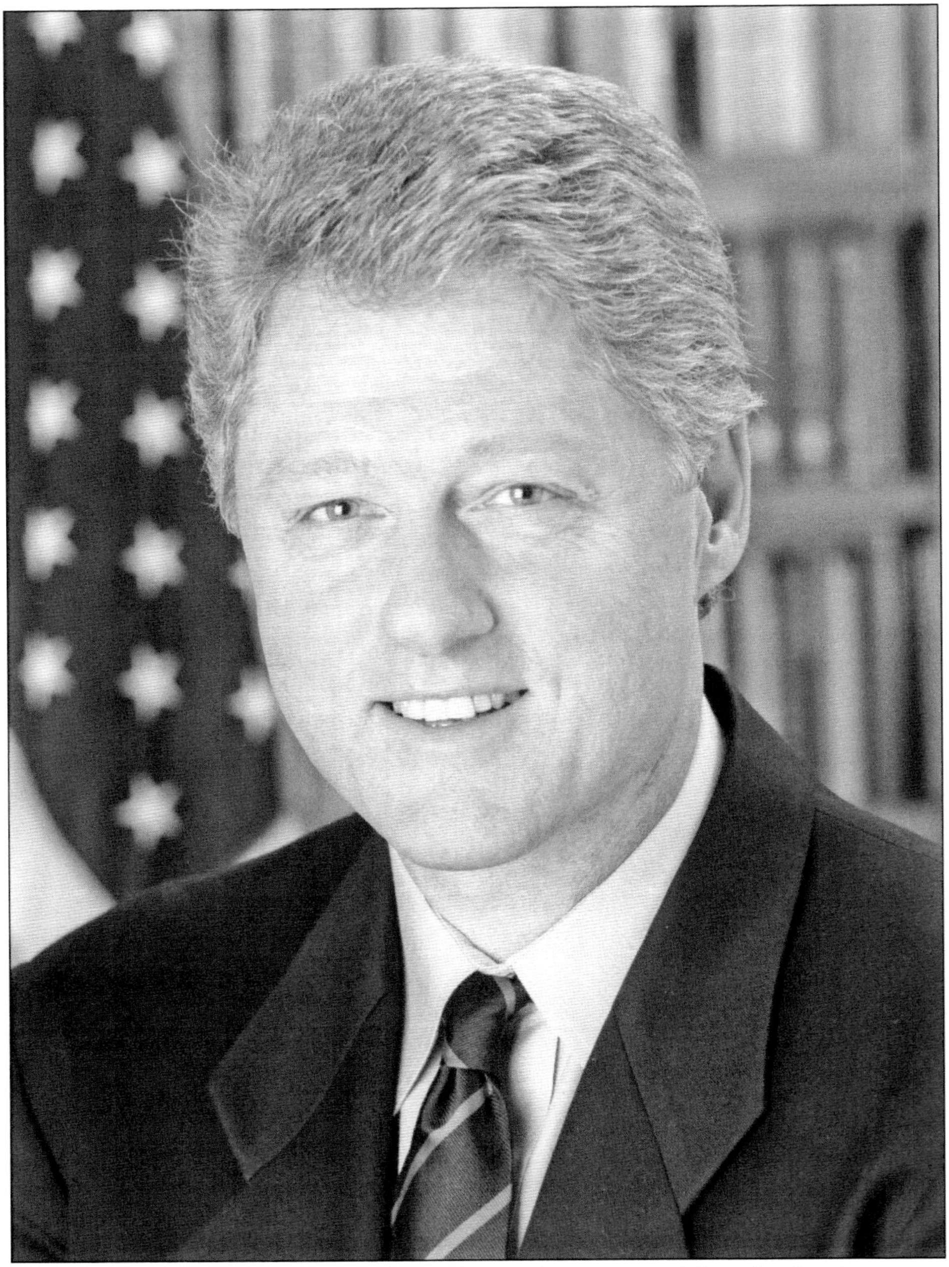

On May 16, 1997, Pres. Bill Clinton apologized to study victims and their families in a ceremony at the White House. Herman Shaw introduced him. The following is an excerpt from his apology: "The United States government did something that was wrong—deeply, profoundly, morally wrong. It was an outrage to our commitment to integrity and equality for all of our citizens. To the survivors, to the wives and family members, the children and the grandchildren, I say what you know: No power on earth can give you back the lives lost, the pain suffered, the years of internal torment and anguish. What was done cannot be undone, but we can end the silence. We can stop turning our heads away. We can look at you in the eye and finally say on behalf of the American people, what the United States government did was shameful, and I am sorry." (Photograph by Bob McNeely, White House photographer, 1993.)

Eight

CIVIL RIGHTS

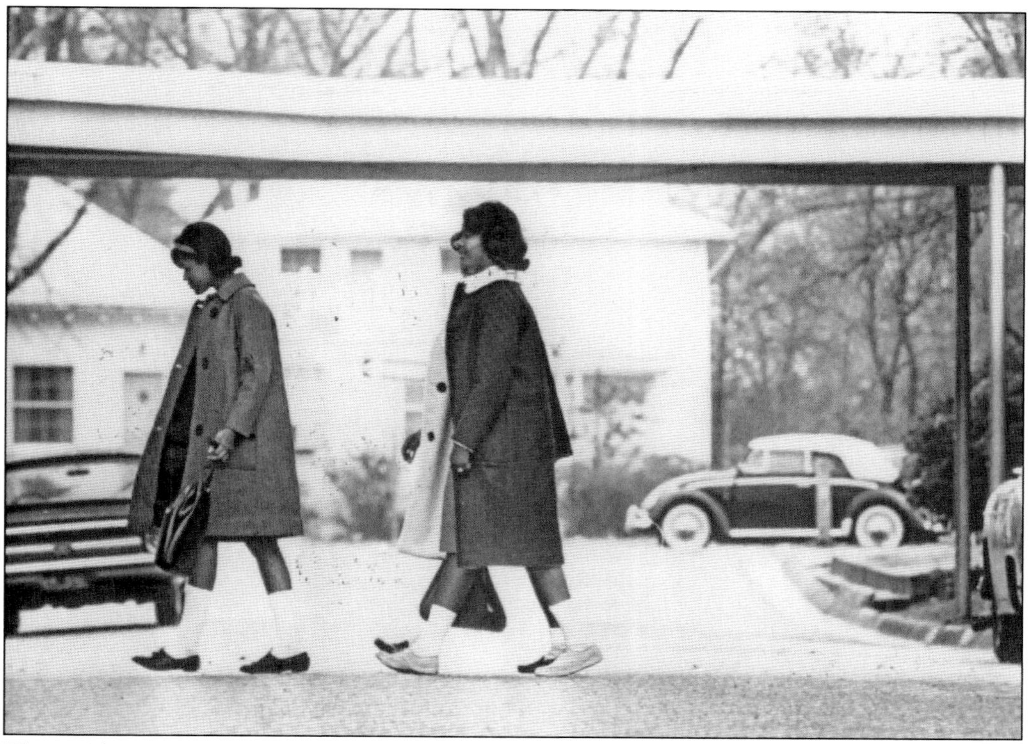

Three African American students at Tuskegee High School return to class from lunch in 1963, the year that white students boycotted. At the time, 13 African American students had just desegregated the high school. After the boycott, the state board of education ordered it closed.

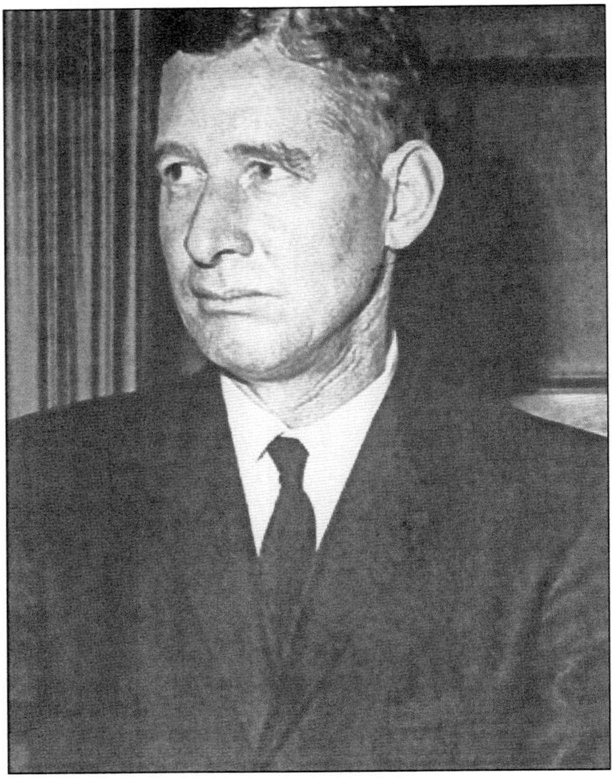

On August 13, 1963, judge Frank Minis Johnson Jr. (1918–1999) ordered the Macon County School Board to desegregate Tuskegee High School on September 2 and present a plan for the entire system by December. Nine years after the Brown v. Board of Education verdict, no black child in Alabama had attended a public school with a white child. Gov. George Wallace vowed in his 1962 campaign that he would stop any school desegregation attempt. This photograph of Johnson in 1965 was taken by Otto Bettman.

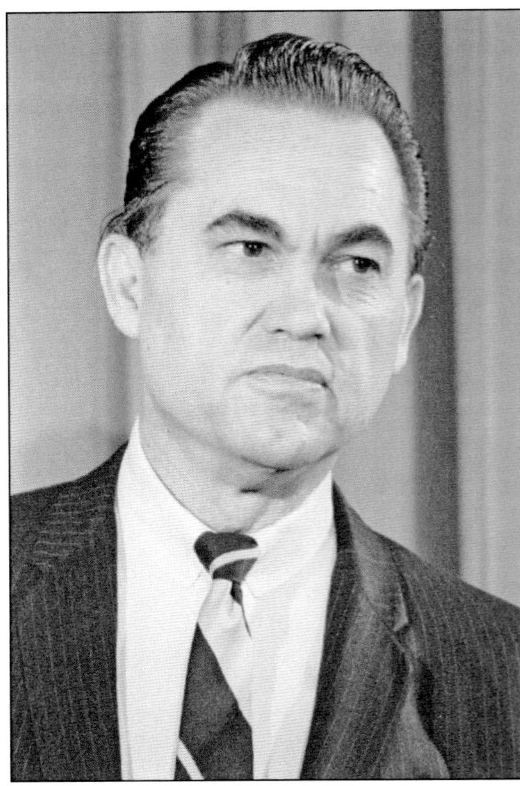

On September 2, 1963, Governor Wallace ordered 200 state troopers to prevent the opening of Tuskegee High School. Troopers turned away the bus bringing 13 African American students to school. On September 9, only 125 of the 565 white students enrolled at the school showed up. On September 10, a group of 150 more whites attended late, fearing violence, and the football team voted to disband. All white students had withdrawn by Thursday, September 11, and Tuskegee High School was segregated again. (Courtesy of the Library of Congress Prints and Photographs Division.)

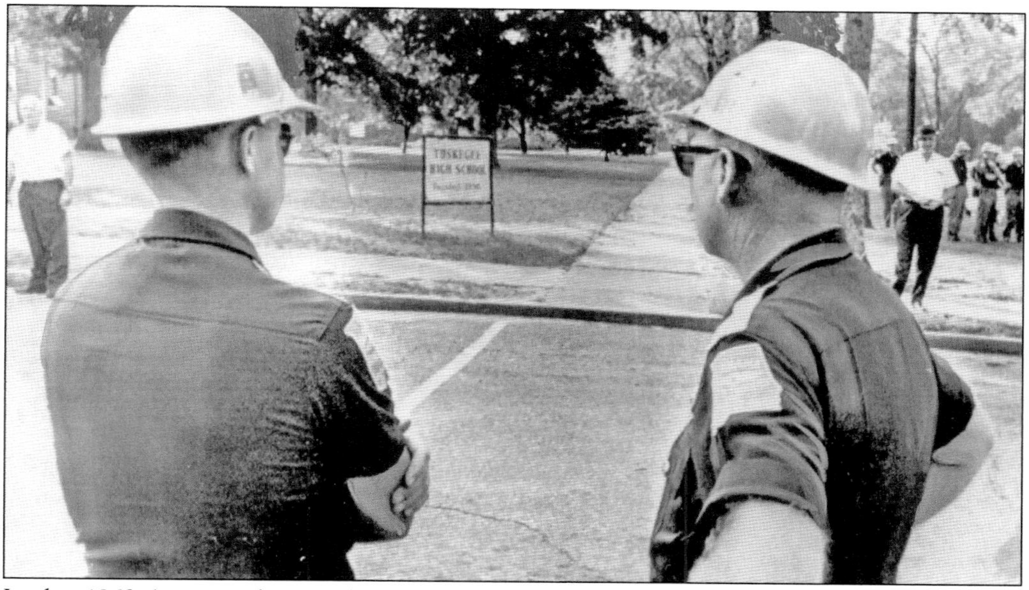

In this 1963 Associated Press photograph, highway patrolmen stand guard at Tuskegee High School, which Gov. George Wallace ordered not to open for another two weeks in an attempt to block integration of the school. The school board announced it would open the school as scheduled despite Governor Wallace's order.

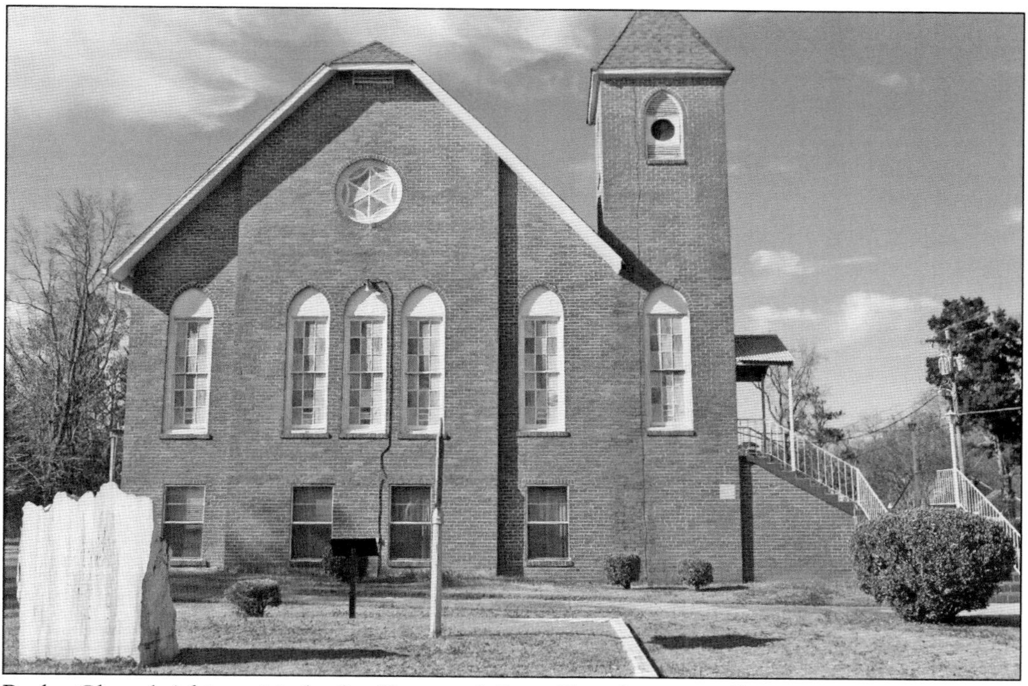

Butler Chapel African Methodist Episcopal Zion Church, originally constructed of wood in 1877, was sided with brick in the 1940s. Perched on a hill west of downtown, it is a prominent landmark in the historically black neighborhood of Zion Hill. When the state legislature re-drew district lines in 1957, placing most African Americans outside the Tuskegee city limits, Butler Chapel was a central gathering place during the four-year grassroots campaign that restored original boundaries.

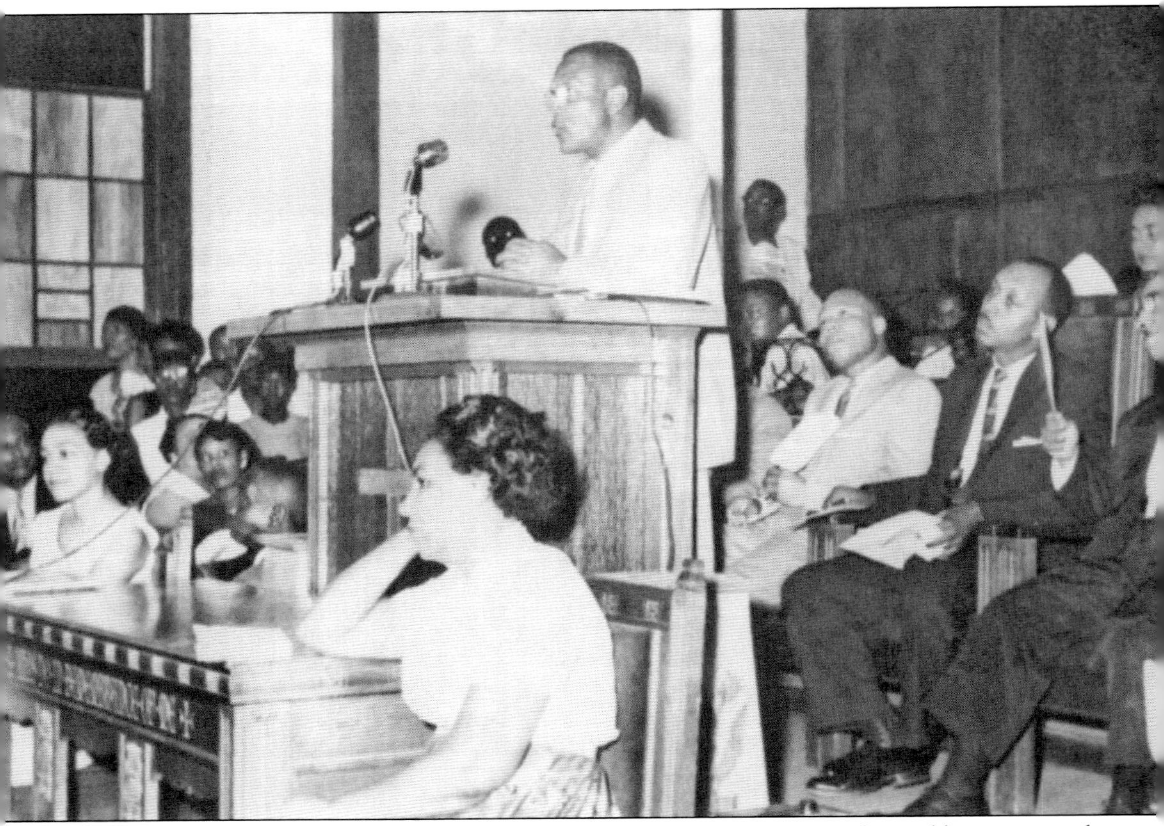

Professor Charles Gomillion, with the Tuskegee Civic Association, is seen here addressing attendees of the first meeting of the Trade with Your Friends campaign in 1957. Gomillion (1900–1995) was the driving force of the all-black civic association. He led a Trade with Your Friends boycott of local white merchants when redistricting was proposed in 1957, urging African Americans to only patronize "those who recognize us as first-class citizens." The boycott ended in 1961 when the Supreme Court ruled: "When a legislature thus singles out a readily isolated segment of a racial minority for special discriminatory treatment, it violates the Fifteenth Amendment."

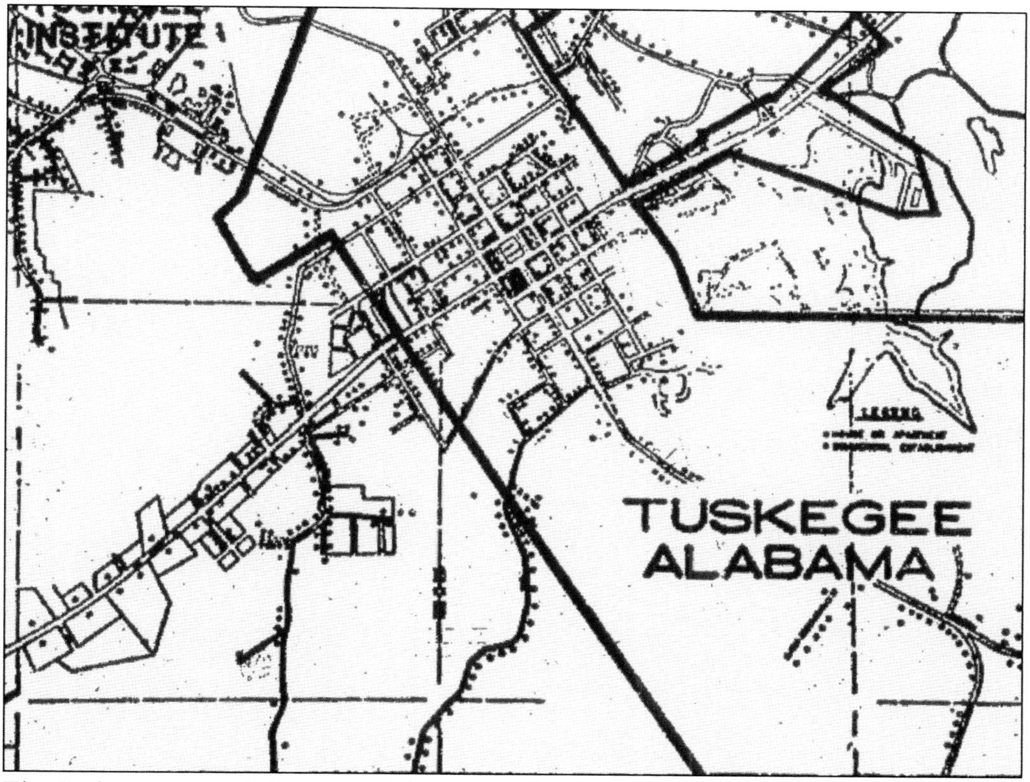

This is the gerrymandering map of the proposed redrawing of boundary lines for the city of Tuskegee, which was an effort to place the majority African American voting populations outside city limits in 1957. With the predominant African American population in Tuskegee, the white officials who proposed the redistricting plan had as part of their goal to prevent this majority from determining election outcomes.

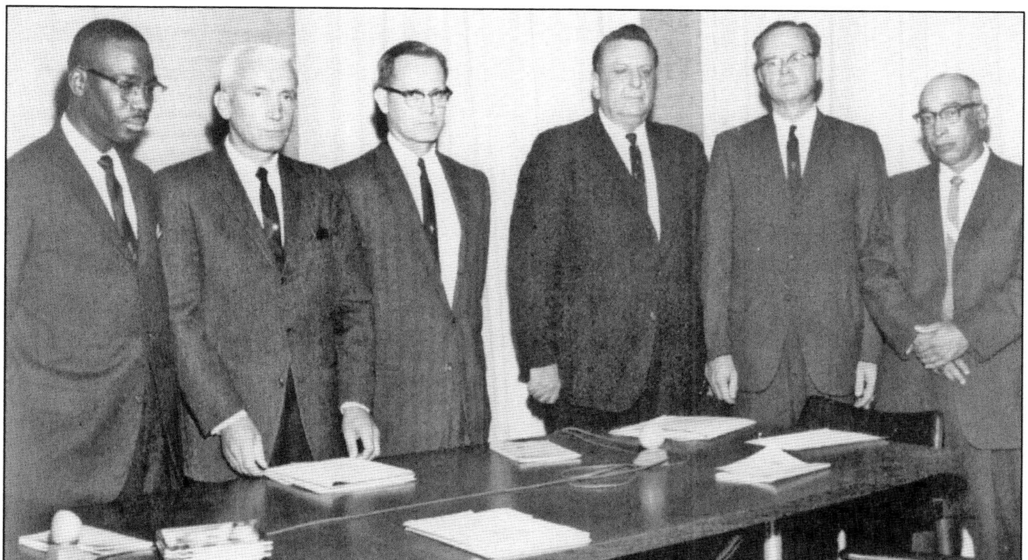

The first integrated Tuskegee City Council, in 1964, included, from left to right, Stanley Smith, L.M. Gregg, Allan Parker, Johnnie L. Sides, Mayor Charles M. Keever, and K.L. Buford.

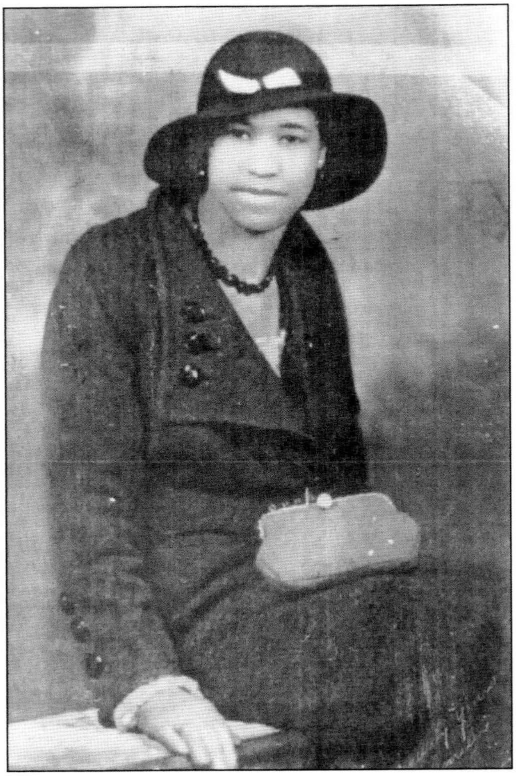

Civil Rights legend Amelia Platts Boynton Robinson (1911–) played a leading role in the activism that led to the passage of voting rights legislation in 1965. Called the Matriarch of the Voting Rights Act, she worked with her late husband, Samuel W. Boynton, on voter registration in Selma from 1929 to 1963 on behalf of the NAACP, until the organization was outlawed. She is best known as the woman at the front of the March 7, 1965, "Bloody Sunday" march in Selma, where she was gassed, beaten, and left for dead on the Edmund Pettus Bridge. Her home and office became headquarters for civil rights operations, and, in 1964, she was the first African American woman to run for Congress in Alabama and the first woman to run on the Democratic ticket in the state. Today, Robinson is the oldest living Tuskegee Institute (now University) graduate, and has lived in Tuskegee since the late 1970s. She is seen at left at age 15, after she entered Tuskegee Institute, and below lying injured on the Edmund Pettus Bridge in 1965. (Both courtesy of Amelia Boynton Robinson.)

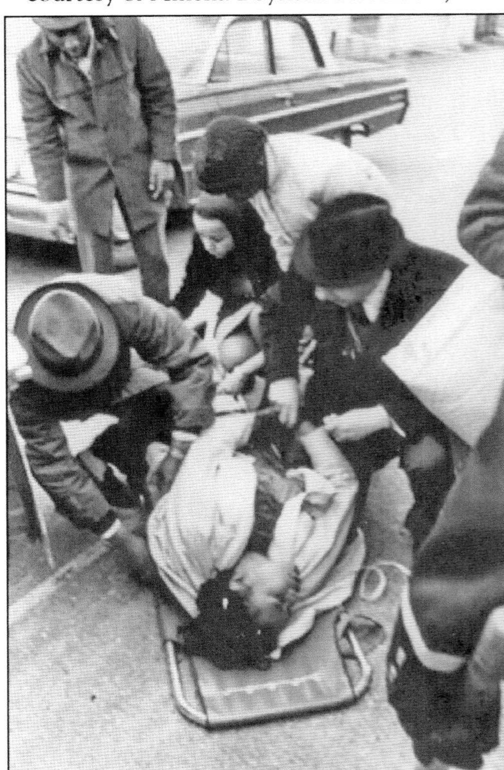

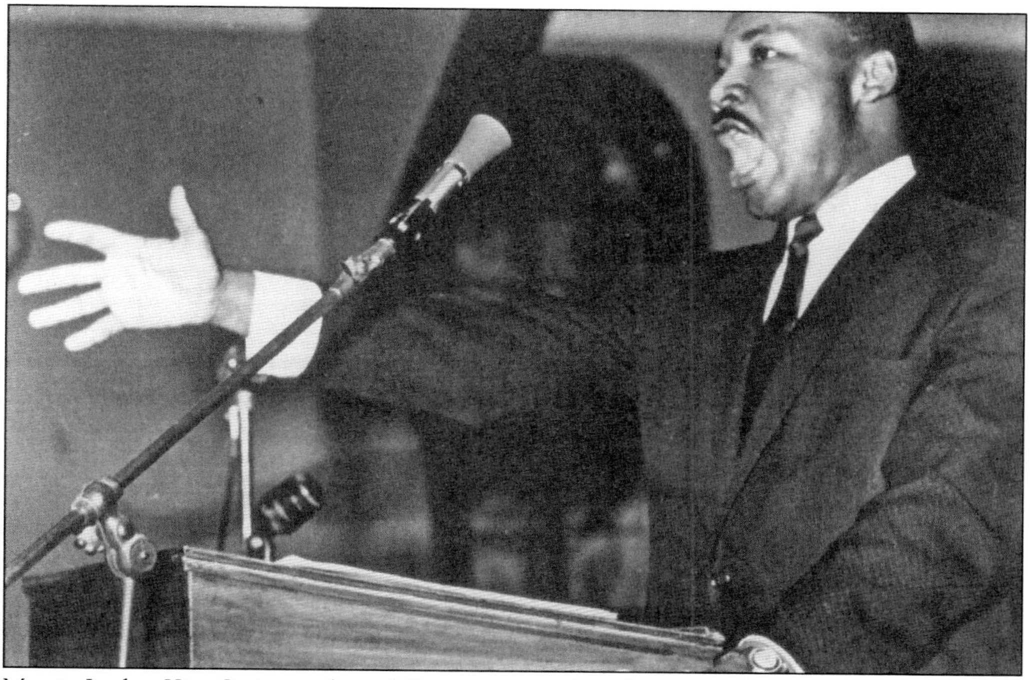

Martin Luther King Jr. is seen here delivering a speech to faculty, students, and other attendees at Tuskegee Institute in 1955. P.H. Polk captured this photograph when King was at the height of his delivery. King was the pastor of Dexter Avenue Baptist Church in Montgomery at the time, and the Montgomery bus boycott began just weeks after this speech. (Courtesy of the estate of P.H. Polk.)

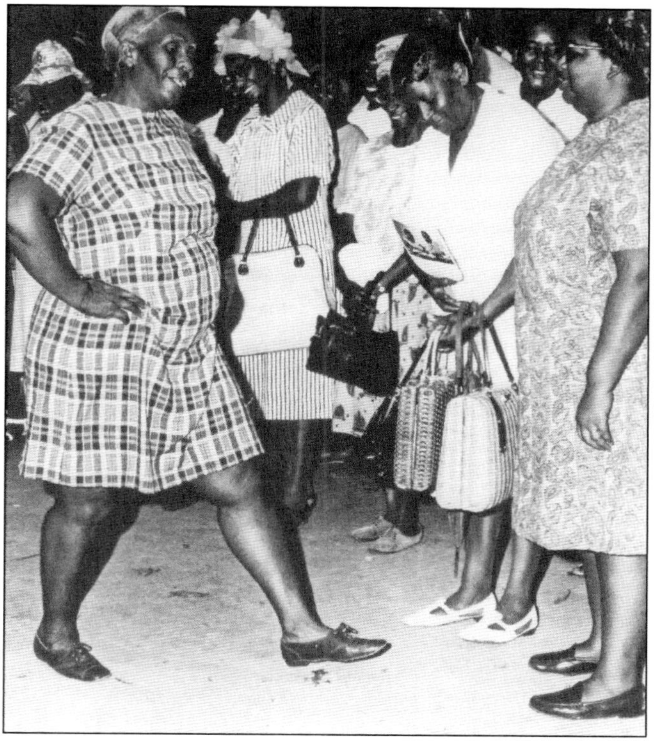

P.H. Polk took this photograph of an unidentified woman as she broke into a spontaneous dance during a civil rights gathering in Tuskegee related to the passage of the Voting Rights Act. He titled the photograph *Freedom Dance, 1965.*

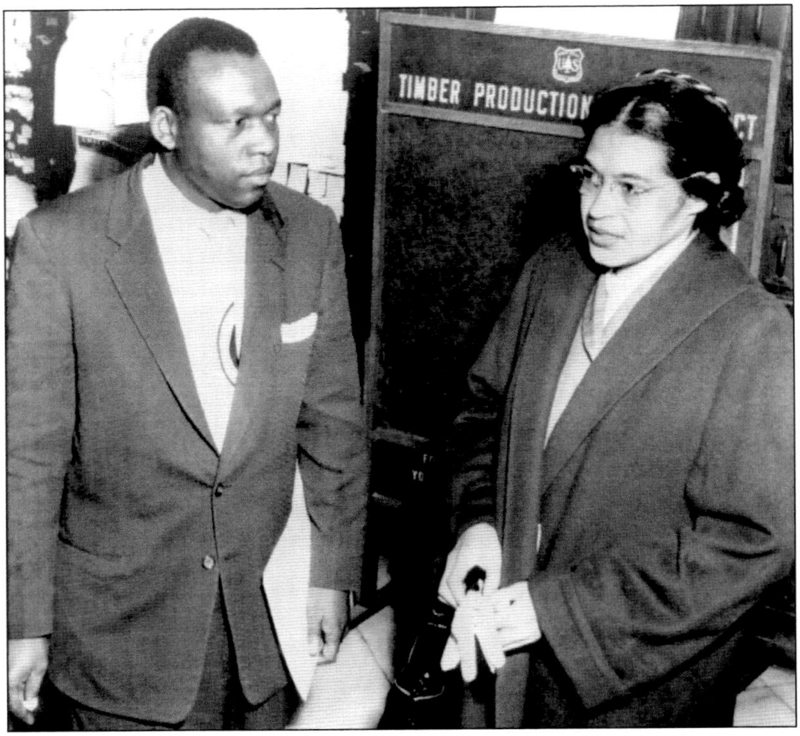

Rosa Louise McCauley Parks (1913–2005) was a civil rights activist born in Tuskegee whose refusal to surrender her seat on a Montgomery bus to a white man on December 1, 1955, led to a 13-month bus boycott. Assisted by the NAACP and Martin Luther King Jr., the Montgomery bus boycott forced the Montgomery Bus Company to integrate, after loss of revenue and a Supreme Court ruling.

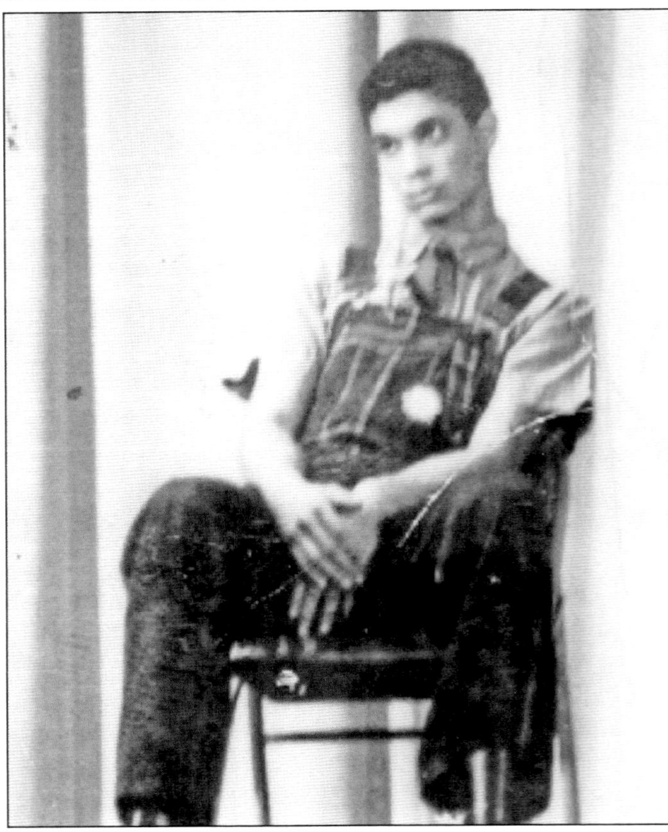

On January 3, 1966, Tuskegee native Sammy Younge Jr., 21, was killed by a white gas station attendant after he refused to use a segregated restroom. Younge had been in the Navy until two surgeries caused him to lose a kidney. He enrolled at Tuskegee Institute and became active in civil rights activities. Younge was the first student to die in the black liberation movement.

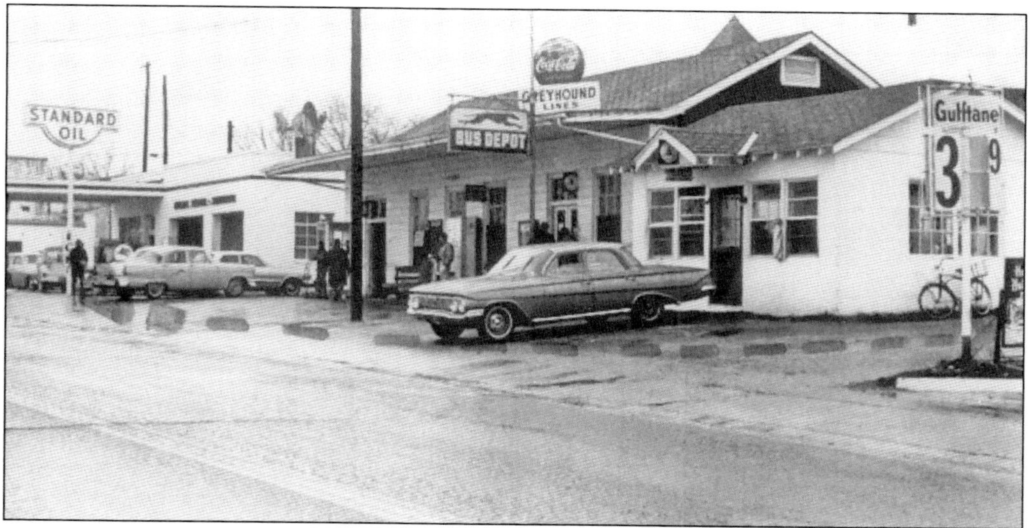

This 1966 photograph shows the site where white service station attendant Marvin Segrest fired the fatal shot to the head of Sammy Younge Jr. Segrest insisted that the incident was personal, not racial.

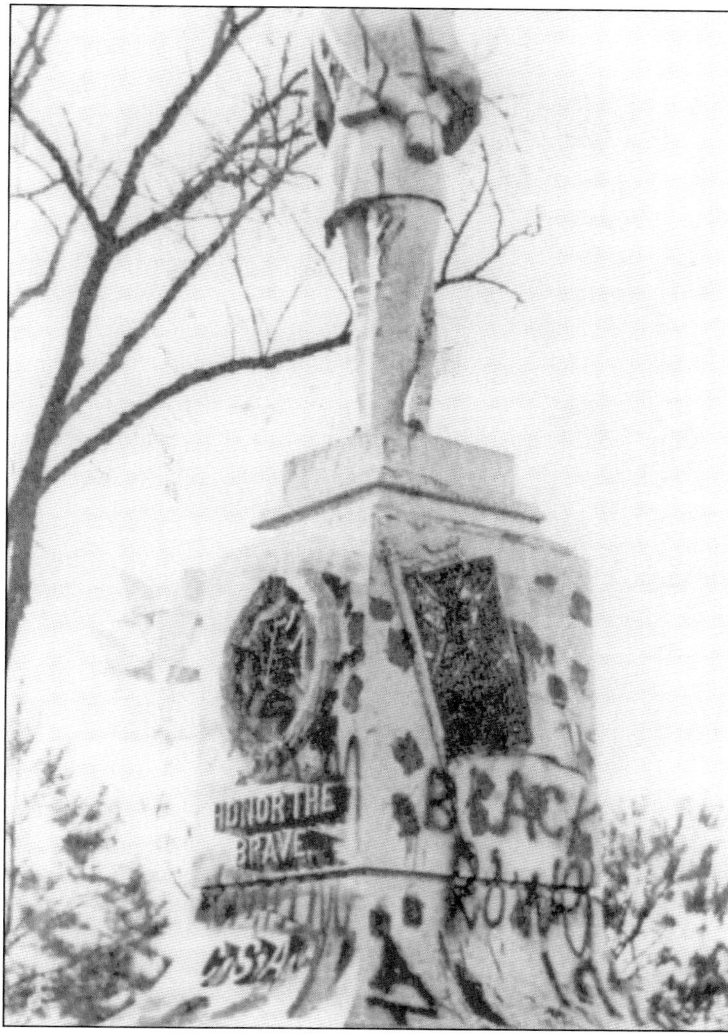

The morning following Younge's death, 3,000 students marched in the rain from campus to downtown, demanding an audience with Tuskegee mayor Charles Keever and the city council. When the mayor and council members appeared, students pressed them about what they planned to do. After rounds of questions, the contingents prayed together and sang "We Shall Overcome" before returning to campus. When Marvin Segrest was acquitted, the Confederate monument downtown was defaced.

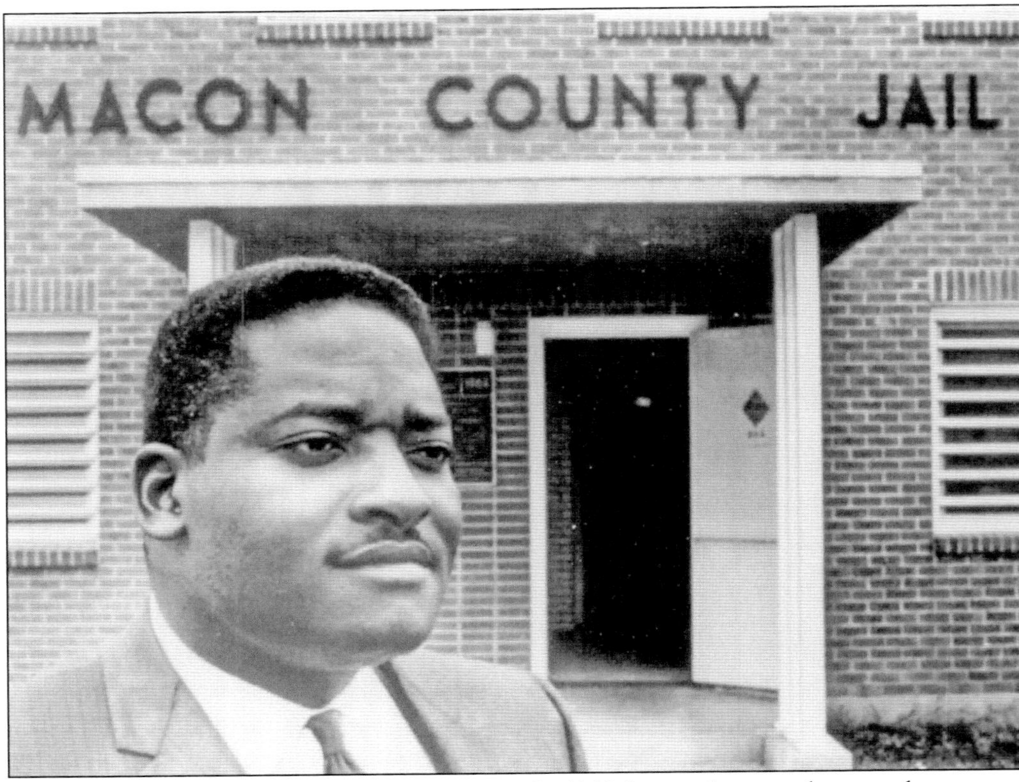

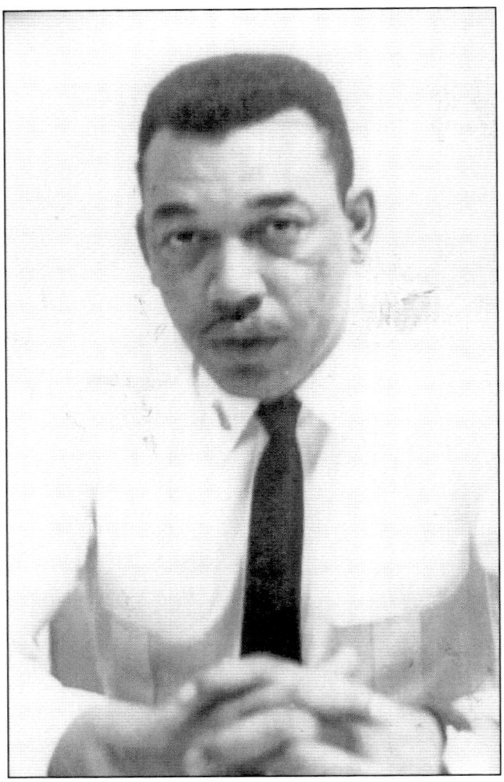

In 1966, Lucius Amerson became the first African American sheriff elected in Macon County, defeating Harvey Sadler. Gov. George Wallace had appointed Sadler in 1964 to complete Preston Hornsby's term after Hornsby resigned to become a probate judge. A Korean War veteran and VA hospital worker, Amerson wanted to become a policeman, but considered the sheriff's position to be a good way into law enforcement since few Alabama police departments hired African Americans.

Eugene Harrison is seen here in an Associated Press wire photograph on January 30, 1968, after his election as police chief. The article, titled "Negro Chief," reported, "Eugene Harrison, 31, a Negro, is the new police chief at Tuskegee, AL. He was named last week by the city's biracial City Council."

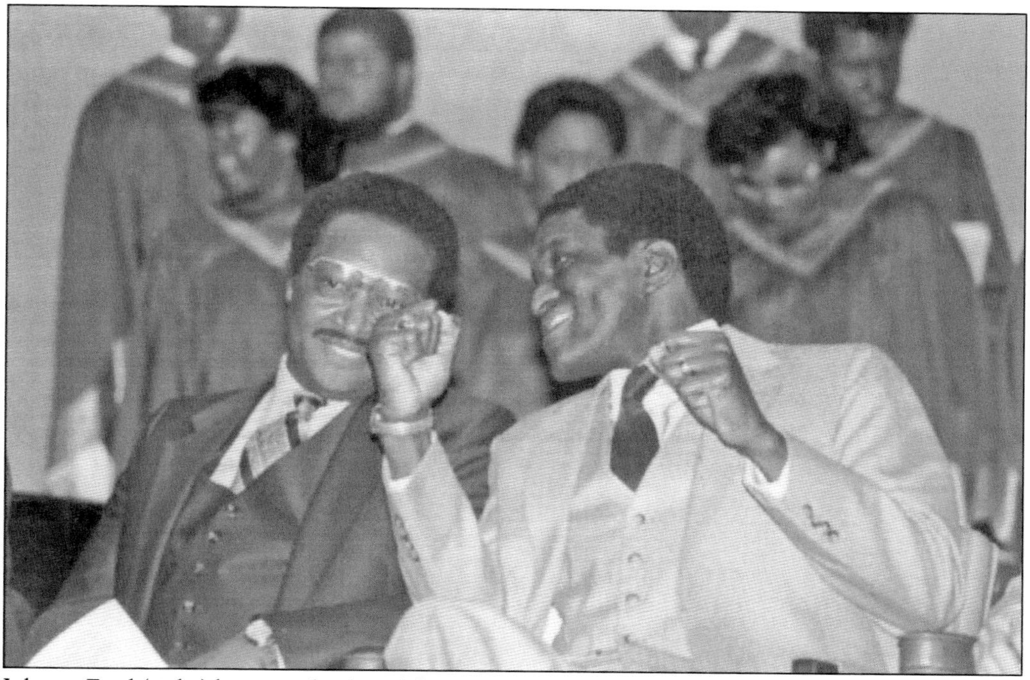

Johnny Ford (right) became the first African American mayor of Tuskegee in 1972, serving until 1996. He then served as a state representative of the 82nd District, which includes Macon County, from 1999 to 2004. Switching to the Republican Party in 2003, he resigned from the legislature and successfully ran for mayor again, serving from 2004 to 2008. He later rejoined the Democratic Party. Ford is seen here with an unidentified man in a church before a speech in 1984.

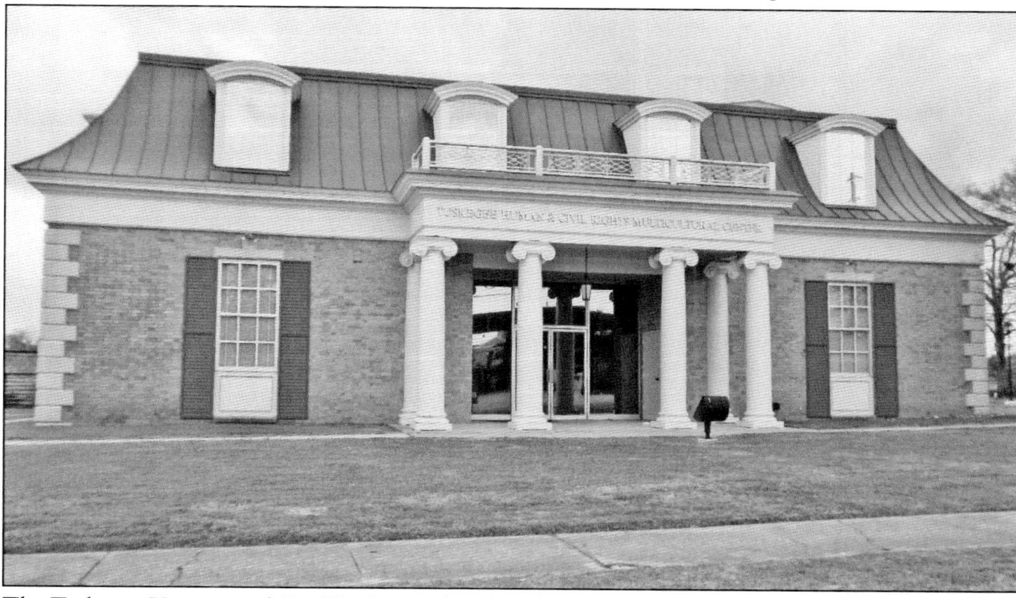

The Tuskegee Human and Civil Rights Multicultural Center highlights the diversity and distinction of Native American, African American, and European American cultures that forms the history of Tuskegee and Macon County. Established in 1997 by executive director Thomas "T.C." Coley Jr., the center's primary mission is to serve as a memorial to the victims of the Tuskegee syphilis experiment. The center continues to broaden its scope.

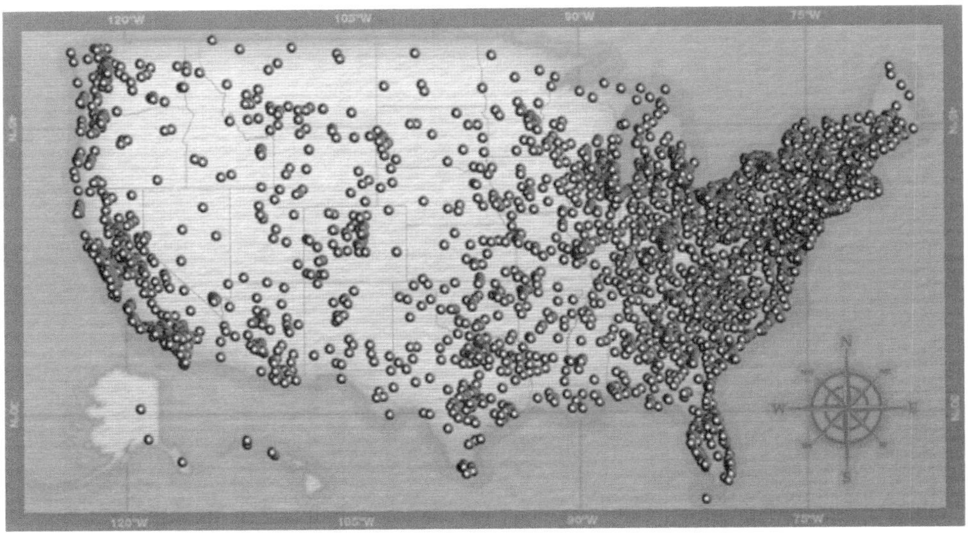

Consistent with our mission to preserve history on a local level, this book was printed in South Carolina on American-made paper and manufactured entirely in the United States. Products carrying the accredited Forest Stewardship Council (FSC) label are printed on 100 percent FSC-certified paper.

MADE IN THE USA